I0126244

Feedback Informed Treatment

Feedback Informed Treatment

A Treatment, Training and Implementation Manual

SCOTT D. MILLER & SUSANNE BARGMANN

© 2025, Scott D. Miller, Ph. D.
All rights reserved.
No part of this volume may be copied or transmitted in whole or in part in printed or digital form without written permission.

ISBN 978-0-9966624-4-4

To the thousands of helping professionals and millions of clients who have helped us understand and relate how best to seek and use feedback to improve behavioral healthcare

ACKNOWLEDGEMENTS

The revised edition of the feedback informed treatment manual is made possible by the input and dedication of scores of researchers, thousands of helping professionals, and millions of clients working or seen in diverse settings around the world. Gratitude also goes to the leadership, board members, and hundreds of ICCE Certified FIT Trainers who have provided feedback and support over the years. Thanks to Rasmus Møller, Mette Gnisa, Jim Reynolds Brooke Mathews, Stacy Bancroft and Layla Davis for their input and suggestions throughout the writing process. A very special thanks to Cynthia Maeschalck who devoted countless hours to the unglamorous tasks of reading, rereading, commenting, formatting, and hunting down references. Completion of the manual would not have been possible without her attention to detail and deep experience and expertise in feedback-informed treatment.

WHAT IS FIT?

Feedback-Informed Treatment (FIT) is a transtheoretical approach for evaluating and improving the quality and effectiveness of behavioral health services. It involves routinely and formally soliciting feedback from consumers regarding the therapeutic relationship and outcome of care and using the resulting information to inform and tailor service delivery. FIT, as described and detailed in these pages, is not only consistent with but also operationalizes the American Psychological Association's (APA) definition of evidence-based practice. To wit, FIT involves "the integration of the best available research ... and monitoring of patient progress (and of changes in the patient's circumstances— e.g., job loss, major illness) that may suggest the need to adjust the treatment ... (e.g., problems in the therapeutic relationship or in the implementation of the goals of the treatment)" (APA Task Force on Evidence-Based Practice, 2006, pp. 273, 276-277).

A PERSONAL PREFACE

This manual on feedback-informed treatment began as a set of six volumes. First published in 2012, the original series was created to provide the most up to date, "how to" information on using Feedback-Informed Treatment (FIT) to inform and improve mental health service delivery. Since that time, much has changed. In 2013, the measurement scales and clinical process described in these pages were reviewed and granted "evidence-based" status by the National Registry of Evidence-based Programs and Practices (Miller, 2013). Scores of randomized controlled trials, meta-analyses and systematic reviews have been published. The results, along with experience implementing FIT in diverse settings around the world, not only confirm early findings documenting the impact of FIT on retention, outcome, and cost of treatment services but also provide a more nuanced understanding of how it works and what is required for successful implementation. When the Third Interdivisional American Psychological Association Task Force recommended all clinicians seek and use the type of feedback FIT provides, the decision was made to publish an update (Norcross & Wampold, 2019a).

That was the plan, at least. Truth is the process took far longer than expected. Committees were formed. Discussions took place. Plans were made, outlines constructed, revisions started. And yet, whenever meetings were held to review progress, it always felt as though the project wasn't coming together. A crucial study had been missed. Some aspect of clinical experience wasn't adequately covered. Old understandings were being stretched to fit new circumstances and challenges rather than rethought or jettisoned altogether. Finally, each change contemplated, like tipping the first domino, led to the identification of other changes needing to be made—to the FIT core competencies, approved statistical indices, training curricula for the FIT intensives, and certification standards for FIT trainers.

For nearly two years, work on the manuals stopped completely. When the world shut down in response to the outbreak of COVID-19, I began meeting regularly with my colleagues Susanne Bargmann and Cynthia Maeschalck. Critically, the time spent not only made it possible to make necessary revisions to the training the International Center for

Clinical Excellence offered, but also to reflect deeply on the research and clinical experience that had accumulated in the decade since the publication of the original manuals in 2012. Ultimately, we decided a rewrite, not revision, was required. Susanne and I started writing, sending documents back and forth and writing together several hours a week via Zoom. Aside from a continuing commitment to improving the outcome of psychological or social care, the content of the current volume is entirely new.

Now, as then, the purpose of the manual is to provide practitioners, administrators, and agencies with a thorough grounding in the knowledge and skills of FIT. While organized in a series of 5 chapters, they do not need to be read from start to finish. Experienced readers can simply turn to the chapter most relevant to their practice or current state of application of FIT. Interested in the role supervisors play? Turn to chapter 3. Wanting to understand the meaning and use of the performance indices made possible via aggregation of individual or agency data? Start with chapter 4. Part of an agency considering how, or whether to implement FIT? Read chapter 5. Just beginning your FIT journey? Read chapters 1 and 2, and then, as experience with FIT grows, use the Table of Contents to identify topics of interest or pursue answers to specific questions. Regardless, take the time to complete the quizzes found at the end of each chapter as well as consult the appendices at the end of the book as doing so will support the successful application of FIT in your practice or treatment setting.

My hope is that FIT will, as intended, help you understand and connect more effectively with the people you serve.

Scott D. Miller, Ph. D.
Director, International Center for Clinical Excellence
Sarasota, Florida
December 2024

TABLE OF CONTENTS

CHAPTER 1

FEEDBACK-INFORMED TREATMENT: EMPIRICAL FOUNDATIONS

THE PRINCIPLES AND PRACTICES of Feedback-Informed Treatment (FIT) are derived from a wide base of empirical findings related to effective psychological care. Understanding the empirical foundations is considered a core element of competence as a FIT practitioner. Five areas of research supporting FIT will be reviewed, including studies on:

1. The efficacy of psychological care
2. The qualities of effective helping relationships
3. The impact of routinely monitoring outcome and relationship on retention and progress
4. Implementation of FIT
5. Factors associated with the development of expert performance

Subsequent chapters will translate these findings into practice.

1. THE EFFICACY OF PSYCHOLOGICAL CARE

For millennia, humans have used conversation in the context of a personal relationship to promote change and improvement in well-being or functioning (Frank, 1961; Miller & Hubble, 2017; Truscott, 2010; Wampold, 2010). Early on, maladies of the body, heart, soul and community were thought to result from the actions of otherworldly forces. Relief, recovery, and a return to health required the intercession of one who could move between the physical and supernatural realms. The success of the "treatments" depended on gaining access to powers inaccessible in the natural world. Ceremonies elaborated in songs, prayers, chanting, dancing, and awe-inspiring demonstrations of power were used to invite spirits, gain their permission and cooperation, and enlist their healing energies. All this occurred in a social context strongly supportive of the beliefs and related practices. The healer, the afflicted, and the community were engaged in a common purpose.

Today's informed practitioners rely on science. All aspects of the care they provide, from start to finish, are explained in the preferred, medicalized language of current times. The role of spirits and other worldly powers have given way to a focus on thoughts, behavior, emotions, and brain chemistry, all believed to provide both a research-based explanation for suffering and pathway to recovery. Helping has become highly specialized, divided into numerous disciplines (e.g., social work, counseling, psychology, psychiatry, education, occupational therapy, case management) and lists of "evidence-based" methods for which extensive training is required in order to practice competently and effectively.

That modern healing practices work is not in question. Fifty years of research on psychotherapy, for example, consistently shows it is effective across populations, age groups, *and* diagnoses (APA, 2012; Barkham et al. 2021). In settings ranging from community mental health agencies to university counseling centers and independent practices, the average person who engages in psychotherapy is better off in terms of their well-being and functioning than 80% of people with similar problems who do not receive care (Wampold & Imel, 2015). Such results are equal to or better than many common and well accepted medical treatments (e.g., chemotherapy for breast cancer, heart bypass surgery) as well as being equal to or more effective than popular psychotropic medications (Cuipers et al. 2013; Kamenov et al. 2017; Lee et al. 2016).

How Psychological Care Works

Over the last 5 decades, the "medical model," as it is termed, has come to dominate the view of how psychological care works (Wampold, 2001). It is perhaps the position held by most people who seek help from professionals. Proponents argue contemporary approaches are similar to medical treatments (Barlow, 2004). Treatment works, they assert because, like penicillin, the methods contain ingredients specifically remedial to the disorder being treated. Consistent with this perspective, emphasis is placed on diagnosis, treatment plans, and experience with, adherence to, and the competent delivery of "empirically supported" treatments (Siev et al. 2009; Huppert et al. 2006; Chambless & Ollendick, 2001).

Less well known is that little empirical support exists for the medical view of contemporary healing approaches. Indeed, researcher Bruce Wampold (2001) argues, adopting such a perspective "distorts the nature of the endeavor" (p. 2), especially services relying on *conversation in the context of a relationship* to promote improvement in well-being and functioning (e.g., psychotherapy, counseling, case management [Hubble et al. 1999; Norcross & Lambert, 2019; Norcross & Wampold, 2019a; Wampold & Imel, 2015]). A variety of research methods further fail to support a host of other related practices and beliefs about what impacts outcome. Figure 1.1 summarizes the types of studies employed in outcome research over the last 70 years—the specific designs, their characteristics and evidentiary value. Figure 1.2 summarizes research findings on factors traditionally considered important, but which have proven to be weak or non-predictors of treatment results.

TYPES OF RESEARCH DESIGNS		
Name	Definition	Evidentiary Value
Case Studies and Examples	An in-depth study of one person.	Limited and prone to the point of view of the writer.
Randomized Controlled Trials (RCT)	A study in which people are randomly assigned to receive one of several treatments. Typically, one of the interventions is a control condition in which participants receive no treatment or treatment as usual.	Considered the gold standard of research designs for prospectively assessing the effectiveness of an intervention or treatment approach. Comparisons of one approach to a no treatment, attentional, relational control or "treatment as usual" cannot be used to determine whether one approach is superior/inferior to another. Direct comparisons of two or more "bona fide" treatment approaches within the same study are needed to determine whether one approach is superior to another (see Figure 1.4).
Systematic Reviews	Attempt to summarize, integrate, and/or synthesize a body of research on a particular topic or area.	Considered the highest level of evidence. Starts with a specific clinical question followed by a comprehensive literature review in which poorly done studies are eliminated. Practice recommendations are made based on well-done experimental and quantitative studies.
Meta-analysis	A statistical method for combining evidence from the results of many independent RCT's addressing a related set of hypotheses.	Stronger evidentiary value than single studies. The strength and meaning of the results depend on the nature and quality of the studies included.

| Dismantling studies | A study investigating which elements within a treatment approach are causally related to change. Generally, parts of the method are compared to the full treatment. | Necessary for determining whether a specific ingredient or element within a treatment is necessary for change or the degree to which a specific component adds to the magnitude of change. |

Figure 1.1: Types of Research Designs

WEAK OR NON-PREDICTORS OF OUTCOME OF CONTEMPORARY HEALING APPROACHES		
Client Factors	Age, gender, diagnosis, prior treatment history.	Bohart & Wade (2013) Clarkin & Levy (2004)
Clinician Factors	Age, gender, licensure, professional discipline, degree earned, theoretical orientation, participation in personal therapy, amount of training, clinical supervision, clinical experience.	Baldwin & Imel (2013) Malouf (2012) Goldberg, Rousmaniere et al. (2016) VanderWal (2015) Whipple et al. (2020)
Treatment/Model/ Technique Factors	Match between helper and client on personal or demographic qualities, match of model to client diagnosis, use of, adherence, or competence in "evidenced-based" approaches, specific or general competence.	Behn et al. (2018) Sakaluk et al. (2019) Wampold & Imel (2015) Williams et al. (2021)

Figure 1.2: Weak or Non-Predictors of Outcome of Contemporary Healing Approaches

What is responsible for the effectiveness of modern healing practices? Researchers have identified a core group of factors. In order of their impact on outcome, these include: (1) the client and their unique life circumstances; (2) the helper/practitioner; (3) the quality of the relationship between the client and helper; (4) hope, expectancy, and belief; and (5) a healing rationale and ritual/method. The role and degree of influence that any one factor plays in the outcome of an episode of care depends on who is involved, what takes place between them, when and where the interaction occurs and, ultimately, whose perspective is being considered.

Figure 1.3 provides a visual representation of the factors affecting outcome, their interaction and percentage-wise contribution to the results of care. As can be seen in the larger circle in the upper left, treatment effects (represented by the smaller circle within) account for a small percentage of the overall results (13-20%) relative to the impact of the client and their unique life circumstances (80-87%), known as client/extratherapeutic factors. Research indicates the latter includes what clients bring to care, and the circumstances and events that take place in their lives that either aid or hinder improvement.

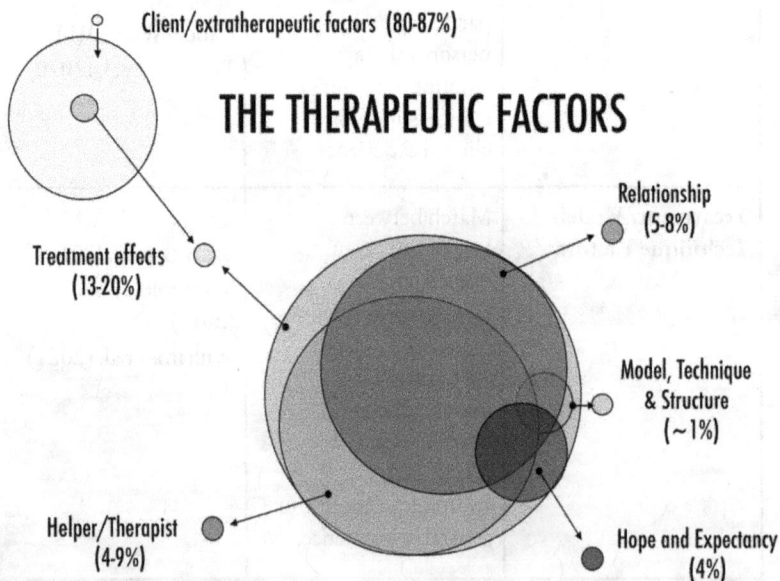

Figure 1.3: Therapeutic factors underlying the effectiveness of contemporary treatment approaches

Given the large impact client/extratherapeutic factors exert on outcome, helpers maximize effectiveness when they continuously adjust and adapt services to fit the individual client. Research presented in section three of this chapter will document how routinely and formally seeking feedback from clients regarding their engagement and progress in care can help practitioners improve their responsiveness thereby increasing retention and effectiveness.

Returning to Figure 1.3, the factor within treatment that contributes most to outcome is the helper/therapist (4-9%). Simply put, who is more important than what. Significant differences in outcome between providers persist even when treatments are highly structured or manualized (Blatt et al. 1996; Project MATCH Research Group, 1998; Wampold & Imel, 2015). Interestingly, most of the difference in outcome (97%) between helpers is accounted for by their ability to form working relationships with a broader range of clients (Baldwin et al. 2007; Del Re et al. 2021). By contrast, age, gender, years of experience, professional discipline, degree, training, licensure, theoretical orientation, amount of supervision or personal therapy, and use of so-called, "evidence-based" methods contribute little or nothing to effectiveness (see Figure 1.2). Such findings challenge traditional beliefs and practices regarding professional development activities (e.g., hours of clinical supervision, training in specific methods, attendance at continuing education events). Section five of this chapter will present the latest research findings on expertise, noting what's required for helpers to improve their effectiveness.

The quality and strength of the relationship between client and helper is the next largest contributor to outcome (5-8%). More research exists documenting the impact of the relationship on the effectiveness of care than any other therapeutic factor (Norcross & Lambert, 2019; Wampold & Imel, 2015). Making the case for monitoring the client's experience of the relationship from the outset, researcher Wampold (2010) notes, "except for initial severity of the client, there is no other variable that has been assessed early in therapy that predicts final outcome better" (p. 97).

Hope and expectancy are critical to effective psychological care, accounting for up to 4% of the variance in outcome (Greenberg et al. 2006; Snyder et al. 1999; Wampold, 2010). For both client and professional, faith in the potency of care—including, the helper's healing rationale, specific skills and methods—fosters engagement in behaviors consistent with the expectation of positive results. The significant role hope and expectancy play in outcome can be seen in robust research findings documenting improved well-being following the simple act of making an appointment with a helper (Baldwin et al. 2009; Simon et al. 2012; Weiner-Davis et al. 1987).

The last of the therapeutic factors is model, technique and structure, accounting for 1% or less of the variance in outcome. All contemporary approaches to psychological care contain: (1) a conceptual framework (e.g., theory) for understanding client problems; and (2) procedures believed to foster problem resolution (e.g., methods or techniques) involving both the helper and client.

Contrary to popular belief, decades of research find little evidence that the success of care depends on matching treatment to the client's presenting complaint or diagnosis (Duncan et al. 2010; Wampold & Imel, 2015; Wampold et al. 2017). Neither does research designed to investigate the elements within treatment models considered responsible for effectiveness support the notion that certain ingredients are necessary for the remediation of clients' problems (Ahn & Wampold, 2001; Roehrig et al. 2006; Spielmans et al. 2013; Wampold & Imel, 2015). Indeed, research comparing "bona fide" (see Figure 1.4) treatment methods—those specifically developed to be helpful—show little or no difference in outcome when compared directly to one another in the same study (Benish et al. 2008; Imel et al. 2008; Miller et al. 2008; Wampold, 1997; Wampold & Imel, 2015; Wampold et al. 2017).

CHARACTERISTICS OF BONA FIDE PSYCHOLOGICAL TREATMENTS	
Qualities	Indicators
Intended to be therapeutic	- Theoretical base and associated techniques. - Employment of psychological principles and processes. - Identification of the factors believed responsible for therapeutic impact.

Considered viable by the professional community	- Documented to be in use in professional publications.
Delivered by trained practitioners	- The existence of a training program, manual or protocol for administering the treatment. - Meetings between client and practitioner in which the treatment is delivered.

Figure 1.4: Qualities of Bona Fide Psychological Treatments

So, how do models and techniques help? As stated earlier, they contribute to outcome by providing a coherent and convincing structure for both creating positive expectations and engaging the client in taking steps to resolve their difficulties. Studies have found, for example, that a lack of structure and focus in treatment are reliable predictors of a negative outcome (Lambert, 2013; Mohr, 1995; Sachs, 1983). Ultimately, helpers should choose an approach they believe in and feel confident about and which, most importantly, engages the individual client and facilitates progress. Regardless of the model or technique used, the responsibility of the helper is to routinely monitor the client's experience of outcome and helping relationship, adjusting on an ongoing basis to improve the fit.

When Psychological Care Does (and Does not) Work

As noted above, a significant number of people experience a measurable and meaningful improvement in their functioning prior to their first meeting with a helper (Baldwin et al. 2009; Simon et al. 2012; Weiner-Davis et al. 1987). Once in care, research shows many experience early improvement, with 30 to 40% reporting positive change in the first handful of visits, and 60% to 65% by session seven—changes which most maintain at two year follow up (Haas et al. 2002; Howard et al. 1986; Lutz et al. 2009; Lutz et al. 2014). Although the rate of client change differs from person to person, early response in care is a good indicator of eventual outcome.

While many are helped, the data also show psychological care does not work for every client, every time. Data reveal a sizeable number of people who start care, dropout (i.e., discontinue unilaterally) prior to experiencing a measurable improvement in their functioning or well-being. Meta-analytic evidence puts the percentage of adults who dropout at 22% (Swift et al. 2017). Children and adolescents, it turns out, are at even greater risk, being 30% more likely to end services without benefit (Fernandez et al. 2015; Garcia & Weisz, 2002; Kazdin, 1996).

Of those who remain in care, evidence indicates many continue without benefit, and a smaller percentage worsen. Researcher Michael Lambert (2017) observes, "Even when an evidence-based treatment is offered to carefully screened individuals who have the same disorder and see helpers who have been carefully selected, monitored, and supervised, 30-50% of patients fail to respond" (p. 81). Estimates from clinical trials suggest between 5 and 10% of adults, and twice as many children and adolescents, deteriorate while in care (Lambert, 2013; Warren et al. 2009).

In Chapter 2, step-by-step instructions are provided for using evidence-based benchmarks—known as "Treatment Response Trajectories" and "Success Probability Index"—to evaluate client progress and enable the identification of and response to clients at risk for a negative or null outcome.

2. THE QUALITIES OF EFFECTIVE HELPING RELATIONSHIPS

In a review of 50 years of process-outcome research, Orlinsky et al. (2004) conclude, "the quality of the patient's participation ... emerge[s] as *the* most important determinant in outcome" (emphasis added, p. 324). Simply put, people who are more involved and engaged in the helping process are more likely to benefit from the care offered. One of the best predictors of engagement is the quality of the helping relationship as experienced by the client (Bachelor, 2013; Bartholomew et al. 2022; Bedi & Hayes, 2020; Horvath et al. 2011).

Figure 1.5 illustrates the components of effective helping relationships. The depiction as a three-legged stool is purposeful, emphasizing both the importance of the relationship in keeping clients "comfortably and securely seated" for the duration of the work but also the fragility of their engagement should one or more of the elements be missing or askew. The four are: (1) agreement on the goals, meaning or purpose of care; (2) agreement on the means/ methods used; (3) a relational bond (e.g., empathy, warmth, genuineness) including agreement on the role of the helper in the change process; and (4) sensitivity to and accommodation of client preferences and identity (Bargmann, 2017; Norcross & Lambert, 2019; Norcross & Wampold, 2019a).

WITH "WHOM?"
Client preferences, values, identity, culture/worldview

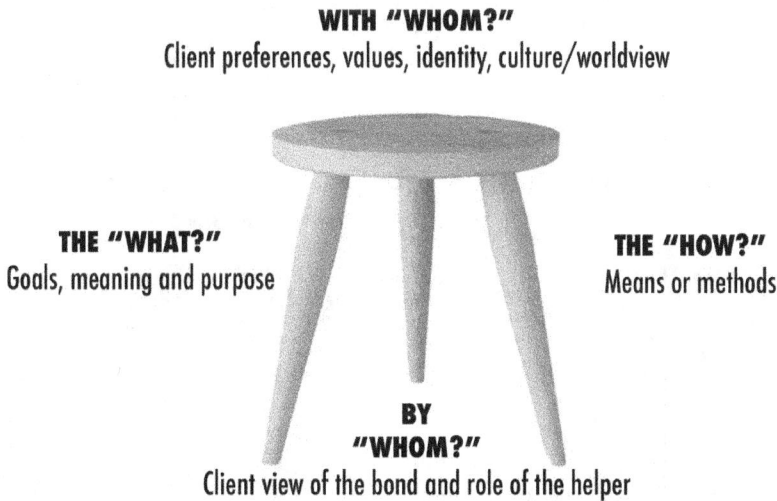

THE "WHAT?"
Goals, meaning and purpose

THE "HOW?"
Means or methods

BY "WHOM?"
Client view of the bond and role of the helper

Figure 1.5: The Helping Relationship

The impact of the helping relationship on outcome cannot be overstated. Consider results displayed in Figure 1.6 comparing the effect size of relational elements to those of treatment-specific factors. In the graphic, the width of the bars represents the number of studies and the height, the contribution made to outcome. As can be seen, one of the most researched areas in psychotherapy is treatment models (listed as, "treatment differences"). And yet, the impact of adhering to, competence in, differences between, and any specific ingredients contained within, pales by comparison.

Little wonder then that next to the level of functioning at intake, the client's rating of the helping relationship/alliance is the best predictor of treatment outcome.

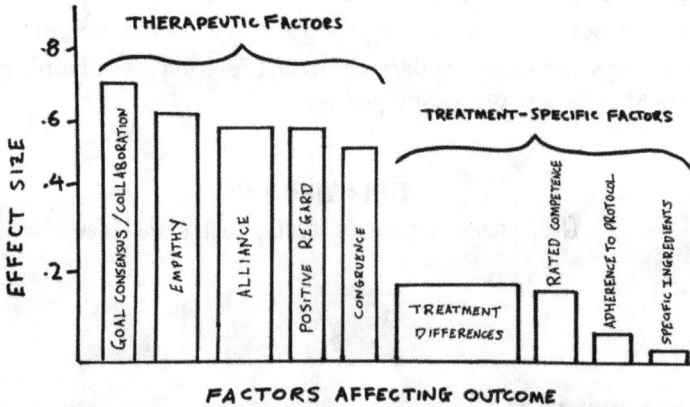

Figure 1.6: The Effect Size of Factors Affecting the Outcome of Psychotherapy. (Note: Width of bars reflects the number of studies reflecting effect sizes for each therapeutic factor. [Adapted with permission from "The Great Psychotherapy Debate," by Wampold & Imel, 2015, p. 258])

When combined with other findings about the helping relationship—namely, that: (1) client ratings tend to be more highly correlated with outcome than clinician ratings; (2) poorer ratings are associated with higher dropout rates and poorer outcomes; and (3) improved scores (from intake to termination) are associated with better outcomes and lower dropout rates—a strong case can be made for monitoring the client's experience of their connection with the helper on an ongoing basis (Bachelor, 2013; Harmon et al. 2005; Horvath & Symonds, 1991; Lambert, 2010; Martin et al. 2000; Miller et al. 2007; Norcross & Wampold, 2019a, b; Owen et al. 2016). Research shows routinely monitoring the relationship not only enables helpers to intervene early with clients at risk of dropout and poor outcome, but also identify specific professional development opportunities most likely to lead to improved effectiveness of the individual helper (see section 5).

3. THE IMPACT OF ROUTINELY MONITORING OUTCOME AND RELATIONSHIP ON RETENTION AND PROGRESS

In 2006, the APA Task Force on Evidence-Based Practice concluded, "Providing clinicians with real-time patient feedback to benchmark progress in treatment and clinical support tools to adjust treatment as needed" was one of the "most pressing research needs" (p. 278). Since that time, scores of validation studies, randomized controlled trials, and meta-analyses have confirmed routinely monitoring progress and the quality of the helping relationship, and using the resulting information to inform care: (1) improves the amount of reliable and clinically significant change clients experience; (2) reduces dropout; (3) decreases the risk of deterioration; (4) shortens the length of care episodes; (5) lowers the rate of hospitalizations; and (5) results in an overall reduction in the cost of care (Brattland et al. 2018; de Jong et al. 2021; de Jong et al. 2024; Delgadillo et al. 2021; Østergård et al. 2018; Shimokawa, 2010; Schuckard et al. 2017; Slade et al. 2006; Whipple et al. 2003).

Routinely seeking feedback from clients about their progress and experience of the helping relationship (i.e., feedback-informed treatment [FIT]) is not only consistent with, but operationalizes the American Psychological Association's (APA) definition of evidence-based practice. To wit, FIT involves "the integration of the best available research ... and monitoring of patient progress (and of changes in the patient's circumstances—e.g., job loss, major illness) that may suggest the need to adjust the treatment ... (e.g., problems in the therapeutic relationship or in the implementation of the goals of the treatment)" (APA Task Force on Evidence-Based Practice, 2006, pp. 273, 276-277). In so doing, FIT provides the only evidence that truly matters, *practice-based*; that is, evidence the service delivered engages and helps the client, or not (Drisko & Friedman, 2019). Figure 1.7 lists and defines three terms commonly used in professional discourse to categorize the evidence for psychotherapy.

EVIDENCE-BASED PRACTICE, EMPIRICALLY-SUPPORTED TREATMENTS, AND PRACTICE-BASED EVIDENCE		
Type	**Definition**	**Application**
Evidence-based practice	Use of the best available evidence, combined with clinical expertise, in the context of client preferences, situation, values, culture, and background.	A philosophical stance regarding the integration of research findings in clinical practice.
Empirically supported treatments	Specific treatment methods for specific populations/ disorder(s) shown to be effective in experimental research.	The use of specific psychological treatment approaches that have been tested in randomized clinical trials and shown to work better than control conditions (e.g., no treatment, waitlist, and treatment as usual).
Practice-based evidence	Measurement of the actual impact of services.	Involves the administration of valid[1], reliable[2], and feasible[3] outcome and relationship measures throughout care.

Figure 1.7: Evidence-based Practice, Empirically-supported treatments, and Practice-based Evidence

---

1 *Validity* refers to how well a scale measures the variable it purports to measure. With outcome and alliance scales, this is most often accomplished by correlating a scale with other well-established or documented scales (known as concurrent validity), testing whether the measure can accurately differentiate between clinical groups and non-clinical groups (discriminate validity), or reviewing and estimating whether the scale measures what it purports to measure (face validity).

2 *Reliability* refers to the degree to which a scale consistently measures the variable it purports to measure. To be reliable, any differences between two administrations of the same measurement tool must be attributable to the changes in the variable being measured.

3 *Feasibility* refers to ease and speed by which a scale can be explained, completed, and interpreted.

Research on FIT—also referred to in the literature as ROM (routine outcome monitoring), MBC (measurement-based care), and PROMS (patient-rated outcome measures)—has accelerated over the last decade (Schuckard et al. 2017). Early studies reporting the process was easily implemented and required minimal training to achieve medium to large effects, generated a great deal of hope and interest among researchers and practitioners. For example, Anker et al. (2009) reported a "moderate to large effect size" for feedback (0.5) in a randomized controlled trial of couple's therapy following only minimal training (11 hours). Ten years later, Tilden et al. (2019), working in the same country with a similar sample, found feedback had no impact!

When individual studies are combined and analyzed in systematic reviews and meta-analyses, they consistently find significant, yet more modest effects on outcome (de Jong et al. 2021; Kendrick et al. 2016; Lambert et al. 2018; Østergård et al. 2020). The most recent research has focused on identifying how and under what circumstances FIT works best. At present, the results indicate:

- Both of the most widely used feedback measures—the brief Outcome and Session Rating Scales (Miller et al. 2005) and longer Outcome Questionnaire 45 (Lambert et al. 1994)—have similar impacts on outcome (Lambert & Shimokawa, 2011; Lambert et al. 2018).

- The effect of FIT depends on the degree to which the feedback obtained fosters improvement in the relationship between the helper and the client (Mikael et al. 2016; Brattland et al. 2019).

- Seeking feedback at each session—as opposed to less frequent intervals (e.g., every third visit, pre and post)—is more effective in terms of improving outcome and reducing dropouts (Bickman et al. 2011; Warren et al. 2009).

- The impact of FIT varies depending on the helper's openness and willingness to adjust services in response to feedback (de Jong et al. 2012; Miller et al. 2015).

4. IMPLEMENTATION OF FIT

One hundred sixty years have passed since Hungarian-born physician Ignaz Semmelweis published research documenting the importance of handwashing for preventing the spread of infections in hospital settings (Madsen et al. 2023). And yet, today, poor hand hygiene remains one of the leading causes of serious complications and death in intensive care units (Gawande, 2007). The disconnect between Semmelweis's groundbreaking discovery and its consistent application in real world settings is not an isolated event. Indeed, available evidence indicates such implementation failures are the rule rather than the exception. In both medicine and mental health, years often pass between the time new ideas are introduced and their integration into practice (Brownson et al. 2018; Ogden et al. 2012; Morris, 2011)

In recent years, an entirely new field of scientific inquiry known as "implementation science" has emerged to identify effective strategies for facilitating the application of the latest research in real world settings. What is clear is that the process extends far beyond providing information and skills training, requiring a significant investment of time, planning, and leadership. Bertram, King et al. (2014) note, "Successful program implementation requires examination and alteration of organizational structures, culture, and capacity as well as development of new staff competencies" (p. 481).

Research in this area confirms the degree of implementation increases from 14% (over a 17-year period), to 80% (in 3 years), when a series of evidence-based steps and methods are followed (Fixsen, Blase, Metz et al. 2013). The specific steps and respective tasks for successful implementation of FIT will be described in detail in Chapter 5. In the meantime, available research indicates:

- The effectiveness of FIT varies depending on the status of the implementation process. It is clear one-and two-day workshops focused on learning how to administer, score and interpret feedback tools (e.g., measures) result in minimal or no effects (Davidsen et al. 2017; Østergård et al. 2020; Pejtersen et al. 2018).

- FIT will not have an impact when treatment protocols and organization rules prevent adjusting the type, modality, timing, or provider of service in response to client feedback (Davidsen et al. 2017; van Oenen et al. 2018).

- Successful implementation requires a change in practitioner attitude and agency culture, away from a focus on measurement/evaluation and toward responsiveness to individual client engagement and progress. Consistent with the broader implementation science literature (Fixsen et al. 2019), at least three years of consistent planning and support (e.g., coaching, training, case review, management involvement and oversight) are required for the benefits of FIT to be realized (Brattland et al. 2018).

5. FACTORS ASSOCIATED WITH THE DEVELOPMENT OF EXPERT PERFORMANCE

Although the effectiveness of psychological care is well established, the field's outcomes have remained flat for more than five decades (Prochaska et al. 2020; Thomas, 2013; Wampold & Imel, 2015). Access to continuing education, regular supervision, and training in "empirically supported treatment" approaches has not altered this fact (Neimeyer et al. 2009; Rousmaniere et al. 2014; Whipple et al. 2020; Watkins, 2011; Webb et al. 2010). Even more sobering, some studies show the effectiveness of the average helper declines as time and experience in the field lengthens (Goldberg, Rousmaniere et al. 2016; Norton et al. 2014).

Recently, research from outside the field has provided inspiration for new lines of thinking and research aimed at improving clinical effectiveness (Miller et al. 2007; Miller & Hubble, 2011). In particular, direction was found in the extensive scientific literature bearing on the development of expertise (Colvin, 2008; Ericsson, 2009; Ericsson et al. 2006). Such research is less concerned with the particulars of a given performance domain (e.g., medicine, music, sports, psychological care) than how mastery of any human endeavor is acquired by continuously reaching for performance objectives just beyond an individual's current abilities. The process, known as deliberate practice (DP), includes: (1) determining one's baseline level of performance; (2) setting individualized improvement targets; (3) engaging in focused, systematic practice; and (4) obtaining regular, ongoing progress feedback (Miller et al. 2018).

In 2015, Chow et al. found highly effective helpers devote 2.5 more hours to DP than average helpers and 14 times as many than the least effective. Goldberg, Babins-Wagner et al. (2016) reported increases in individual helper effectiveness over time when an agency systematically applied the four components of DP to daily clinical work. It is important to note the growth in effectiveness was not only consistent with the size of improvements seen in other performance domains (e.g., elite athletes), it was also the first time in the history of the field a particular training approach enhanced individual practitioner outcomes.

Detailed instructions for using DP to improve effectiveness are available in two recently published books, *Better Results* (Miller et al. 2020) and *The Field Guide to Better Results* (Miller et al. 2023). As noted in each volume, the first step of the process is determining each individual helper's baseline level of effectiveness. Doing so requires practitioners measure their work and use the resulting data to identify individualized performance improvement objectives. To accomplish this end, two well-validated scales in use in diverse settings around the world are introduced in the next chapter (Bargmann, 2016; Prescott et al. 2017). Later, in chapter 4, a variety of statistical indices derived from the routine administration of the scales are defined and described. Taken together, they allow helpers and agencies to both determine their baseline level of effectiveness and track and refine DP efforts.

SUMMARY

Feedback Informed Treatment (FIT) involves routinely seeking feedback from clients about their progress and experience of the helping relationship. The process is based on several key research findings from the helping literature including: (1) psychological care has an impact equal to or better than most medical treatments; (2) a significant percentage of people do not improve or worsen while in care; (3) traditional training activities are not sufficient for improving helper effectiveness or individual client outcomes; (4) responding to client feedback regarding the quality of the relationship or lack of progress improves retention and outcome for "at risk" clients; and (5) implementation of FIT requires time and planning.

QUIZ

1. Research consistently shows that people who in engage in psychotherapy:

    a. Are no better off than those who receive no psychotherapy

    b. Most often are worse off at the end of treatment

    c. Are better off in terms of their well-being and functioning than 80% of people with similar problems who do not receive care

    d. Only benefit if the correct "evidence-based" approach is applied

2. Primary factors responsible for effective psychological care do not include:

    a. The client and their unique life circumstances

    b. The helper/practitioner

    c. The quality of the relationship between the client and helper

    d. The client's psychiatric diagnosis

3. Based on empirical evidence:

    a. The treatment approach needs to be matched to the specific client problem

    b. The helper's approach has no relationship to outcome

    c. The best approach is one that engages the client and facilitates progress

    d. Adherence to a treatment manual improves outcome

4. Next to the level of functioning at intake, the client's rating of the helping relationship is:

    a. Of little importance

    b. The best predictor of outcome

    c. Not as important as the helper's rating of the client functioning

    d. Not as important as the helper's rating of the helping relationship

5. Why should helpers routinely monitor the effectiveness of treatment and the helping relationship?

    a. Research indicates it improves the amount of reliable and clinically significant change

    b. Research indicates it can decrease dropouts and risk of deterioration

    c. Research indicates it can result in reduced lengths of care and an overall reduction in the cost of care

    d. All of the above

6. What is considered the "gold standard" of research methodology?

    a. Case studies

    b. Random controlled trials

    c. Meta-analysis

    d. Dismantling studies

7. What other factors are responsible for the effectiveness of modern behavioral health practices?

    a. Hope, expectancy, and belief

    b. A healing rationale and ritual/method;

    c. Both 1 and 2

    d. Neither 1 or 2

8. Most of the difference in outcome among helpers is accounted for by:

    a. Their ability to form working relationships with a broader range of clients

    b. Age, gender, years of experience

    c. Professional discipline, degree, training, licensure

    d. Theoretical orientation and use of "evidence-based" methods

9. Research has identified which of the following as being related to better treatment outcomes?

    a. Hours of clinical supervision

    b. Training in specific methods

    c. Attendance at continuing education events

    d. None of the above

10. Early response in care is a good indicator of eventual outcome because:

    a. Research shows that once in care not many people experience early improvement

    b. 30 to 40% of clients demonstrate improvement in the first handful of visits

    c. 60% to 65% do not experience improvement

    d. Such clients tend to have fewer problems/difficulties

Answers: *1. C, 2. D, 3. C, 4. B, 5. D, 6. B, 7. C, 8. A, 9. D, 10. B*

CHAPTER 2

FEEDBACK-INFORMED TREATMENT: THE BASICS

IN THIS CHAPTER, THE basics of working feedback-informed are described and illustrated. It details how to introduce the Outcome Rating Scale (ORS) and the Session Rating Scale (SRS) in clinical work as well as how to use the two measures to improve engagement and outcome. Information is divided into eight sections:

1. Psychometrics and predictive indices of the ORS and SRS

2. Creating a "culture of feedback"

3. Administering the ORS

4. Administering the SRS

5. The FIT Service Delivery Agreement and Progress Note

6. FIT with children, families and couples, clients scoring at or above the clinical cut off (e.g., mandated, involuntary), in groups, residential, and inpatient settings, and when delivering services online

7. Understanding and processing client feedback over time

8. When and when not to use FIT

1. PSYCHOMETRICS AND PREDICTIVE INDICES OF THE ORS AND SRS

The ORS and SRS are brief, practical measures for tracking client progress and the quality of the therapeutic alliance, taking less than a minute each for clients to complete and for clinicians to score. The ORS has proven sensitive to change among those receiving services (Miller et al. 2003; Andrade-Gonazalez et al. 2021; Lambert & Shimokawa, 2011). Numerous studies have documented concurrent, discriminant, criterion-related and predictive validity, test-retest and internal-consistency reliability for both measures (Schuckard et al. 2017). The significant impact of these scales on the outcome of services has been well documented by numerous researchers (de Jong et al. 2021; de Jong et al. 2024; Lambert & Shimokawa, 2011; Østergård et al. 2018; Schuckard et al. 2017).

The Outcome Rating Scale

The Outcome Rating Scale (ORS) is a brief, client-rated, four-item visual analogue scale that measures the client's experience of well-being in four different areas: individual, interpersonal, social, and overall. The ORS is designed and normed for adults and adolescents (ages 13+). The Child Outcome Rating Scale (CORS) was developed and has been normed for ages 6-12. The Young Child Outcome Rating Scale (YCORS) is for children ages six or younger. The YCORS is not scorable. It is best viewed as a clinical "engagement" tool designed to provide preliterate children with a way to communicate about their well-being. Versions of the ORS are available in many different languages, as well as a script for oral administration.

Clinical Cutoff of the ORS: Determining the clinical cutoff for an outcome measure accomplishes two related objectives: (1) it defines the boundary between a clinical and non-clinical range of distress; and (2) it provides a reference point for evaluating the severity of distress for a particular client or client sample. Using the method described by Jacobson and Truax (1991), Miller et al. (2003) established a clinical cutoff score of 25 for the adult version of the ORS—a figure confirmed in other studies and across several different cultures (Andrade-Gonazalez et al. 2021; She et al. 2018). The clinical cutoff for adolescents (age 13-18) is 28, and for children (age 6-12) is 32 (Casey et al. 2019; Duncan et al. 2006). Figure 2.1 illustrates the clinical cutoff for adults, adolescents, and children on the paper and pencil graph that accompanies the packet of measures when downloaded from www.scottdmiller.com.

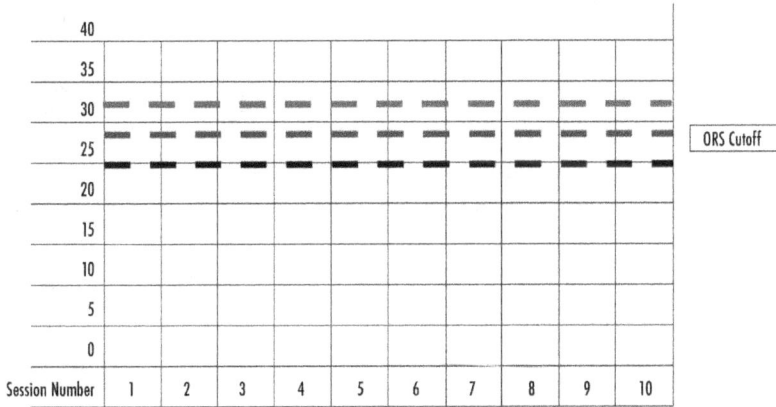

Figure 2.1: The dotted lines on the graph represent the clinical cutoff for adults (25 [bottom line]), adolescents (28 [middle line]), and children (32 [top line]) on the ORS.

Treatment Response Trajectories: Multiple web-based applications are available for tracking clients' ORS and SRS scores[4]. In addition to administering and scoring the measures, each system uses normed algorithms to establish benchmarks—known as "treatment response trajectories" (TRTs)—for assessing individual client progress over the course of treatment. The benchmarks are based on a large and growing international sample of clients and helpers working in diverse settings. To date, comparisons of datasets over different time periods and across cultures and countries have revealed little or no difference in the reliability and validity of the benchmarks (Miller, 2011).

An example of the type of feedback generated by the web-based systems can be found in Figure 2.2. The graph displays two TRTs for a client whose initial score on the ORS is 15. The topmost line

4 Authorized software systems are described in detail in section 3 of Chapter 4 and online at: http://www.scottdmiller.com/fit-software-tools/ Images of graphs and the measures appearing in this chapter used with permission of Performance Metrics, LLC, Myoutcomes.com and Fit-outcomes.com.

(represented in green in the three computerized systems) is the TRT
for successful treatment. All scores falling at or above this line from
session to session are indicative of clients who are on track for a positive
outcome at the conclusion of treatment. The lowest curved line
(represented in red in the three computerized systems) is the TRT for
unsuccessful treatment. Scores falling at or below this line are indicative
of clients who are not on track and at risk for a negative or null outcome.
Finally, the area inbetween the two lines (represented in yellow in the
electronic systems) represents scores that are indeterminant of either
success of failure). In sum, by comparing the client's scores at each
session to the TRTs, practitioners and clients receive feedback in real
time about the effectiveness of services being offered: green = on track,
red = off track, yellow = uncertain.

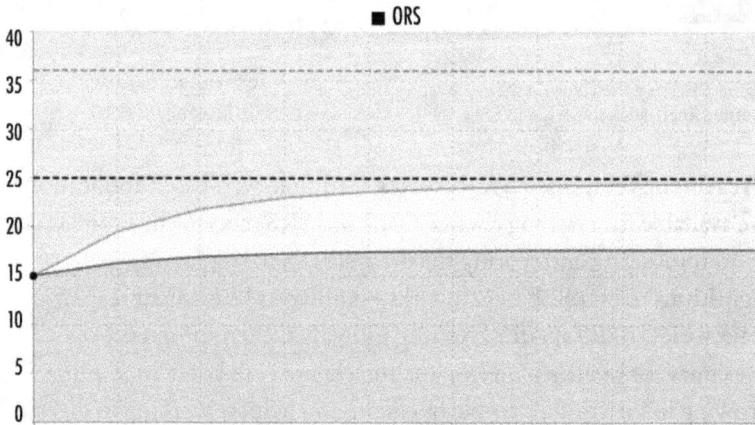

Figure 2.2: Treatment Response Trajectory for a Client with an Initial ORS Score of 15

The Session Rating Scale

The Session Rating Scale (SRS) is a brief, client-rated visual analog
measure of the helping relationship. Like the ORS, the SRS takes less
than a minute to administer and score. Items on the scale reflect the
classic definition of the therapeutic alliance first proposed by Bordin
(1979). The scale assesses four interacting elements, including the

quality of the relational bond, as well as the degree of agreement between the client and helper on the goals, methods, and overall approach of care. The SRS is designed for ages 13 and older, the CSRS (Child Session Rating Scale) for those between the ages 6-12, and the Young Child Session Rating Scale for ages 6 and younger. A version of the scale is also available for use in groups with adults (13+). Briefly, the Group Session Rating Scale (GSRS) assesses multiple relationships, including the one between members and group leader as well as members to each other. The versions of the SRS are available in many different languages, as well as a script for oral administration.

Cutoff Score on the SRS: The cutoff score on an alliance measure helps clinicians detect the possibility of difficulties in the therapeutic relationship (e.g., rupture, empathic failure, mismatch, disengagement). Scores below the cutoff are at increased risk for client drop out and negative or null outcome from treatment. The cutoff for the SRS is 36. Studies of different language versions conducted in different countries show fewer than 25% of adult clients score lower than 36 at any given session and, therefore, are considered cause for concern and discussion (Miller & Duncan, 2004; Andrade-Gonazalez et al. 2021; Anker et al. 2009; Cazauvieilh et al. 2022; Janse et al. 2014; Moggia et al. 2020). Clinical experience shows the scores of younger clients are both more variable and reactive than adults (e.g., wider variation from session to session and more extreme values). Until research identifies a specific cutoff for adolescents and children, the score of 36 should be used to alert clinicians to the need for discussing the quality of therapeutic relationship.

Success Probability Index (SPI): The SPI provides a prediction of the likelihood of success based on the pattern of SRS and ORS scores. Unlike the static TRTs, the SPI is dynamic, updating at each session. As such, the index is designed to prompt helpers to act as early as possible with clients who may be at risk for negative or null outcome. The data used to generate the SPI at any given session varies depending on what most accurately predicts success at the end of care (e.g., the average of scores, their slope, and change in scores since the prior visit or across sessions). As can be seen in the screenshot below, despite similar start scores, the different patterns of progress represented in the two graphs result in different predictions. Specifically, the first case is on track (a positive SPI [coded in green in the electronic systems]), while the one below (a negative SPI [coded in red]), is about 16.5% below the average successful client. More detailed information about understanding and integrating the SPI into care will be provided in Chapter 3.

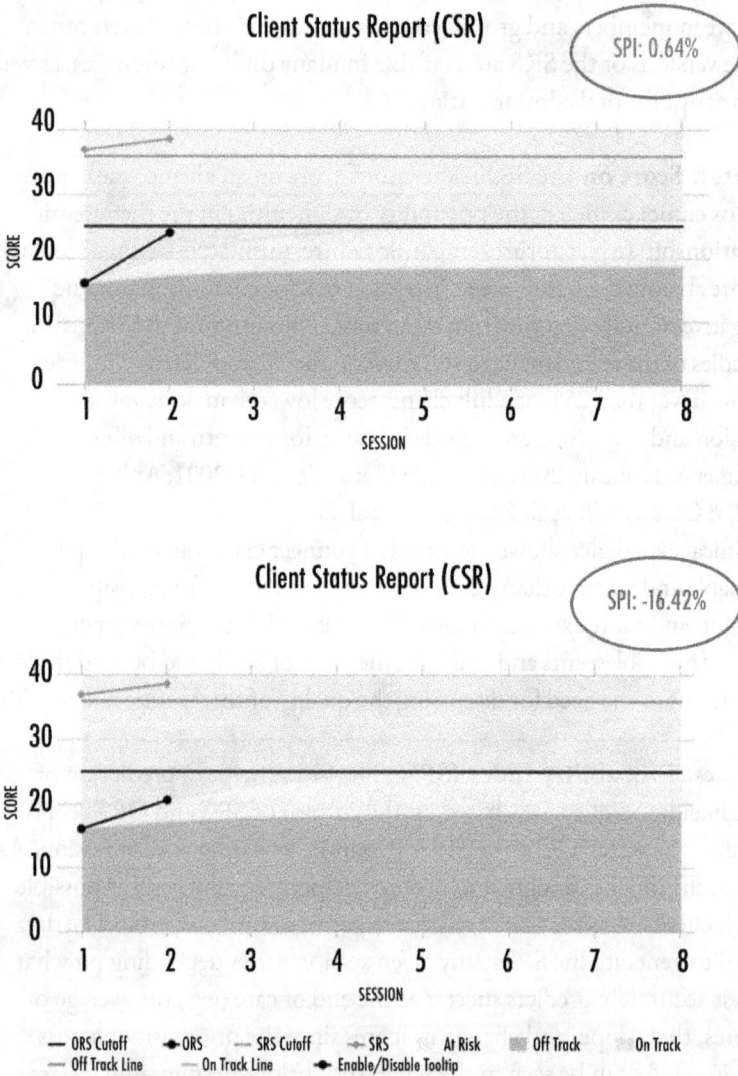

Client Status Report (CSR)

SPI: 0.64%

Client Status Report (CSR)

SPI: -16.42%

— ORS Cutoff   ◆ ORS   — SRS Cutoff   — SRS   At Risk   ▓ Off Track   On Track
— Off Track Line   — On Track Line   ● Enable/Disable Tooltip

Figure 2.3: The SPI in Two Different Cases

2. CREATING A "CULTURE OF FEEDBACK"

Administering the ORS and SRS is not sufficient for obtaining useful feedback from people in treatment. Research shows clinicians must create an atmosphere in which those receiving services feel free to rate their experience of the process and outcome: (1) without fear of retribution; and (2) with a hope of having an impact on the nature and quality of services delivered (Brattland et al. 2018). Beyond displaying an attitude of openness and receptivity, creating a "culture of feedback" demands clinicians spend time introducing the measures in a thorough, thoughtful, and engaging manner. Providing a rationale for seeking feedback on an ongoing basis is also critical, as is explaining how the information gathered will be used to guide treatment delivery (e.g., enabling practitioners to identify and repair problems in the therapeutic relationship and determining when progress is not being made so that services can be adjusted to better meet client needs).

Research on highly effective practitioners underscores the importance of establishing "a culture of feedback." The evidence shows practitioners who consistently elicit more negative feedback (e.g., lower SRS scores) during the initial phase of treatment achieve better outcomes overall (Miller et al. 2007; Owen et al. 2016; Chow, 2014; de Jong et al. 2012). Obtaining and responding to negative feedback, even about apparently trivial matters, appears to strengthen the helping relationship, thereby improving the chances for positive treatment results.

Experience using the measures shows clients are more likely to be engaged and provide feedback when:

- Time is taken to introduce and explain how to complete the measures
- A believable, succinct, and coherent explanation is provided for why the questions on the tools are important
- They are told tracking clients' experience of progress, and the quality of the relationship helps because: (1) early improvement is predictive of successful outcomes; and (2) clients' experience of the relationship impacts engagement which, in turn, is highly predictive of outcome

- They believe the helper will treat all feedback seriously and work to adjust services accordingly (e.g., the focus, intensity, type, location, or the provider of services)
- The helper is clear about both when and what steps will be taken in the absence of progress and when problems arise in the helping relationship.

The following introduction is an example of what might be said at an initial contact to facilitate the creation of a "culture of feedback." Look at the principles stated above, considering what adaptations might need to be made to fit your style and treatment context:

I work a little differently than some (helpers, social workers, counselors). I want to make sure that you get what you've come for, that you benefit from our work together and achieve the results you want. In order to do this, we'll be tracking your experience of progress from visit to visit using two simple tools, one at the beginning and the other, at the end. Here's what we know from research. People who feel engaged in care and experience improvement early on are more likely to end treatment feeling helped. Using these tools will help ensure we are on the right track from visit to visit.

Naturally, if what we do works, we can continue as long as you like. However, if it doesn't help—if the feedback you give indicates that the way we are working isn't a good fit or you're not making the progress you hoped for—it's important to know because that will give us the chance to make a change, to try something else. We could, for example, change what we are doing together. We could also add other resources. And finally, in some cases, we may decide it might be more helpful to refer you to another provider or agency. Does this make sense to you?

3. ADMINISTERING THE ORS

The ORS is administered at the beginning of each session and as early as possible. During the initial encounter, it is important to complete the measure prior to any formal assessment, intake, or treatment. The reason is that interactions with clients risk influencing their scores.

Completing the measure in the presence of the practitioner is also highly recommended, especially while the culture of feedback is being established. Experience shows the farther "removed" measurement is from the provider, the less likely they are to use client feedback to inform care. Certain circumstances do exist when having clients and allied health professionals complete the scale before the session facilitates both the planning and efficiency of treatment (see section 6). When clients are seen more intensively (e.g., several times a week or in residential and inpatient settings), the scale should be administered no more than once per week, preferably at the first clinical contact.

Outcome Rating Scale (ORS)

Name _____ Age (Yrs):____ Gender_____
Session # ____ Date: _____
Who is filling out this form? Please check one: Self_____ Other_____
If other, what is your relationship to this person? _____

Looking back over the last week including today, or since your last visit, help us understand how you have been feeling by rating how well you have been doing in the following areas of your life, where marks to the left represent low levels and marks to the right indicate high levels. *If you are filling out this form for another person, please fill out according to how you think he or she is doing.*

Individually
(Personal well-being)

I--I

Interpersonally
(Family, close relationships)

I--I

Socially
(Work, school, friendships)

I--I

Overall
(General sense of well-being)

I--I

International Center for Clinical Excellence

www.scottdmiller.com

© 2000, Scott D. Miller and Barry L. Duncan

Figure 2.4: The Outcome Rating Scale

As can be seen in Figure 2.4, the ORS contains four questions, each representing a different area of well-being: individual, interpersonal, social, and overall. On the paper and pencil versions of the scale, clients place a mark on each line representing their experience along a continuum from low levels of well-being (to the left) to high levels (on the right). A mouse or touch screen is used to answer the items in the computerized versions (see Figure 2.5).

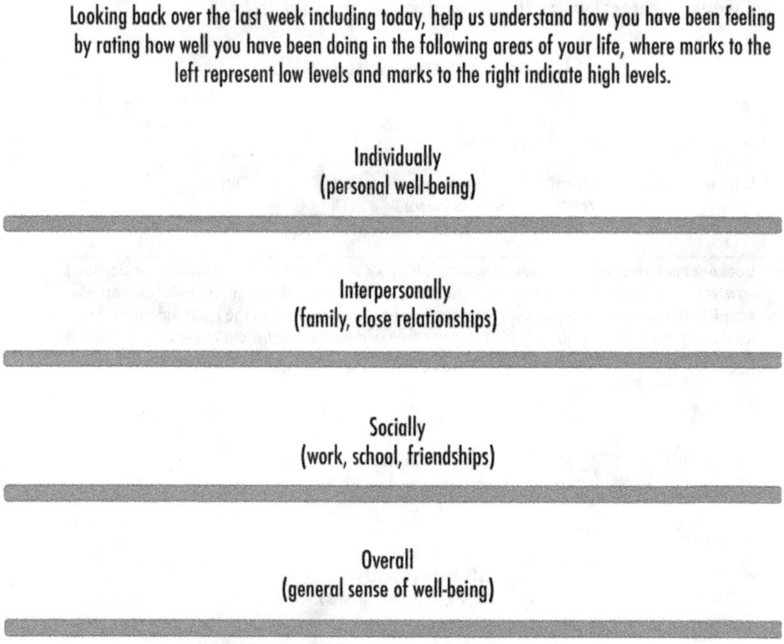

Looking back over the last week including today, help us understand how you have been feeling by rating how well you have been doing in the following areas of your life, where marks to the left represent low levels and marks to the right indicate high levels.

Individually
(personal well-being)

Interpersonally
(family, close relationships)

Socially
(work, school, friendships)

Overall
(general sense of well-being)

Figure 2.5: Sample Electronic version of the Adult ORS

As indicated in the instructions, clients are asked to think back over the preceding week (or since their last visit) before completing the measure. Encouraging clients to take a few moments to reflect on their experience ensures the resulting score represents their overall experience rather than the present moment. Experience shows some clients (e.g., children, adolescents, people in crisis, those with emotional or cognitive challenges) benefit from the practitioner facilitating a discussion about the time between visits prior to completing the scale, a strategy termed "process recall" (Bertolino & Miller, 2012). For example:

Today is Thursday, so if we look back over the week, what was going on at the end of last week, Friday? (allow the client to answer). *And how about the weekend? What did you do? Who did you spend time with?* (again, allow time to answer) *And Monday? And what about yesterday?* (and so on, giving the client a chance to refresh their memory before completing the ORS).

The following is one example of how to introduce the ORS. Once more, the specific language can be adjusted to fit your style and treatment context:

This is the first scale. It is called the ORS and it tells us how you are doing in your life. As you can see, it contains four questions. How are you doing? How are your relationships—family and loved ones? How are you doing socially—work and friendships? And finally, how is your life overall? We will complete this every time we meet to track progress and determine whether our work together is helping. As you can see, the instructions ask you to look back on this last week, including today, and rate how you have been feeling on each of the four items. Does this make sense to you? (If yes, then say, so, take a moment to reflect on the last week before filling it out).

When introducing the scale, care should be taken to avoid overexplaining the measure and defining the meaning of the individual items. Should a client ask for clarification, a detailed and validated script for answering questions accompanies the packet of measures downloaded at the time of licensing (https://tinyurl.com/5n8dn6kj). Guidance for addressing questions for each item is also found below:

Individually: "This refers to how you, as an individual, yourself, are doing, your personal functioning."

Interpersonally: "This is about how you are doing in your family and close relationships." (Note this item contains multiple, different relationships. As a result, some clients may express confusion about how to give a single score. In such instances, the client should be encouraged to score the item based on the relationship that is causing them the most distress).

Socially: "This refers to your life outside the home, in your community, with friends, work, school, church." (Note this item contains multiple, different social contexts and interactions. As a result, some clients may express confusion about how to give a single score. In such instances, the client should be encouraged to score the item based on the context or interaction that is causing them the most distress).

Overall: "This includes all of the above, plus any other parts of your life not included in the other three areas."

At the initial visit, it is better to take more time introducing the scale to minimize the risk that clients misunderstand its purpose or the instructions. The same process should be repeated at subsequent visits, albeit in an abbreviated fashion, to ensure clients recall why and how the ORS is used.

Scoring the ORS

With the computerized systems, scoring is automatic. As noted previously, scores from session to session are plotted on graphs containing the treatment response trajectories (TRT) and success probability index (SPI) thereby enabling practitioner and client to quickly assess progress (see Figures 2.2 and 2.3). When using or making paper copies of the ORS, care should be taken to ensure the lines representing the four different domains of well-being are 10 centimeters in length. To score, simply measure the distance in centimeters (to the nearest millimeter) between the left pole and the client's mark on each item. Add the four resulting numbers together to obtain the total score. The score, in turn, can be plotted on the paper graph provided in the packet of measures downloaded at the time of licensing (see Figure 2.1).

Understanding the initial ORS score: After administration, scoring, and graphing, attention turns to understanding, or making sense of, the client's score. In this regard, the helper engages in an open, transparent, collaborative, and matter-of-fact discussion about: (1) the client's score in relationship to the clinical cutoff; (2) the level of distress or severity indicated by the client's initial ORS score; and (3) the accuracy of the score according to the client.

The first step in interpreting the client's initial ORS score is determining where it falls in relationship to the clinical cutoff. For example, adult clients with scores 25 or above are more like people who are not in treatment and who are saying their life and sense of well-being are satisfactory (within the "non-clinical" range). By contrast, scores below 25 are typical for people who are in treatment or saying aspects of their life or well-being exist that they would like to change (within the "clinical range").

Consider the following example of an adult client who has a total ORS score of 15 at the first session (see Figure 2.2). The helper would first share the graph, noting the initial score and say:

> *Here's your score today, a 15. You can see from the graph that it's below this dashed line at 25. That line is called the clinical cutoff. The cutoff line is based on having given this measure to many people and finding that those whose scores fall below the line are more like people who are seeking treatment and feeling, "There are things in my life I would like to change, that are bothering me." People who score above the line are more like a broad range of people who are not in treatment and who are saying, overall, their life is fine. So, looking at your score, it indicates you're in the right place, that you are hoping for a change in your life. Does that make sense to you? Does this match your experience?*

In typical outpatient mental health settings, between 25 and 33% of clients will score *above* the clinical cutoff at intake (Miller et al. 2003). Being mandated into treatment is the most common reason for such high scores. Suggestions for using the ORS in a meaningful way with mandated clients will be covered in more detail in section 6 of this chapter. Having a specific problem (e.g., phobia, exam anxiety, relationship issue, vocational matter, etc.) is another reason why some clients score above the cutoff at the initial visit. In essence, the score indicates, despite being troubling, the problem does not affect the client's overall quality of life or functioning. The best practice in such cases is to help the client maintain their current level of well-being while using the least invasive and intensive methods needed to resolve the problem at hand. Given that high scorers are at a heightened risk for deterioration, clinicians are advised against expanding the focus of the clinical work via exploratory or depth-oriented techniques.

One more observation about interpreting initial ORS scores in relationship to the clinical cutoff. In addition to falling above and below, some clients' scores fall at or near the clinical cutoff. Experience indicates such clients generally fall into one of two groups: (1) those with many, and relatively longstanding, problems to which they have become accustomed; and (2) clients transitioning from a higher to a lower, less intensive form of care. Consider the graph in Figure 2.6, displaying the TRTs for a client with a first session score at the clinical cutoff. As can be seen, the slope of topmost line (typically in green in the electronic systems and representing progress consistent with being on track for a positive outcome) increases at a relatively slow rate. It is not unusual for people with such scores to appear hesitant or ambivalent about making changes in their lives as the risk of deterioration (the lowest curved line represented in red line in the computerized systems) is the same as the chance of improvement. As such clients are not likely to change rapidly, or maintain any dramatic improvements, practitioners are advised to consider adjusting the intensity of services downward and spreading contact out over a longer period of time.

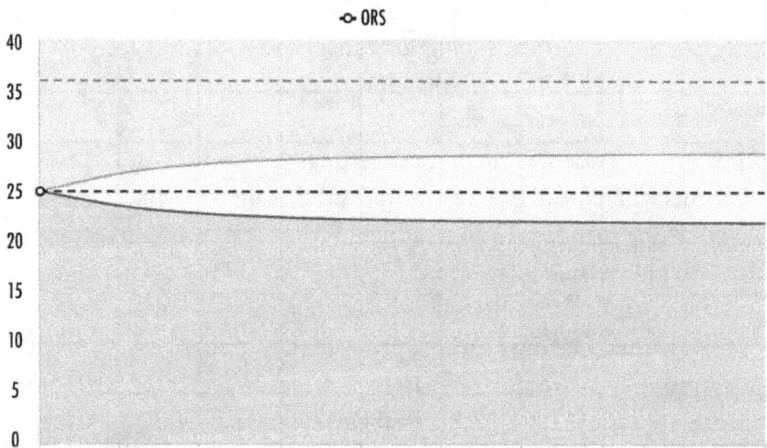

Figure 2.6: Treatment response trajectory with an initial ORS score of 25

The second step in understanding the initial ORS score is assessing the client's level of distress, functioning, or well-being. In general, lower scores are indicative of higher levels of distress. Using real world data gathered electronically by the authorized computer systems, the average, cross-cultural first session ORS score of adults seen in outpatient settings scoring in the clinical range (e.g., 25 or lower) falls between 15 and 16. The average, cross-cultural first session ORS score of adolescents seen in outpatient settings falling in the clinical range (e.g., 28 or lower) is 20, and for children (e.g., 32 or lower), 23.5. Across all age groups, scores of 12 or lower are rare and should be explored as they may be indicative of crisis and, in some instances, a risk of harm to self or others.

With regard to accuracy, it should be noted that, although rare, clients occasionally express surprise or disagreement with their resulting ORS score. Any large discrepancy should be explored with the client. Given that engagement in the process is essential for obtaining meaningful feedback, if found not to match their experience, completing the measure a second time is acceptable.

4. ADMINISTERING THE SRS

The SRS is administered by the helper near the end of each session, leaving a few minutes for reflection and discussion. Since the entire point of the scale is to identify and address any problems in the helping relationship at the "time of service," having an assistant or administrative personnel administer the SRS after the visit is not recommended. Similar to the ORS, the SRS should be completed no more than once a week. In more intensive treatment settings (e.g., residential, inpatient), the best practice is administering the measure at the end of the week, with the ratings reflecting the client's experience of all interactions and services (see section 6).

Session Rating Scale (SRS V.3.0)

Name _____ Age (Yrs):____
ID# _____ Gender:_____
Session # ____ Date: _____

Please rate today's session by placing a mark on the line nearest to the description that best fits your experience.

Relationship

I did not feel heard, understood, and respected.

I--I

I felt heard, understood, and respected.

Goals and Topics

We did *not* work on or talk about what I wanted to work on and talk about.

I--I

We worked on and talked about what I wanted to work on and talk about.

Approach or Method

The therapist's approach is not a good fit for me.

I--I

The therapist's approach is a good fit for me.

Overall

There was something missing in the session today.

I--I

Overall, today's session was right for me.

International Center for Clinical Excellence

www.scottdmiller.com

© 2002, Scott D. Miller, Barry L. Duncan, & Lynn Johnson

Figure 2.7: Session Rating Scale (Adult)

As can be seen in Figure 2.7, the SRS contains four questions, each representing an element of the helping relationship: emotional bond, agreement on goals, agreement on approach and method, and overall. On the paper and pencil versions, clients place a hash mark or "x" on each line representing their experience along a continuum from negative (to the left) to positive (on the right). A mouse or touch screen is used to answer the items in the computerized versions (see Figure 2.8).

Please rate today's session by placing a mark on the line nearest to the description that best fits your experience.

Relationship

| I did not feel heard, understood and respected. | | I felt heard, understood and respected. |

Goals and Topics

| We did not work on or talk about what I wanted to work on and talk about. | | We worked on and talked about what I wanted to work on and talk about. |

Approach or Method

| The therapist's approach is not a good fit for me. | | The therapist's approach is a good fit for me. |

Overall

| There was something missing in the session today. | | Overall, today's session was right for me. |

Figure 2.8: Sample electronic version of the Adult SRS

As noted previously, a number of studies show lower initial scores that improve over time are associated with better outcomes than either consistently high scores or scores that decline (Brattland et al. 2019; Goldberg et al. 2020; Owen et al. 2016; Miller et al. 2007). Given these results, successful helpers work purposefully to create an atmosphere where negative feedback is not only tolerated but valued as an important part of an effective working relationship.

The following is one example of how to introduce the SRS. Of course, the wording should be adjusted to fit your style and context:

> Remember, at the beginning of the session, I told you I'd be asking for feedback about your experience of the time we've just spent together. A great deal of research shows that you feeling understood, able to talk about and work on what you want, in a way that fits for you, is critical to success. For this reason, at the end of each time we meet, I will ask you four questions. I want you to know, I'm not looking for "high marks." The point is to get your input about even the smallest things—trivial or otherwise—that would make this experience more useful. Like a tailor asking whether the garment fits, I won't take it personally. Actually, I'll be thankful you took the time to let me know. Does this make sense?

It is not uncommon for practitioners to express concern about the ability of some clients to provide critical feedback. Some of the most frequent reasons given are: (1) cultural barriers, traditions, history regarding interactions with authority figures; (2) the power imbalance inherent in the helping relationship; and (3) client traits (e.g., acquiescent, dependent, manipulative, dishonest). Several factors are important to keep in mind when administering and interpreting the SRS. First, most people score high on scales measuring similar constructs. On the SRS, for example, 75% of people score above the cutoff (36) at any given session. Second, research shows practitioners have a far greater impact on determining whether negative feedback is shared than any reasons noted above (Baldwin et al. 2007). Indeed, the most effective helpers receive and are more receptive to critical feedback, especially early in care (Miller et al. 2007; Slone & Owen, 2015). It is critical, therefore, that helpers learn to administer the SRS in a way that facilitates an open and transparent discussion of the strengths and weaknesses of the relationship.

Scoring the SRS

Scoring of the SRS is automatic when one of the authorized computerized systems is employed. Feedback is also provided comparing the score to the cutoff for the measure and identifying when clients are at increased risk for drop out or a negative or null outcome (in the electronic systems a red signal dot appears next to SRS).

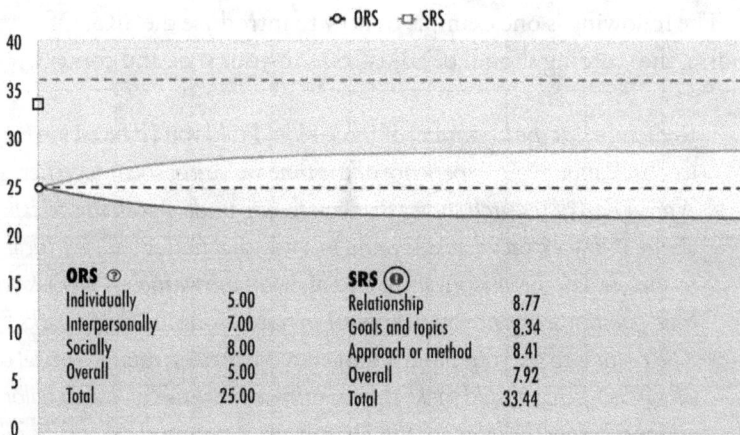

Figure 2.9: Client first session SRS score and system feedback indicating problems in the helping relationship

When using or making paper copies of the SRS, care should be taken to ensure the lines representing the four different elements of the relationship are 10 centimeters in length. To score, simply measure the distance in centimeters (to the nearest millimeter) between the left pole and the client's mark for each item. Add the four resulting numbers together to obtain the total score. The score, in turn, can be plotted on the paper graph provided in the packet of measures downloaded at the time of licensing. As can be seen in Figure 2.10, the dotted line at 36 identifies the cutoff on the scale.

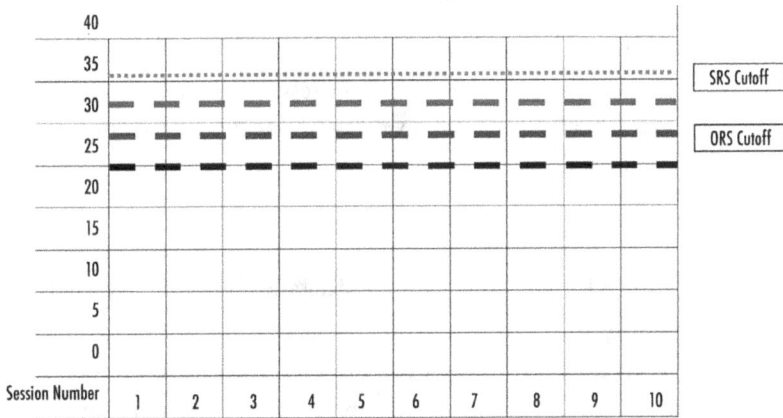

Figure 2.10: Paper and pencil graph for the ORS and SRS including the cutoff on the SRS (red/top line)

Understanding the SRS Score: As mentioned previously, 75% of adult clients will score above the SRS cutoff at any given session. It is important to note such scores are not necessarily indicative of a strong helping relationship. Clients score above the cutoff for a number of reasons, including not feeling safe enough to provide negative feedback. Recall, research shows improving SRS scores are associated with better outcomes. Therefore, should a provider's or agency's average intake SRS score fall above the cutoff, or a preponderance of clients give perfect scores (e.g., 40), clinicians should review how the scale is being introduced, paying particular attention to creating a culture of feedback.

Prior to ending each session, an invitation to reflect on the client's experience should be offered whenever the total score:

- Falls at or below 36.

- Declines a single-point or more compared to the previous session (Miller et al. 2007).

Research and clinical experience document five principles that increase the likelihood of clients providing meaningful, negative, and actionable feedback in response to helper inquiries (Miller et al. 2020). Questions are more likely to be successful when they are descriptive rather than evaluative in nature, are based on observations rather than inferences, ask for specifics instead of general reflections, focus on quantities instead of qualities, and are task rather than person oriented. As examples, consider the difference between the following questions, each representing one of the five principles:

- "What was good about today's session?" (evaluative) versus "Was there a particular time in the session when the score was (higher/lower)? What were we doing during that time?" (descriptive)

- "You seemed less engaged during the visit today" (inference) versus "You gave very short answers when we were speaking about (X). Can you help me understand this?" (observation)

- "How was the session today?" (general) versus "What would have to be different to move from a score of 5 in terms of your feeling heard, understood, and respected, to a 6?" (specific)

- "Can you tell me more about how your feelings of low self-esteem might be affecting your scores?" (inference and quality) versus "Several times during the visit you were on the verge of saying something and stopped yourself. I was wondering if there was something you wanted to say, but didn't?" (quantity)

- "What can I do different to improve the session for you?" (person-focused and evaluative) versus "What would be different next time if your score on the SRS was just one point higher?" (task and specific)

As an example of putting these principles into practice when addressing a total score falling below the cutoff, the helper could say:

Thanks for taking the time to complete the SRS. On this measure, we compare your score to the dotted line at 36. That line is called the cutoff. People who score above that number typically feel the session went well and would like to continue working in a similar way in the future. As you can see, your score is below that line. People who score this way often have some specific ideas or suggestions for small changes that could be made in the therapy. What specifically came to mind about the session as you answered each of the questions?

When the total score has decreased a single point compared to the prior visit, the helper could say:

Thanks for completing the scale. Recall, this form is about how you experienced the session. As you can see, last week (using the graph to display the results), *your marks totaled* (X). *This week, the total is* (X – 1). *While that may seem small, research has actually shown that a decrease of a single point can be important, with some peoples' ORS scores declining in the weeks following and sometimes an increased risk of people not wanting to return. Any thoughts or ideas about what might have been different today? Can you think of anything we've not given enough attention to today that could be challenging in the weeks ahead?*

Finally, one item on the SRS being scored lower relative to the others is another opportunity for reflection and exploration. The helper could look for more specific information by asking:

I notice that (relationship, goals and topics, approach and method, and overall) *is a bit lower than* (the others). *What specifically were you thinking about that resulted in your marking this item lower than* (the others)?

Of course, not all requests for feedback will result in detailed, meaningful information for improving care. The purpose of the conversation is to identify and address any barriers to the client returning for their next visit, including the client's experience of the helper and the session just completed (e.g., simple misunderstandings, goals or topics to be addressed at the next session, the method or approach). As a general rule, any inquiries should be limited to two or three follow-up questions and last no more than a few minutes. Should a serious problem in the relationship be identified that requires more time to address, a call should be scheduled as soon as possible following the session. Occasionally, a low SRS score is best resolved by referral to another provider or agency. Experience shows such occurrences typically happen early in care (e.g., first three visits) and follow a client's expression of serious doubt regarding their ability to relate to, communicate with, or be helped by the helper (see case example 2.3).

As already noted, the majority of clients will score at or above 36 at any given session. In such instances, helpers should:

- Thank the client for completing the measure
- Be open to the possibility of the client providing feedback
- Encourage the client to share (e.g., call, email, or recall and share at the next session) any feedback that might occur to them when they reflect on the session on following the visit

In sum, the SRS helps clinicians identify problems in the working relationship (e.g., misunderstandings, disagreement about goals and discussion topics, and approach and method) early in care, thereby preventing client dropout or deterioration.

CASE EXAMPLE 2.1: USING THE SRS TO ADDRESS PROBLEMS IN THE THERAPEUTIC RELATIONSHIP

Sarah sought counseling to decide whether or not she was going to stay in her marriage. At the first session, she mentioned having been temporarily separated from her parents and siblings as a teen while her parents divorced. During that time, she stayed with an uncle and aunt. In a later session, the helper referred back to the separation from her family, spending about half of the hour exploring whether this event might be impacting her current situation. In response, Sarah maintained she had not felt abandoned or harmed by the experience and had even come to value her siblings and parents more as a result. At the end of the visit, the helper administered the SRS. Turns out, Sarah's score was lower than in previous visits (e.g., 34.5 versus 38 or higher), with most of the loss of points resulting from a change on the "relationship" item (e.g., 8 versus 9.8).

The helper engaged Sarah in a discussion about the decline in the total score, pointing specifically to the "relationship" item. After a brief pause, Sarah mentioned the lengthy questioning about the time she had spent away from her parents and siblings. When asked for more details, she went on to explain how the process had made her feel less understood than in prior visits. To her, it seemed the helper assumed the separation was, and even perhaps should have been, unpleasant and traumatic when, in her experience, it was neither. Sarah requested future visits focus more on the present than the past.

On hearing Sarah's feedback, the helper apologized for having persisted with a line of questioning Sarah experienced as irrelevant to her presenting concern and promised future sessions would focus on what she wanted to address. Permission was sought to check in with Sarah if the helper felt the past was having an impact on present circumstances. Sarah agreed. Two more sessions followed during which time the conversation focused on whether to stay in or leave her marriage. Contact was ended by mutual agreement once the decision was made. The SRS scores at both visits were in the 38 to 39 range.

CASE EXAMPLE 2.2: USING THE SRS TO REPAIR PROBLEMS IN THE HELPING RELATIONSHIP

Robert was referred by the courts for a substance abuse evaluation following his arrest for driving while intoxicated. As the ORS was being introduced at the outset of the first session, he sat quietly with a flat, unresponsive facial expression. Uncertain whether Robert understood the purpose of the measure, the helper reacted by reducing her rate of speech, simplifying the words being used, and providing several examples for how to complete the scale.

From the helper's point of view, the session that followed the administration of the scale was unremarkable. Robert was an active participant throughout. At the conclusion of the visit, she introduced the SRS and began explaining why it was being administered and how to complete the scale. Throughout the introduction, Robert once again sat expressionless, prompting the helper to slow down and explain in greater detail.

Robert completed the SRS very quickly and handed the tablet back to the helper, both eyebrows now raised. Looking at the screen, the helper immediately saw the total score fell well below the cutoff, with the "relationship," "approach and methods," and "overall" items accounting for the largest loss of points (see Figure 2.11). In the box summarizing the client's responses to the individual items, a red dot (see circle in graph) prompted the helper to open a discussion about the scores.

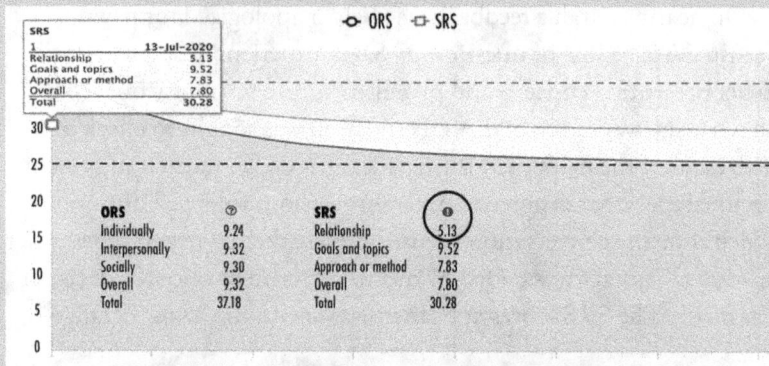

Figure 2.11: Robert's ORS and SRS scores

Robert responded to the inquiry with a question, "I'm just wondering if you think I'm stupid or something?" Completely taken by surprise, the helper simply sat and stared. In truth, no such thought had ever crossed her mind. A few seconds followed, after which the helper regained her composure and asked for clarification. Robert pointed directly to the slow, lengthy, detailed explanations and examples given while introducing the scales, leading him to feel the helper thought him incapable of understanding simple instructions or worse, that he was cognitively compromised. The helper instantly responded, first thanking Robert for the feedback he provided and then acknowledging how her behavior could result in the feelings he described. Realizing her last session with an 8-year-old boy had inadvertently influenced her behavior in the visit with Robert, she apologized, promised to be more mindful, and encouraged him to continue to provide feedback in the future.

CASE EXAMPLE 2.3: IDENTIFYING A "BAD MATCH" WITH THE SRS

Silvia and Ted presented for couple's therapy to address longstanding issues related to trust. Over the years, Silvia had caught Ted in "many lies"— some serious (e.g., finances, job loss), others trivial (e.g., where he was at a particular time). Although she had asked many times, until recently, Ted had refused to seek professional help. He reluctantly agreed to attend sessions with Silvia when a close, personal friend of his highly recommended the present helper.

From the helper's point of view, although Ted did not initiate dialogue on his own, the first meeting went smoothly. He answered all questions respectfully and did not dispute Silvia's accounting of his behavior. As can be seen in Figure 2.12, both partners scored significantly below the clinical cutoff on the ORS. They explained their scores as having reached a "crisis point" in their relationship following an argument in which Silvia threatened to divorce Ted after catching him in another lie.

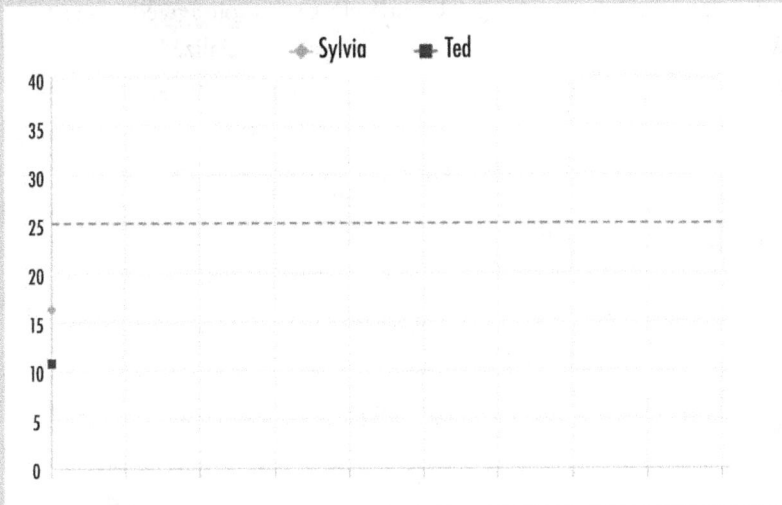

Figure 2.12: ORS scores of Silvia and Ted at first session

Given the seemingly positive and open exchange, the helper was surprised by Ted's score on the SRS at the end of the session (see Figure 2.13). In fact, it was the lowest score they had ever received from a client. Clearly, Ted was very unhappy about something. When asked for clarification, he expressed strong reservations about being able to confide in a practitioner who was so much younger than him. "You're nice enough, but look like you're fresh out of school," he said, "how much experience can you have? Have you even ever had a relationship?" Before the helper could reply, Silvia jumped in, defending the helper and attacking Ted. "It's always something with you," she stated emphatically, "like always, you're just deflecting from the issues."

The helper interrupted the two as they began to quarrel. "Can I just stop you two for a moment?" Looking at Silvia, "I know you are serious in wanting to address the impact of Ted's behavior on your relationship. I know that's why you are here, and I haven't heard Ted dispute or deny these problems." Directing attention to Ted, "I'm wondering how we will get there, if you are feeling like you can't trust me, that I don't have the experience or know-how to work successfully with people who've been together for so many years?"

When Ted agreed, the helper began exploring the qualities a counselor would need to have for Ted to feel confident in their abilities. As the conversation continued, Silvia's concern that Ted would not find any helper acceptable softened. Ultimately, the couple agreed to meet with an older, more experienced colleague with specialized training in creating secure and connected relationships.

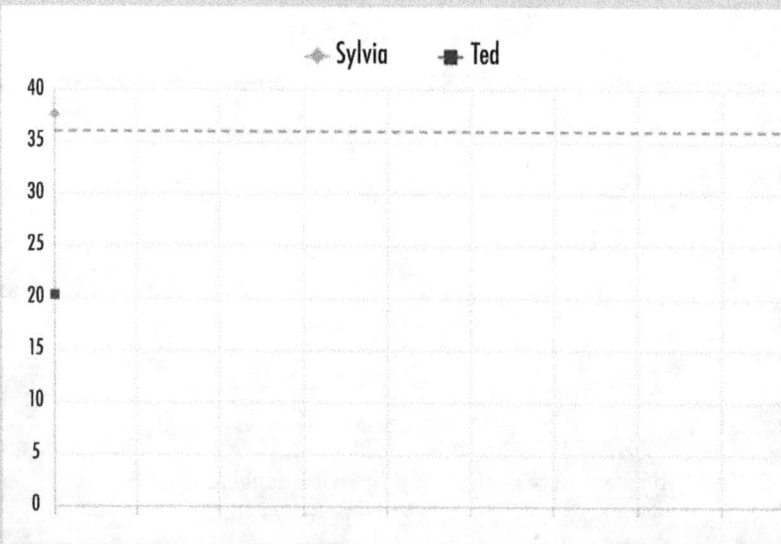

Figure 2.13 SRS scores of Silvia and Ted at first session

5. THE FIT SERVICE DELIVERY AGREEMENT AND PROGRESS NOTE

The ORS and SRS, respective cutoff scores, TRTs and SPI provide helpers with real-time feedback from clients regarding their experience of the process and outcome of care. Two additional tools ensure such feedback is integrated into planning and clinical decision making over the entire course of treatment: the FIT Service Delivery Agreement and the FIT Progress Note.

FIT Service Delivery Agreement (SDA)

The FIT SDA is designed to be completed in an open and transparent manner together with the recipient of care at the initial visit. Unlike traditional treatment plans, the FIT SDA uses the language and exact verbal utterances of the client instead of professional terminology, interpretations, or objectives. Giving the client a copy and placing the original in the official record makes it possible to consult and update throughout the course of care. In doing so, the tool ensures treatment is continuously organized around and responsive to the client's interests, motivations, goals, and outcome (see Figure 2.14 [also Appendix A]). Unlike the ORS and SRS, the FIT SDA is not copyrighted. As such, clinicians and agencies are free to integrate the elements into their existing healthcare documentation.

WITH "WHOM?"
Client preferences, values, identity, culture/worldview

THE "WHAT?"
Goals, meaning and purpose

THE "HOW?"
Means or methods

BY "WHOM?"
Client view of the bond and role of the helper

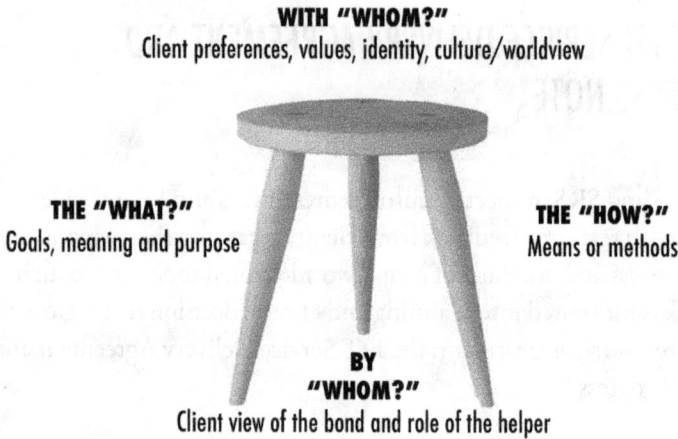

Name:	
Date:	
Client's stated reasons or motivation for seeking services:	
Agreed upon goals, meaning or purpose for services:	
Agreed upon means and methods (including type, frequency, provider):	
Feedback informed process explained (routine outcome and alliance measurement): Yes No	
Clinician signature	Client signature

Figure 2.14: The FIT Service Delivery Agreement

As an example of the SDA in practice, consider a man who presents for treatment to a substance abuse clinic. When asked why he has sought service at that time, he readily reports drinking is "an issue," but maintains his primary reason for seeking help is to "prevent his wife from ending their marriage." While traditional treatment planning might place drinking at the center of services, the FIT SDA would give primacy to helping the client "keep his wife from leaving." The goals and methods employed would, in turn, be framed around helping him achieve that specific objective. For example, in identifying the man's goals, the helper might ask, "What do you understand your wife would like to see change in order to be willing to stay?" Should he respond, he would need to decrease his drinking, that exact verbiage would be entered into the box labelled, "agreed upon goals, meaning or purpose for services." Methods might include, "Weekly individual sessions focused on harm reduction and controlled drinking strategies" or "abstinence and attendance at Alcoholics Anonymous meetings." Alternately, if the man responded his wife would want him "to stay up later in the evening so they could have more time to talk and be together after work," this would be considered an equally valid approach and written in the appropriate section of the FIT SDA. Methods, in such a case, might include, "cutting back on drinking during the evenings" or "setting aside time when he is committed to being fully present" with his wife. As is hopefully clear, the point of FIT SDA is to ensure care is centered on the client's interests and motivations, and therefore, engages them.

Please note two additional items on the tool. The first is a checkbox the helper must tick indicating they have explained how formal client feedback will be used to guide and inform service delivery. The second is signature lines for both the client and helper. The purpose of both is to guarantee the client is an informed and active partner in both the planning and execution of care.

The FIT Progress Note (FIT PN)

Take a moment to review the FIT PN in Figure 2.15 (also Appendix B). In contrast to traditional formats for documenting treatment details of individual clients (e.g., S.O. A. P. or D. A.R.T.), the FIT PN is organized around the client's experience of the process and outcome of care. The structure prompts the clinician to integrate the feedback-informed process (e.g., administering the ORS and SRS, responding to the feedback the client provides via the measures, and altering the course of care when indicated) into the help they are providing. As with the FIT SDA, the FIT PN is designed to be completed in an open, transparent, and collaborative manner together with the recipient of care at the time the service is delivered.

With regard to the specific elements on the FIT PN, the helper indicates whether the ORS (and/or collateral score on the measure [see section 6]) is administered at each visit and the nature of any change that has taken place between administrations. For example, if scores have gone up since the prior measurement, the provider would circle the arrow pointing up and then detail the nature of the improvement as well as how the progress was processed during the visit. The key is documenting the reason for the results in concrete and specific terms, using the client's language. Moving down the page, the "between-session plan" box is the place to summarize what the provider and client have agreed to do to reinforce progress, maintain gains, or address deterioration. The FIT PN concludes with the SRS score, indicating whether it falls above or below cutoff, and is increasing, decreasing, or unchanged. A place is available to record any feedback derived from the discussion of the measure. As with the FIT SDA, the progress note is signed by both client and helper.

Feedback Informed Progress Note

Name:	Date:
ORS Administered: Yes No	Outcome:
Collateral Score: Yes No	
Outcome addressed in session by:	
Between session plan (eg. maintain & consolidate gains/address deterioration/revise approach):	
SRS Administered: Yes No	Score is: Above 36 Below 36
	Score is: Increasing Same Decreasing
SRS scores addressed directly before the end of the session: Yes No	
Client feedback (if any):	
Clinician signature	Client signature

Figure 2.15: FIT Progress Note

6. FIT WITH CHILDREN, FAMILIES AND COUPLES, CLIENTS SCORING AT OR ABOVE THE CLINICAL CUT OFF (E.G., MANDATED, INVOLUNTARY), IN GROUPS, RESIDENTIAL, AND INPATIENT SETTINGS, AND WHEN DELIVERING SERVICES ONLINE

Up to this point, the use of FIT has primarily been described in the context of services delivered to adults voluntarily seeking individual outpatient treatment. Since first being developed, use of the measures has been extended to families, children, couples, people who are mandated into care or being treated in residential or rehabilitation settings, groups as well as services delivered online (Maeschalck et al. 2019; Prescott et al. 2017; Bargmann, 2017). Several developments facilitate the successful application of FIT in such contexts and service settings, including age and context-specific measures, use of collateral scores, guidelines regarding the timing and frequency of measurement, and use of computerized administration and scoring systems.

While considering each of the specific recommendations that follow, it is important to remember the purpose of routinely seeking feedback remains the same, "To ensure consumers have both 'choice and voice' in the services they receive" (p. 73, Duncan et al. 2006). For this reason, whether a service involves one or many participants (e.g., couples, groups, families), is conducted in an outpatient or inpatient setting, involves one or more helpers, with clients who come voluntarily or involuntarily, the fundamentals of FIT practice described previously apply. Feedback regarding each client's experience of the process and progress of care must be solicited, discussed, and used to inform and guide service delivery (Gleave et al. 2017; Obbekær et al. 2017; Robinson, 2017; Vinther & Davidsen, 2016). The case example below illustrates a common challenge in working with couples and families associated with poorer outcomes and higher dropout rates. Known as a "split alliance," it occurs when participants' experiences of the helping relationship differ. In such instances, helpers must work to find common ground between the participants, connecting with each individual without alienating others, and actively attending to anyone with a low alliance score (Bargmann & Robinson, 2012; Bartle-Haring et al. 2012; Friedlander et al. 2011; Glebova & Woolley, 2019).

CASE EXAMPLE 2.4: USING FIT IN COUPLES WORK

Linda and Stefan presented for couple's therapy to address "intimacy issues." Following the birth of their second child, Linda suffered a lengthy period of postpartum depression. During that time, the two grew apart both emotionally and physically. Although they had tried on their own, every attempt to resolve the difficulties had failed, often ending up in heated arguments magnifying the distance between them.

At the outset of the first visit, the helper administered the ORS. Linda scored 14, Stefan 21 (see Figure 2.16). As both fell below the cutoff, the helper began by acknowledging both were experiencing distress. An open question followed about what they hoped would change as a result of entering treatment. Stefan nodded as Linda described their lack of closeness and intimacy. She characterized their sex life as "non-existent," explaining how her depression, and the stress of having two small children at home, made intercourse impossible. When asked what she was looking for from Stefan, she sighed, immediately dismissing the possibility of him changing, "You know, he's a 'typical man.' If we hold hands or he rubs my back, he expects it to lead to sex." For his part, Stefan listened, occasionally expressing disagreement with Linda's perspective. "I miss being close," he offered at one point, a comment Linda replied to saying, "Yeah, but like all men, your kind of 'closeness' is just about getting me into bed." Stefan grew more and more quiet as the visit continued.

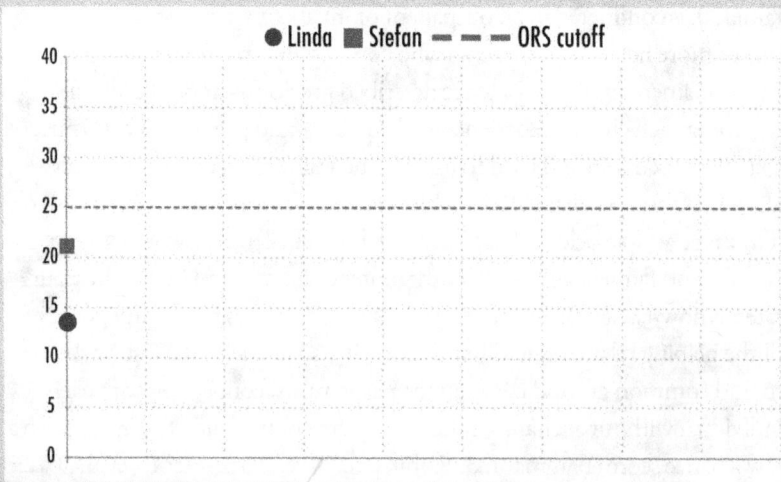

Figure 2.16: Combined ORS Graph of Linda and Stefan

At the conclusion of the session, Linda and Stefan completed the SRS. As can be seen in Figure 2.17, their scores diverged significantly, with Stefan's falling far below the cutoff. When asked about her score, Linda expressed satisfaction with the visit, specifically having been able to talk about their issues without arguing. When the helper expressed concern about Stefan's experience, he replied, "I agree, I'm glad we've been able to talk without fighting."

Sensing Stefan was holding back, the helper pointed to his SRS score, tentatively asking, "Of course, I'm glad to hear that, but your score suggests there might be something in our work here today that, if changed, would make the experience better for you?" After a short pause, Stefan shared, "Well, I know my wife has certain ideas about men and sex, including that we all just want to satisfy our physical needs, but … that's not me. I'm not some kind of he-monster driven by primitive urges, only caring about getting my 'rocks off.'" With little prodding, he added, being physical—touching, holding hands, sitting close, kissing, and intercourse—was a form of deep connection, times he truly felt loved. With these words, Linda's tone softened. Turning to Stefan, "I think I've forgotten that … I've lost touch with you, seeing that you love me and that you need and deserve to be loved back." Linda and Stefan agreed to return for a second session focused on reconnecting with one another. As Stefan stood to leave, he said, "I actually don't think I would have agreed to come back again had we not talked about this—I would have left here feeling that neither of you understood how I felt. Now, I'm looking forward to next time."

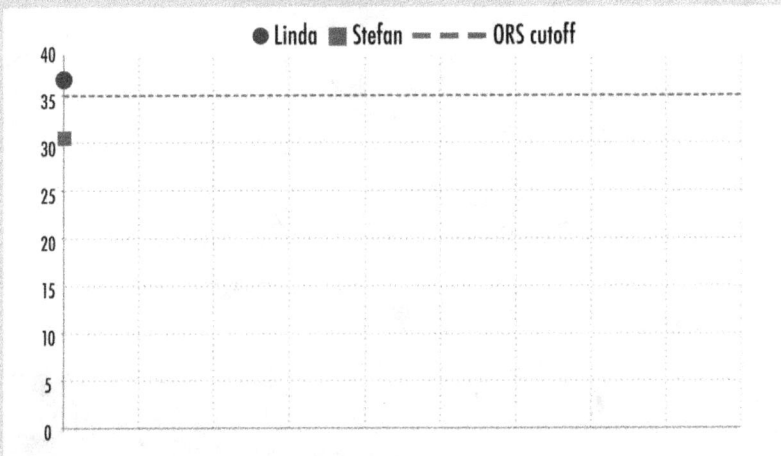

Figure 2.17: Combined SRS Graph for Linda and Stefan

Age-specific measures

As mentioned previously, versions of the ORS and SRS are available for use with adults, adolescents, and children. The content of the ORS and SRS falls at the 7th grade reading level (ages 13 and up) and is appropriate for adults and adolescents 13 years of age and older (see Figures 2.4 and 2.7, respectively). The CORS and CSRS are designed for children ages 7 to 12 (see Figures 2.18 and 2.19). The content of these scales falls at the 2nd grade reading level (ages 7 and higher).

Child Outcome Rating Scale (CORS)

Name _____Age (Yrs):____
Gender:_____
Session # ____ Date: _____
Who is filling out this form? Please check one: Child_____ Caretaker_____
 If caretaker, what is your relationship to this child? _____

How are you doing? How are things going in your life? Please make a mark on the scale to let us know. The closer to the smiley face, the better things are. The closer to the frowny face, things are not so good. *If you are a caretaker filling out this form, please fill out according to how you think the child is doing.*

Me
(How am I doing?)

I---I

Family
(How are things in my family?)

I---I

School
(How am I doing at school?)

I---I

Everything
(How is everything going?)

I---I

International Center for Clinical Excellence

www.scottdmiller.com

© 2003, Barry L. Duncan, Scott D. Miller, & Jacqueline A. Sparks

Figure 2.18: Child Outcome Rating Scale

Child Session Rating Scale (CSRS)

Name _____ Age (Yrs):____
Gender:_____
Session # ____ Date: _____

How was our time together today? Please put a mark on the lines below to let us know how you feel.

Listening

did not always
listen to me.

I--I

listened to me.

How Important

What we did and
talked about was not
really that important
to me.

I--I

What we did and
talked about were
important to me.

What We Did

I did not like
what we did
today.

I--I

I liked what
we did
today.

Overall

I wish we could do
something different.

I--I

I hope we do the
same kind of
things next time.

International Center for Clinical Excellence

www.scottdmiller.com

© 2003, Barry L. Duncan, Scott D. Miller, Jacqueline A. Sparks

Figure 2.19: Child Session Rating Scale

The YCORS and YCSRS are pictographic versions of the outcome and alliance measures and are appropriate for preliterate children ages 6 and younger (see Figures 2.20 and 2.21). Unlike the other versions, these two measures are not scorable. Their purpose is to support having a structured conversation with younger children regarding their well-being and experience of the session.

Young Child Outcome Rating Scale (YCORS)

Name _____ Age (Yrs):____
Gender:_____
Session # ____ Date: _____

Choose one of the faces that shows how things are going for you. Or, you can draw one below that is just right for you.

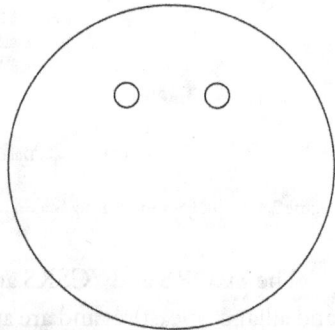

International Center for Clinical Excellence

www.scottdmiller.com

© 2003, Barry L. Duncan, Scott D. Miller, Andy Huggins, and Jacqueline A. Sparks

Figure 2.20: Young Child Outcome Rating Scale

Young Child Session Rating Scale (YCSRS)

Name _____ Age (Yrs):____
Gender:_____
Session # ____ Date: _____

Choose one of the faces that shows how it was for you to be here today. Or, you can draw one below that is just right for you.

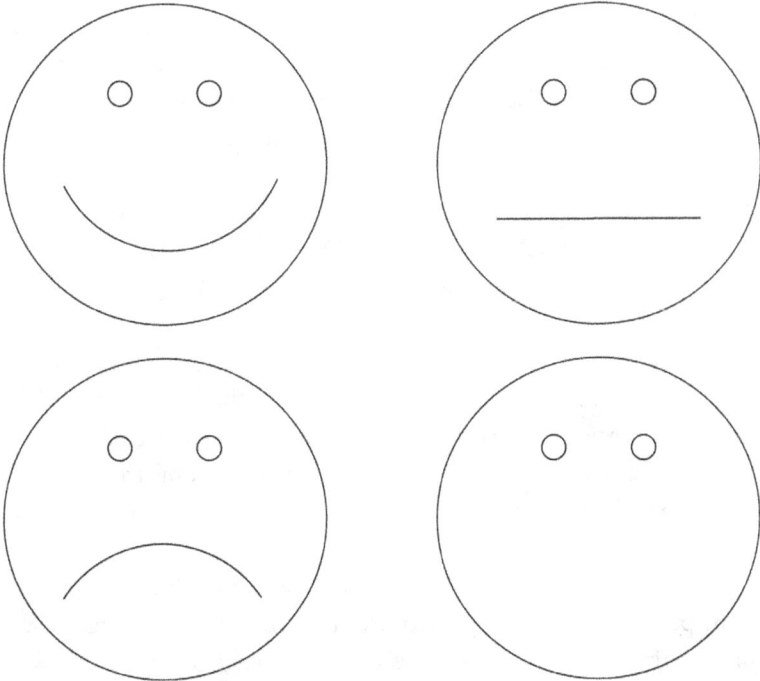

International Center for Clinical Excellence

www.scottdmiller.com
© 2003, Barry L. Duncan, Scott D. Miller, Andy Huggins, & Jacqueline Sparks

Figure 2.21: Young Child Session Rating Scale

In most instances, the actual age of the client is the most reliable guide for choosing the version of the measures to be used. However, in certain situations, using a version from a different age group may increase the likelihood of eliciting meaningful feedback.

For example, a young child (e.g., age 6 or younger) seen in the context of family therapy may want to complete the same version of the tools as their older siblings. Experience shows simply having someone read the items out loud often makes it possible for the child to complete the CORS and CSRS. Alternately, an adult who struggles with the concepts or words on the ORS and SRS, may find the simpler language and visual symbols of the CORS and CSRS, easier to complete. When uncertain, choice of version can always be made in collaboration with clients.

CASE EXAMPLE 2.5: USING THE MEASURES WITH YOUNG CHILDREN

The Petersons are being seen as a family in a local mental health clinic. They were referred for therapy following the mother's diagnosis of multiple sclerosis. In the last year, she had experienced several falls in the home requiring her children—ages 6 and 9—to come to her rescue. In addition, all family members had noticed and been impacted by her fluctuating mood and energy levels.

As the first meeting began, the ORS and SRS were introduced, and the helper worked to create a culture of feedback. Tablets containing computerized versions of the scales were eventually handed to the two parents and 9-year-old child. A paper version of the YCORS was offered to the 6-year-old, along with handful of colored pencils.

"Pick a face," the helper explained, "that shows me how you have been feeling." Pointing to each in turn, "This one has a smile and looks a bit happy. The next one has a flat mouth and is neither happy nor sad. Here, you can see, the mouth is frowny. It could be sad or angry or upset. And this last one, it has no mouth. Using these pencils, you can circle or color the face that best fits you—how you are feeling—or color the last one and make your own mouth. Do you understand?"

The child nodded in agreement, but then leaned over and whispered in her mother's ear. In response, Mom pointed to the YCORS, telling her daughter, "No, this one is for you. The iPads are for us."

At this point, the helper intervened. Speaking directly to the child, "You would like to use one of the iPads too, wouldn't you?"

Nodding in agreement, she replied, "I don't want to do a coloring book and, anyway, I know how to use the iPad."

The helper responded by first opening a CORS on a tablet—the version of the tool normally applicable for ages 7 to 12—and then handed the device to the child. "Mom," she asked, "Could you please read the instructions?" Turning to the child, "And you, since you know how to use the iPad, you touch the line in between the frowny and smiley faces to show how you've been feeling." At this juncture, and throughout the sessions that followed, all family members completed the computerized versions of the measures.

Context-specific measures

The versions of the measures previously discussed are specifically designed to be applicable across client presenting concerns (e.g., diagnosis, goals), practitioner professional discipline (e.g., social workers, substance abuse counselors, occupational therapists, case managers, psychotherapists, pharmacists, and psychiatrists) and practitioner theoretical orientation (e.g., psychodynamic, humanistic, cognitive-behavioral, trauma-informed, energy-based, eclectic). Two measures have been developed for application in specific contexts: (1) the Group Session Rating Scale (GSRS); and (2) the Leeds Alliance in Supervision Scale (LASS).

GSRS: Adapted from the SRS, the GSRS is a four-item visual analogue measure designed to assess the multiplicity of relationships characteristic of services delivered in a group format (e.g., the individual to the group and the leader, and the relationship between group members [see Figure 2.22]). Research to date shows the tool demonstrates adequate reliability and validity, correlating well with established group measures and enabling helping professionals to identify and attend to relationship problems between group members and the facilitator (Davidsen et al. 2017; Quirk et al. 2012; Vinther & Davidsen, 2016; Slone et al. 2015).

The GSRS is designed to be used in combination with the ORS. As always, time is taken at the outset of each meeting to foster a "culture of feedback," ensuring that group members feel invited and safe to share their experience. Sessions begin by using the ORS to establish a baseline measure of client well-being or assessing progress since the last meeting. Some group leaders choose to administer the measure prior to starting their group, noting it allows more time for discussing results. Members can either complete the scale in the waiting room or a link from one of the authorized computer systems can be emailed allowing them to complete the measure in advance. Similar to services delivered to individuals, the GSRS is then administered near the end of the group leaving enough time for processing of the feedback provided by the participants.

Group Session Rating Scale (GSRS)

Name _____ Age (Yrs):____
ID# _____ Gender_____
Session # ___ Date: _____

Please rate today's group by placing a mark on the line nearest to the description that best fits your experience.

Relationship

I did not feel understood, respected, and/or accepted by the leader and/or the group.
I---I
I felt understood, respected, and accepted by the leader and the group.

Goals and Topics

We did *not* work on or talk about what I wanted to work on and talk about.
I---I
We worked on and talked about what I wanted to work on and talk about.

Approach or Method

The leader and/or the group's approach is a not a good fit for me.
I---I
The leader and group's approach is a good fit for me.

Overall

There was something missing in group today—I did not feel like a part of the group.
I---I
Overall, today's group was right for me—I felt like a part of the group.

International Center for Clinical Excellence

www.scottdmiller.com

© 2007, Barry L. Duncan and Scott D. Miller

Figure 2.22: Group Session Rating Scale

It is important to note that the practices and principles characteristic of effective use of feedback apply when administering the ORS and GSRS in groups; namely, clients must believe: (1) they can share feedback about their progress and experience of the group, it's members and leader, without fear of retribution and (2) that their feedback can and will impact the nature and quality of services delivered. With regard to the latter, in a study of group treatment of people with eating problems, Davidsen et al. (2017) found that use of the ORS and GSRS had no impact on outcome or engagement when helpers were prohibited by protocol from changing or adjusting services in response to client feedback. Given such results, prior to adopting the ORS and GSRS, mental health professionals are strongly advised to consider whether the context and nature of the service being delivered permits them to respond to the feedback provided. As in individually delivered services, engagement and responsiveness are fundamental to successful care. Indeed, as will be reviewed in section 8, being able to respond to client feedback is one of the three principles for determining when and when not to use FIT.

LASS: Inspired by the SRS, the Leeds Alliance in Supervision Scale (LASS) is a three-item visual analogue measure designed to assess the quality of the supervisory relationship (see Figure 2.23). To date, only two studies of the measure have been published (O'Donovan et al. 2017; Wainwright, 2010). Originally developed as part of a doctoral dissertation by Wainwright (2010), the evidence shows the tool demonstrates acceptable reliability and validity, correlating well with similar measures. At present, no normative data (including a cutoff score) exist. For this reason, an electronic version is not included in any of the authorized computer systems. Extrapolating from research on the SRS, it is recommended that a score of 9 or lower on any single item be discussed with the supervisee at the end of the supervision session.

Leeds Alliance in Supervision Scale (LASS)

Supervisee Name _____

Date of supervision session: _____

ATTENTION: TO <u>INSURE</u> SCORING ACCURACY PRINT OUT THE MEASURE TO INSURE THE ITEM LINES ARE 10 CM IN LENGTH. ALTER THE FORM UNTIL THE LINES PRINT THE CORRECT LENGTH. THEN ERASE THIS MESSAGE.

Instructions:

Please place a mark on the lines to indicate how you feel about your supervision session

| This supervision session was not focused | (Approach) I---I | This supervision session was focused |

| My supervisor and I did not understand each other in this session | (Relationship) I---I | My supervisor and I understood each other in this session |

| This supervision session was not helpful to me | (Meeting my needs) I---I | This supervision session was helpful to me |

International Center for Clinical Excellence

www.scottdmiller.com

©Wainwright, N. A. (2010). *The development of the Leeds Alliance in Supervision Scale (LASS): A brief sessional measure of the supervisory alliance.* Unpublished Doctoral Thesis. University of Leeds

Figure 2.23: Leeds Alliance in Supervision Scale

Similar to the state of empirical evidence, clinical experience with the LASS is limited. Some supervisors report that using the tool in group supervision enables them to detect differing needs of individual group members as well as negotiate how to structure supervision time to optimize engagement in future meetings (Bargmann, 2017). Others have noted that use of the scale helps to model the culture of feedback necessary for implementing FIT (Bargmann, 2017; Chow, 2017).

Collateral scores

Typically, clients complete the ORS by and for themselves. In certain circumstances, it may be useful, or necessary, to have information about how others might rate the well-being or functioning of the client. "Collateral scores," as they are termed, can either be collected from an external or internal source. In the first instance, the helper asks another person (e.g., parent, teacher, partner/spouse, referrer) to complete the measure about the client. An internal collateral, by contrast, is when clients complete the scale based on how they believe another person might rate them (e.g., parent, teacher, referrer). Either way, the guiding principle is administering the ORS in a manner that captures the distress or concern responsible for a person being in care.

External Collaterals: As may be obvious, the primary purpose of gathering ORS scores from collaterals external to the treatment process is to understand the concerns and assessment of progress of different stakeholders in the client's life. Simply put, many people do not seek out services on their own. Children, for example, are most often brought to treatment by their parents or at the request of social services, school teachers, or the family physician. Similarly, parents may be mandated into care by government agencies to address worries about the welfare of their children. Employers and family members are another reason why some clients present for treatment. Finally, courts frequently require the participation of people in services who do not readily admit to having problems or see themselves as needing help (e.g., substance abuse, domestic violence, aggressive or criminal behavior). In all such instances, the stakeholder's assessment is central to determining the type, length, intensity, and success of services offered. More, as the case below illustrates, integrating external collateral scores into care can improve engagement of clients by fostering an open and transparent negotiation regarding treatment objectives between all parties involved.

CASE EXAMPLE 2.6: EXTERNAL COLLATERAL SCORES IN MANDATED TREATMENT

Fourteen-year-old Thomas was ordered into family therapy with his mother by the local social services agency. Over the last several months, he had committed a series of petty thefts as well as being chronically truant from school. Feeling powerless in her efforts to parent her son, mother readily agreed to treatment. While acknowledging others were concerned, Thomas maintained he did not need, nor was he interested in receiving any help. At the initial visit, his score on the ORS was significantly above the clinical cutoff (see Figure 2.24).

Hoping to facilitate a conversation regarding the purpose of the visit, and consistent with the principle stated above, the family worker decided to collect external collateral scores from Thomas's mother and the social worker. "OK, Thomas," she began, "from your perspective, everything is fine. To better understand why your Mom, and (the social worker), wanted us to meet, I'm going to ask them to fill out the same form you've just completed, sharing how they think you are doing."

Handing a tablet to Mom and the social worker, "Would each of you take a moment, recalling the last week, and rate how you think Thomas has been doing in each of these four areas?"

As can be seen in the graphs below, scores provided by Thomas's mother and social worker were significantly lower, with each falling below the clinical cutoff (see Figures 2.25 and 2.26 [Note: when an adult completes the scale about a child or adolescent, the adult cutoff score is applied]). Clearly, both were concerned about Thomas.

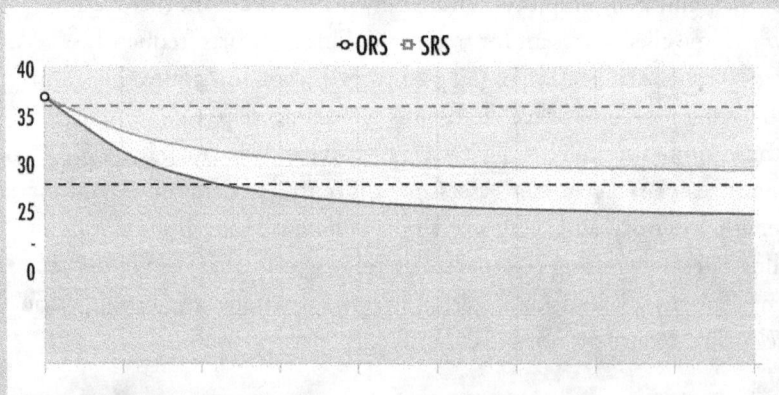

Figure 2.24: ORS Score for 14-year-old Thomas

Using the computer program to display the three ratings on a single graph, the family helper invited Mom and the social worker to explain the meaning of their respective scores and explore the connection between their concerns and the purpose of meeting together in family therapy (see Figure 2.27). When asked to share his thoughts, Thomas readily acknowledged the concerns of both—admitting to the thefts and truancy—but maintained he did not need any help. He promised to attend school and stay out of trouble as long as he was not forced to participate in family therapy.

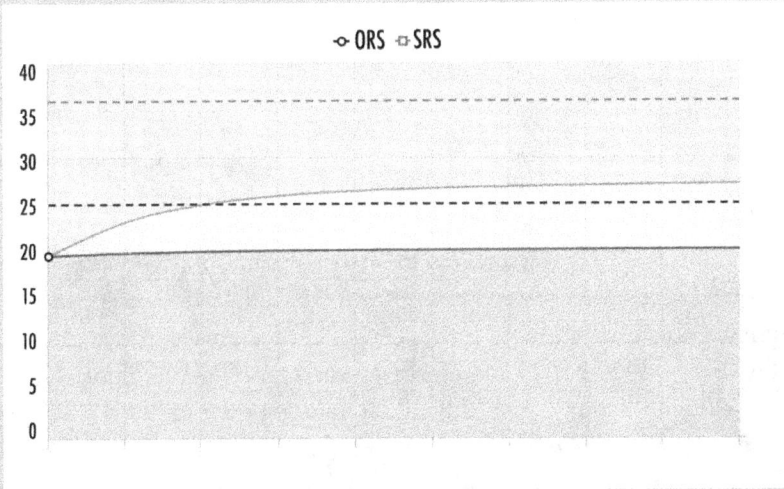

Figure 2.25: Mother's ORS Score for Thomas

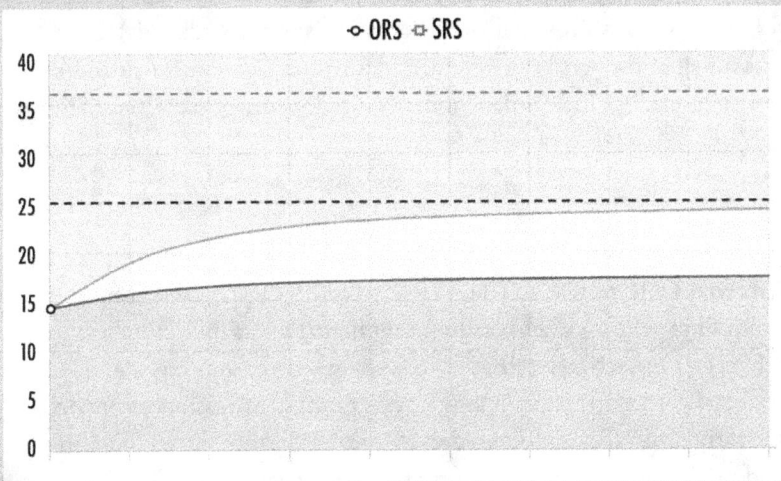

Figure 2.26: Social Worker's ORS Score for Thomas

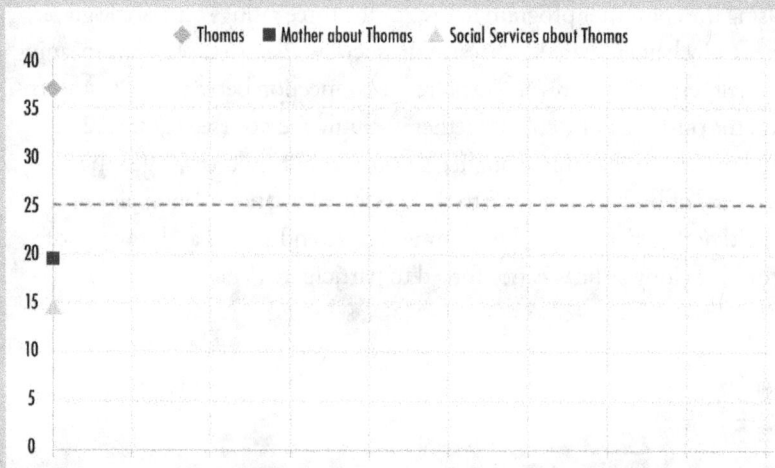

Figure 2.27: Combined ORS Graph

Accepting Thomas's statement as the starting point for negotiating mutually acceptable treatment objectives, the family worker engaged him in a conversation about small changes he could make to address the worries of his mother and the social worker so, "he would not have to come here anymore." Initially, Thomas spoke in all-or-nothing terms (e.g., "I'd have to be a straight-A student," "I couldn't have any friends," "I could never go out"). With skill and persistence, by the end of the visit, the family worker had managed to help him identify several small, achievable objectives (e.g., making it to school every morning the following week, shift socializing with friends to the weekends). Each was noted in the "goals, meaning, and purpose" section on the SDA (see Figure 2.14), including Thomas's ultimate purpose, "to end family therapy as quickly as possible."

Internal Collaterals: Asking clients to complete the ORS from the point of view of another person rating them (e.g., parent, teacher, referrer) is a practical alternative to seeking scores from external collaterals. In many cases, it may not be possible or feasible to obtain the ratings of various stakeholders. More, experience shows soliciting and using internal collateral scores frequently works as well or better than the ratings of external collaterals when it comes to facilitating client engagement in addressing stakeholder concerns. As the 17th century philosopher Blaise Pascal observed, "people are generally better persuaded by the reasons which they have themselves discovered than by those which have come into the mind of others." Case example 2.7 illustrates how internal collateral scores can be used to establish strong working relationships with people who are sent to treatment by others.

CASE EXAMPLE 2.7: USING INTERNAL COLLATERAL ORS SCORES

A man was referred to counseling by his family physician. At the first session his score on the ORS was 28, placing him above the cutoff and in the nonclinical or functional range of scores. Pointing to the graph, the helper said, "As you can see, your score falls above this dotted line, called the clinical cutoff. Scores above that line are more like people who are not in treatment and saying life is generally pretty good." The man readily agreed. Continuing, "That's great, of course. What I'm wondering is, given that, why did you come to see me today?" On hearing the man had been referred by his physician due to concerns about prolonged grief following his wife's death, the helper replied, "OK, I get it. You are fine, but your doctor sees things differently, is concerned about you?" The man nodded in agreement, adding an emphatic, "yes!"

Following the guiding principle of administering the ORS in a manner that captures the distress or concern responsible for a person being in care, the helper asked for an internal collateral rating. Opening a new ORS form on the tablet, "Would you mind filling this out one more time? This time as if you were your doctor? Putting yourself in her shoes, right after your last appointment, the one that led to this referral, how would she rate you?" After completing the scale, scores from the two administrations were plotted on the same graph. Pointing at the first, the helper said, "As you can see, you're up here, at 28. You are, just like you said, doing all right." Moving to the second, "but your doctor has a different opinion. She's at a 15." When the man said nothing, the helper asked, "Do you have any idea, based on what happened when you met, why she might think seeing me would be a good idea?"

Angrily, at first, the man related what he had told the physician. In particular, how, since his wife's passing, he had lost touch with family and friends. That said, weight loss was the primary reason he gave for making an appointment to see the doctor, fearing he might have cancer or some other disease. "They are running some tests," he added, "but I'm pretty sure she thinks this is 'all in my head.'" A change in tone began to occur when the helper acknowledged the man felt his concerns had not been taken seriously by the physician. "What you wanted," the helper said, "the reason you went to see your doctor was to make sure you were OK physically." When the man agreed, the helper continued, "As those tests are being done, and you find out what might be going on physically, do you think being connected with your family and friends would be of help?" With a laugh, the man replied, "Well, at least she (the doctor) would be happy!" Together, the two then explored how reestablishing connections with family and friends would not only satisfy the physician but also help establish the support he would need in case of physical illness or disability. Feeling that meeting with the helper would help him achieve his goal of ensuring his physical well-being, the man agreed to return for more sessions focused on helping him get started reaching out.

Timing and Frequency of Measurement

As previously discussed, it is generally recommended the ORS be administered as early as possible during the initial encounter and prior to any formal assessment, intake, or treatment. The SRS should be completed at the end of each visit including any formal intake and assessment meetings. Routine administration of the measures (e.g., weekly versus monthly or quarterly) has been shown to enhance the impact of feedback on outcome, particularly among youth and children (Bickman et al. 2011; Nelson et al. 2013; Warren et al. 2010).

In intensive service settings (e.g., residential, inpatient, day treatment, or when multiple providers are involved in an episode of care), completion of the measures should be limited to once a week to avoid measurement fatigue and ensure any feedback provided is meaningful. The ORS is given at the start of the week, the SRS at the end. Many settings have found it helpful to designate a particular provider or group for administering and discussing the measures (Frølich, 2017; Gleave et al. 2017; Obbekær et al. 2017). Scores and critical feedback are then recorded in the client record to facilitate communication among all care providers.

In certain circumstances, clients and providers may interact over periods of time far longer than typical mental health services (e.g., court mandated treatment, probation, custodial supervision/oversight, case management, disability services, medically assisted treatment [e.g., methadone, suboxone], supported employment and housing). Research shows the average number of sessions for people in outpatient psychotherapy is 5, with 90% receiving 20 sessions or less (Miller & Hubble, 2023). Hospital stays are equally brief, with 10 plus-or-minus-three days being the average (Lee et al. 2012). The TRT and SPI used to assess and predict client progress reflect these typical patterns of service utilization. More, as noted in Chapter 1, research consistently finds the greatest amount of change occurs early in treatment.

The ORS and SRS can be helpful in longer episodes of care to assess maintenance of gains, identify potential risks (e.g., single-point declines in SRS scores [Miller et al. 2007]), and address any setbacks (e.g., drops in ORS scores in response to life events [Schilling et al. 2020]). As contact with clients lengthens, the amount of time between administrations (e.g., from weekly to monthly, monthly to quarterly, and so on) can be increased to prevent measurement fatigue. Decisions about frequency are best informed by considering the amount of expected change between visits predicted by the TRT. In principle, feedback should be sought more often when the probability of change is high and decrease as the expected amount of progress declines.

Measurement Technology

When first developed, the ORS and SRS were administered in paper and pencil format. Clients completed the scales. The helper then used a ruler to measure in centimeters to the nearest millimeter of their marks on each item, adding the four together to obtain the total score. This number, in turn, was plotted on a graph and a comparison was made to the clinical cutoff and prior scores. Change between visits was deemed "significant" if and when it exceeded a statistical indice known as the reliable change index (RCI). Reported as 5 points, it was the average difference in scores (from the first to the most recent) needed to be confident improvement was attributable to treatment versus chance variation in the client's experience or measurement error (Miller et al. 2006).

Technological developments, in combination with the accumulation of data from widespread use of the tools in diverse practice settings and cultures, has made it possible to provide much more precise and individualized feedback regarding client progress. The TRTs described earlier have replaced the original static, average RCI with a client-specific estimate of the amount of change necessary to be deemed reliable and "on track" from session-to-session. On the graphs produced by the web-based applications, change can be attributed to treatment when client scores fall at or above the green line of the TRT (see Figure 2.2). At this time, the static RCI is no longer considered best practice when evaluating client progress.

A list of the authorized software applications can be found on the International Center for Clinical Excellence (ICCE) website (www.iccexcellence.com). Each allows users to administer, score, and display individual client results in relationship to the TRTs in real time. Additionally, all are compatible with online service delivery (e.g., teletherapy, remote services). As already noted, validated scripts are available for oral administration of the scales. When used, client responses can simply be added to the system by hand, thereby enabling them to use the TRTs and other statistical indices (e.g., SPI) in exactly the same way as when clients complete the scales in person on a computer. The systems also allow helpers to send a secure link to clients to complete the scales on their own device either before the scheduled meeting or in real time.

Collecting outcome scores ahead of time is an efficient way of administering the scales when services involve multiple participants (e.g., groups, meetings involving multiple stakeholders). It is important, however, to ensure that any time saved does not come at the expense of creating and maintaining a "culture of feedback." Whether completed before the visit or in real time, the same suggestions for introducing the measures reviewed in section 2 of this chapter apply. Meeting in person the first time the tools are introduced is optimal as it allows for discussion and clarification with participants regarding the purpose of gathering feedback. However, when such a meeting is not possible, experienced FIT practitioners have found it helpful to send a detailed written description of the purpose of the scales together with the link for remote administration.

Finally, in addition to improved efficiency and more precise feedback regarding client progress, the systems aggregate practice data and report a number of empirically supported, ICCE-approved descriptive and outcome statistics (e.g., demographics, treatment length, retention and discontinuation rates, and effectiveness). Such information is useful for identifying individual and agency professional development opportunities and reporting to funders and statutory authorities. A detailed review of these indices can be found in Chapter 4. It is important to note access to the TRTs, SPI, and aggregated performance indices is essential for securing the full benefit of using the ORS and SRS. For this reason, no digitalization of the scales in any form is permitted outside of these systems.

7. UNDERSTANDING AND PROCESSING CLIENT FEEDBACK OVER TIME

Routinely reviewing clients' experience of progress and the quality of the relationship is a fundamental aspect of working feedback informed. Such monitoring enables helpers to detect when clients are at risk and make adjustments to the type, frequency, and provider of services. The two key principles for understanding and processing client feedback are:

1. Transparency; and
2. Timing

Transparency

Without exception, each time a measure is administered, the results should be shared and discussed openly with the client. Indeed, from a FIT perspective, interpretation of the scores is not possible without client input. Detailed instructions for fostering transparent, session-by-session conversations about SRS scores were provided in section 4 above. With regard to the ORS, following the completion of the measure, FIT practitioners show the computerized graph of the client's scores containing the TRTs and SPI, provide a basic description of the results, and then solicit client feedback:

> *Since last time we met, you can see that your scores have* (increased, decreased, stayed the same). *Does that fit with your experience? Can you help me understand what's been happening?*

Timing

As noted in chapter 1, research shows the likelihood of continued engagement in therapy, and a successful outcome, are greatest when clients experience improvement in the early stages of treatment (Baldwin et al. 2009; Howard et al. 1986; Lambert & Ogles, 2004). While the rate of progress varies for individual clients, between 30 and 40% will experience significant, enduring improvement within the first 5 weeks. A lack of improvement by the twelfth week is associated with a higher risk of a negative outcome at termination (~90% [Brown et al. 1999; Owen et al. 2015; Miller, 2014]). Up to 25% of people will continue in care despite a lack of measurable benefit (Miller, 2014).

Ongoing monitoring provides clinicians with an opportunity to respond to a lack of progress or problems in the relationship early enough to forestall dropout, or long-term, unsuccessful treatment (Reese et al. 2009). Given the research cited above, in the absence of progress by weeks 3 or 4, helpers should speak with clients about their goals and expectations, exploring what might be changed within the service being provided for it to be more helpful. Consultation with a colleague or supervisor is also highly recommended—a step, research shows, few helpers take, but which has been documented to increase the chances of eventual success (Lutz, 2014; Reese et al. 2009).

When progress fails to occur by weeks 7 or 8, practitioners should consider making more substantive modifications to the care being offered (e.g., increasing the dose or intensity of current services, adding different services). If they have not already done so, consultation with colleagues or their supervisor is strongly advised.

When a lack of progress continues through weeks 10 to 12, serious consideration should be given to making more significant changes to service delivery including, referral to: (1) a different provider; (2) another type of help or outside agency; or (3) a specialist for in-depth medical or psychological evaluation. Another option is engaging the client in an open discussion about whether or not further services are needed or likely to prove useful (Miller, Hubble, Valla et al. 2020). Whatever changes are considered, the likelihood of clients feeling abandoned or rejected is significantly reduced when the helper has: (1) taken the time at the outset of treatment to clearly and transparently explain how the measures will be used to guide decision-making; and (2) reviewed and discussed the lack progress at each meeting. Ultimately, the main objective is to end ineffective care or facilitate exploration of alternatives when the probability that a particular helper or service will succeed has been exhausted. Doing so has, in the FIT literature, been referred to as, "failing successfully" (Duncan et al. 2004; Miller et al. 2004).

CASE EXAMPLE 2.8: FAILING SUCCESSFULLY

Stacy was a college student in the first semester of her freshman year. From the age of 15, she had struggled on and off with anorexia. When her symptoms returned and began to affect her energy level and social life, she made an appointment with a helper at the university counseling center. At intake, her score on the ORS was 13, well below the clinical cutoff. When no change had occurred by session 3, the helper initiated a conversation with Stacy about the lack of progress, exploring the quality of the relational bond and what might be added to the counseling to make it more helpful (e.g., change of approach or goals). Stacy immediately suggested changing the focus of the sessions, leaving behind stress management (e.g., mindfulness, meditation) and addressing her increasingly restrictive eating habits more directly. As can be seen in Figure 2.28, despite the adjustment in approach, Stacy's ORS scores did not improve over the next three visits. More, her physical condition continued to deteriorate (e.g., weight loss, difficulty concentrating, sleep disruption).

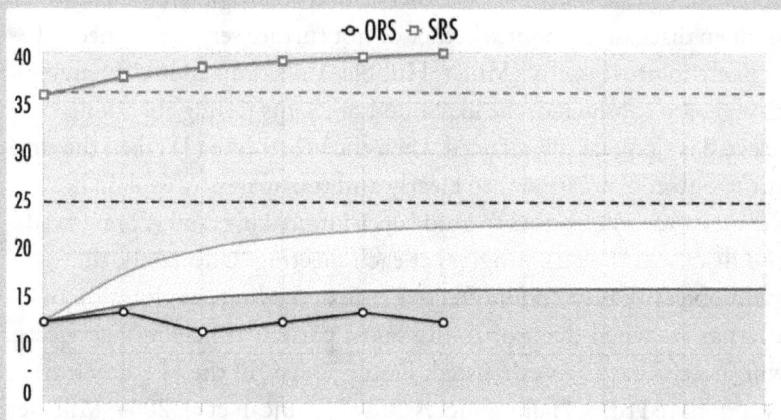

Figure 2.28: Stacy's ORS and SRS Scores

After expressing concern about the lack of change in ORS scores, and Stacy's physical condition, the helper initiated a conversation about how best to proceed. As noted above, it was time to consider making substantive modifications to the care being offered (e.g., increasing the dose or intensity of current services, adding different services). Pointing to the graph, "If you look here, your score today is almost exactly the same it was the first time we met."

Nodding, Stacy replied, "Yeah, it's like, we talk about all these great things, but when I get home, anorexia hits me, and everything we talked about here seems to be wrong and I just end up thinking that you are wrong about all the things you say, and I decide not to eat after all."

Looking together at the SRS scores, the helper commented, "Yes, I can see that. At the end of each session, it always seems that you felt they go well, but then ... "

Stacy agreed, "Right. I really like you, and I like coming here, and what we talk about. I always leave feeling inspired and ready to fight the fight."

"And yet ... it, the inspiration, doesn't last ... "

With a laugh, Stacy adds "Well, actually, it lasts for about 12 hours ... but mealtime comes and it all falls apart!"

With that, the helper suggested it was time to consider whether she needed more help than the weekly sessions the student counseling center could provide. Stacy immediately replied, "I really don't like the idea of not coming to see you ... I like talking with you ... I think you really get me."

In response, the helper agreed to continue meeting with Stacy while arranging for a service that provided more ongoing, daily support. When a placement was found two weeks later, services at the student counseling center were ended.

Transparency and timing are two core principles of making sense of ORS and SRS scores from session to session. In Chapter 3, common patterns of ORS and SRS graphs will be reviewed which can enhance helpers' understanding and processing of client feedback.

8. WHEN AND WHEN NOT TO USE FIT

The ORS and SRS are available in many different languages, each translated, reviewed and confirmed by native speakers. Since first being developed, literally hundreds of thousands of helping professionals and millions of clients have used the tools in an effort to improve the quality and outcome of mental health care. Research by Lutz (2016) shows most people "like the idea of ... monitoring the quality of ... therapy" (92.2%), "find it important to monitor the results of ... treatment" (92.9%), and consider the time involved in the measurement and feedback process, "appropriate" (95.5%). Finally, as reviewed in Chapter 1, a large and growing number of studies conducted in different treatment settings and with diverse people around the world show FIT is associated with improved retention, effectiveness, and efficiency of care (Carlier et al. 2012; Chesworth et al. 2017; de Jong et al. 2024; Kopua et al. 2020; Pringle & Fawcett, 2017; Tilsen & McNamee, 2015; Shaw et al. 2019; She et al. 2018).

Despite such generally positive results, as the application of FIT widens, questions naturally arise about its applicability in particular treatment settings, with specific people or diagnostic groups, and across different cultures. On first hearing about FIT, for example, it is not uncommon for helpers to ask, "Can I use FIT with all my clients" (e.g., people in recovery for drug and alcohol problems, those with bipolar illness or schizophrenia, in crisis settings, group or family therapy, long term, inpatient or residential care, people from non-Western, non-majority, marginalized or oppressed countries or cultures)?

The near limitless number of dimensions by which suitability can be assessed ultimately makes it impossible to provide answers about the application of FIT for each specific group, population or circumstance. Think of the panoply of potential parameters one would need to test to be able to say FIT works with everyone, everywhere, all the time. Starting with diagnoses, for example, the latest edition of the Diagnostic and Statistical Manual of Mental Disorders alone contains 297 distinct problem types. More than a decade ago, researchers writing for Scientific American identified 500 different treatment models (Lilienfeld & Arkowitz, 2012), any of which can be delivered in an ever-evolving number of service settings (most recently online). Add to these, considerations regarding client and cultural diversity (e.g., age, race, ethnicity, national/country of origin, social economic status, gender/ sexual orientation and identity, disability, religious/spiritual beliefs and affiliation) and the timeline for determining when and when not to employ any approach, let alone FIT, quickly stretches to infinity.

In chapter 5, studies appearing to show limitations in the effectiveness of FIT in specific settings (e.g., acute psychiatric services, inpatient treatment) and with certain diagnoses (e.g., eating disorders, autism, personality disorders and other severe mental illnesses) are reviewed in detail. Meanwhile, experience indicates approaching such questions in a principle-based manner is a more efficient and effective way for determining when and when not to use FIT. Briefly, should any of the conditions outlined in the principles reviewed below not be met, FIT would not be recommended and likely prove unhelpful. In order of importance, these include:

1. THE SERVICE IS SPECIFICALLY INTENDED TO RELIEVE DISTRESS OR IMPROVE THE WELL-BEING OR FUNCTIONING OF THE PARTICIPANTS

Not surprisingly, the documented impact of FIT on retention and outcome has led to its application in a wide range of settings and contexts. Though well intentioned, in some, it has proven both unhelpful and burdensome to staff and service recipients. For example, after attending an introductory workshop, the manager of a government-supported housing program decided to implement FIT. The mission of the service was to provide housing to young people lacking a stable or safe home environment. Staff were present to assist with practical matters (e.g., arranging furniture, financial management, setting up utilities, fixing a broken pipe, learning how to cook) and to help with the knowledge, skills and resources associated with independent living. Participants could stay in the subsidized apartments for up to 5 years, which most did while finishing their education or taking their first job. Despite the initial attraction to the overall philosophy of FIT, and the possibility of having "data" to show funders, it did not take long for the manager to realize that administering the ORS and SRS on a routine basis to all residents generated little information relevant to optimizing the type of help provided by staff. The majority who lived in the apartments were well functioning and did not require psychological support. Those with mental health concerns could and did seek help elsewhere.

Consider another example. FIT was being implemented at a large, multidisciplinary children's service agency. In an attempt to create a shared language and care philosophy, a decision was made to mandate the use of the ORS and SRS across all programs (e.g., individual mental healthcare, family treatment, youth programs, adoption, disability and child protective services). While most found the process helpful in guiding and improving service delivery, certain programs struggled (e.g., summer youth camps, clubhouse activities, adoption services, postnatal maternal support). It is important to note that the leaders and staff of those services did as they were told, dutifully administering the measures and discussing the results with their clients. However, the purpose seemed to elude all involved. The number of complaints by clients was significantly higher than in other parts of the agency, and staff questioned the value of the time devoted to the process. Eventually, the reason for the difficulties became clear. Despite their diverse nature, and while all could be seen as providing a needed service, none were intended to be therapeutic (e.g., have a beneficial impact on well-being or functioning). The team overseeing implementation ultimately decided to stop using FIT in such programs, opting instead to administer the ORS at the first contact to identify individuals that might benefit from a referral to mental health services.

By contrast, FIT has been successfully implemented in a number of non-mental health settings. For example, Pringle and Fawcett (2017) trained community pharmacists to use the ORS and the SRS to track well-being and foster the pharmacist-patient working relationship. The study showed use of FIT improved adherence across five medication classes aimed at treating chronic health conditions (e.g., calcium channel blockers, oral diabetes medications, beta-blockers, statins, and renin angiotemsin system antagonists). Prior research had shown nearly one-third of prescriptions are never filled and more than 60% not taken as prescribed. In Denmark, Krog (2023) reported improved engagement and outcomes resulting from the integration of FIT into physical therapy. And finally, in New Zealand, Kopua et al. (2020) used FIT to document the effectiveness of a way of working with Maori individuals, families, and communities based entirely on an "indigenous ontology, epistemology and linguistic idiom" (p. 5). Known as Mahi a Atua, it is an approach specifically designed to address social, economic, and health disparities caused by and unresponsive to Western culture and methods. Consistent with the principle noted above, in each, FIT proved helpful because the relationship with the provider (e.g., pharmacist, physiotherapist, indigenous helper) and the recipient's well-being were critical to the outcome of the service offered.

2. THE TYPE, LENGTH, LOCATION AND PROVIDER OF SERVICE ARE MODIFIABLE.

FIT is about using client feedback to inform and tailor service delivery. As such, any barriers to adjusting or altering a course of care will limit its applicability and usefulness. The two most common obstacles encountered are: (1) policies or practice traditions preventing alterations to the focus, length or type of treatment offered; and (2) a lack of alternative providers, services, or settings for clients not benefiting from the help offered. One agency, for example, had implemented a treatment approach known as "Single Session Therapy," strictly adhering to offering clients a single visit. At an introductory workshop, the manager asked how FIT could be used in their setting. The trainer responded with a question highlighting principle #2. To wit, "Are you willing to change your mind about the number of visits your clients are allowed to attend?" When the manager replied, "No, we are known for single session therapy," the trainer advised not implementing FIT. A back and forth followed, with the manager eventually expressing interest in using the ORS to document the effectiveness of their approach. The trainer indicated that the measure could be used to document effectiveness, but at least two administrations would be required. More to the point, measuring outcomes was never the intent of FIT.

In other cases, helpers may be convinced no changes in services are possible or permitted. For instance, most agencies have "repeat clients," a small group of people who show up time and again, see a variety of helpers and participate in most of the available programming, but fail to benefit. Policy and tradition may prevent staff from transferring clients to services outside the agency or terminating contact with those not being helped. Miller, Hubble, Valla et al. (2020) reviewed the challenges associated with implementing FIT in a country where citizens have a legal right to both a diagnosis and continuing mental health services even when neither proves effective. More commonly, agencies who see their purpose or mission as dealing with the most "challenging" or "intractable" problems—people no one else is willing or has been able to help—are similarly unlikely to end services or refer. As will be described in Chapter 5, alternatives to such policies and traditions must be developed for implementation of FIT to succeed.

3. THE PROVIDER AND AGENCY ARE OPEN TO THE FEEDBACK THEIR CLIENTS PROVIDE VIA THE ROUTINE ADMINISTRATION OF OUTCOME AND ALLIANCE MEASURES

As first reported in Chapter 1, the evidence shows feedback provided by clients via standardized measures is effective for helpers who are willing to use the resulting information to guide clinical activities and decision making (Davidsen et al. 2014; de Jong et al. 2012; Kia et al. 2024). Not surprisingly, experience shows helper engagement with feedback is likely to suffer when measurement is primarily implemented to meet agency or practitioner objectives (e.g., documenting treatment services, securing funding). In short, client interest in and support for the measurement process is likely to be high when they perceive it as an ongoing and integrated part of the care that is used in a transparent and non-hierarchical manner to foster communication and collaboration (Lutz, 2016; Solstad et al. 2017).

Almost everyone can think of an experience of being asked for feedback and then having their comments ignored, dismissed or challenged. In their pioneering research on top performing helpers, Chow (2014) and Chow et al. (2015) found the most effective reported being "surprised by client feedback" more times in a typical work-week than their less effective counterparts, indicative of both an awareness of and receptivity towards feedback. In short, it's about attitude, specifically being open and willing to have one's beliefs and interpretations disconfirmed.

On a related note, it is not uncommon for helpers to have questions regarding the validity of scores on the ORS and SRS. Examples include: (1) consistently high or perfect SRS scores (e.g., 40); (2) inconsistencies between ORS scores and client within session behavior (e.g., improving ORS scores but tearful presentation); and (3) differences between scores on the ORS or SRS and the helper's evaluation of progress or the relationship (e.g., helper doubts improving ORS scores). In such instances, the best practice is taking client scores at face value while simultaneously being curious. As a first step, in the case of consistently high SRS scores, the helper would want to review how they introduce the scale, working to ensure the guidelines for creating the "culture of feedback" outlined in the second section of this chapter have been met. Instead of expressing or implying doubt about the validity of a high SRS score (e.g., "I'm not perfect, certainly some of what I did merits a lower score," "Are you sure there isn't anything I can do to improve how we are working together?"), the helper could ask, "Is there anything that would get in the way of you letting me know something was amiss if a concern developed?" Alternately, "After our sessions, do you ever have a thought about what you wish you would have said, but didn't?" A similar, nonjudgemental inquiry can provide valuable context when differences are noted between client scores on the ORS and behavior during the visit. "I hear how difficult this situation has been for you. Can you help me understand how the feelings you are telling me about connect with your (high) score on the ORS?"

Finally, instances where the helper's assessment differs from the client's report can be the most challenging to address in an accepting and nonjudgemental manner. Such situations require a careful balance between maintaining client engagement and approaching difficult subject matter. It might be tempting, for example, to challenge the truthfulness of a client being treated for an eating problem whose ORS scores are improving despite continuing to lose weight. A better approach would include first acknowledging and exploring positive developments and then being curious about the relationship between such improvements and their weight as well as the perspective of concerned others. "I'm happy to hear about these changes," the helper might begin, in time asking, "Can you tell me how your (e.g., parents, family, partner, referring physician) might score the ORS? What might account for the difference?" Bottom line: be open to, nonjudgemental and curious about the feedback clients provide. Treat discrepancies as learning versus treatment opportunities.

SUMMARY

Scores of studies conducted by different researchers in diverse settings and cultures have documented the reliability and validity of the ORS and SRS and predictive indices (i.e., TRTs and SPI). Detailed instructions were provided for when, how, which, where, by and to whom the scales can or should be administered as well as the importance of creating and maintaining a "culture of feedback." Clinical examples showed how to understand and process client feedback over the course of care. In terms of documentation, the FIT SDA and PN ensure feedback is integrated into planning and clinical decision making. Of course, FIT is not applicable in all circumstances. The chapter concluded with the identification of three principles for determining when and when not to use FIT.

QUIZ

1. Which of the following statements is true:

    a. The Outcome Rating Scale (ORS) is a brief visual analog scale that measures four areas of well-being

    b. The Outcome Rating Scale is not valid for use with adolescents aged 13-19

    c. The Young Child Outcome Ratings Scale (YCORS) is scorable in the same way as the ORS

    d. The Child Outcome Rating scale has been validated for children and adolescents ages 6- 19

2. The clinical cut off of the ORS is

    a. The score that indicates when to end service

    b. The score that tells the helper how long they need to continue working with the client

    c. The score that provides a reference point for evaluating the degree of distress a client is experiencing

    d. The score that indicates when services are needed

3. The clinical cut off scores on the ORS for adults, adolescents and children are:

    a. 26, 28 &32 respectively

    b. 25, 30 & 32 respectively

    c. 28, 30 & 32 respectively

    d. 25, 28 & 32 respectively

4. Which of the following statements is FALSE?

    a. When the initial ORS score is much lower than the clinical cutoff, expect rapid improvement

    b. When the initial ORS score is close to the clinical cutoff, expect slow and steady improvement

c. When the initial ORS score is above the clinical cutoff, expect slow and steady improvement

d. Between 25-33% of adults have an initial ORS score above the clinical cut off

5. When analyzing ORS scores that have been entered into web-based applications used for tracking ORS and SRS scores:

   a. ORS scores falling at or above the green line indicate that the client is on track for a successful treatment outcome

   b. ORS scores falling within the red area indicate treatment should be terminated

   c. ORS scores falling within the yellow area indicate more time in treatment is required for a successful outcome

   d. ORS scores that move from red area to the yellow area indicate the client is on track for a successful outcome

6. The clinical cut off of the adult, child and group versions of the Session Rating Scale are:

   a. 25, 28 and 32 respectively

   b. 32, 34 and 36 respectively

   c. 36, 36 and 36 respectively

   d. 32, 32 and 32 respectively

7. When should the ORS be administered?

   a. At the start of service and monthly intervals over the course of treatment

   b. At the start and end of service

   c. After establishing a working relationship with the client and then at the beginning of sessions over the course of treatment

   d. As early as possible at first contact and at the beginning of each session over the course of treatment but no more frequently than once a week.

8. Scores on the SRS that warrant follow up with the client include:

   a. Scores that fall below 36

   b. Scores that fall 1 point or more between sessions

   c. Scores that are perfect every session

   d. All of the above

9. A score on the ORS that is obtained by asking a referrer to complete the ORS based on their impression of how the client they referred is doing is known as:

   a. An internal collateral rating

   b. An external collateral rating

   c. Both an internal and external collateral rating

   d. Referrers usually are asked to complete an SRS not an ORS

10. If there is no progress on ORS scores by the third or fourth visit:

    a. The helper should not be too concerned

    b. The helper should speak to the client about their goals and expectations ad explore possible changes within the service provided that might be helpful

    c. The helper should refer the client to a different helper

    d. The helper should make substantive changes in their approach

Answers: *1. A; 2. C; 3. D; 4. C; 5. A; 6. C; 7. D; 8. D; 9. B; 10. B*

CHAPTER 3

FEEDBACK-INFORMED CONSULTATION

IN THIS CHAPTER, THE feedback-informed approach for helping mental health professionals work more effectively with clients at risk for negative or null outcomes or dropout from care, is described and illustrated. As will be seen, it departs sharply from theories and practices associated with traditional supervision (e.g., supporting the use of a specific model, theorizing about causes of and solutions for client problems, addressing the impact of the work on the helper), providing a structure for helping process client feedback and adjust services to ensure engagement and effectiveness. For reasons to be described, what has long been referred to as, "FIT Supervision," has been renamed the "FIT Consultation" approach. Information is divided into three sections:

1. Research on the effectiveness of supervision

2. Why FIT Consultation versus FIT Supervision

3. The FIT Consultation Approach

1. RESEARCH ON THE EFFECTIVENESS OF SUPERVISION

Supervision has a long and venerated history in the field of mental health. Since the earliest days of the psychoanalytic movement, its methods and mission have remained remarkably consistent. According to Watkins (2015) it is, "the very crux" of practitioner education, contributing to or allowing for:

1. The development and enhancement of ... conceptual and treatment skills;

2. the development and crystallization of [practitioner] identity;

3. the development of conviction about the meaningfulness of [the practitioner's chosen treatment approach] itself;

4. proper monitoring of the [practitioner's] treatment efforts and, where necessary, "gate-keeping" (i.e., not sending an unacceptable candidate forward); and

5. the monitoring and safeguarding of patient care. (p. 231)

Helpers, research indicates, value supervision. In their massive, long-term international study of practitioner development, Orlinsky and Rønnestad (2005) found, "practitioners at all experience levels, theoretical orientations, professions, and nationalities report that supervised client experience is highly important for their current and career development" (p. 188). Indeed, according to supervisees, the relationship between the amount and frequency, and their satisfaction with and perceived helpfulness of supervision, is simple: more is better (Hill & Knox, 2013; Lambert & Ogles, 1997). In terms of sources of influence, it ranks third in importance, exceeded only by direct clinical experience and personal therapy. Evidence shows participating in supervision can enhance helper self-awareness, treatment knowledge, skill acquisition and utilization, and self-efficacy (Hill & Knox, 2013; Knox & Hill, 2021; Lambert & Arnold, 1987; Lambert & Ogles, 1997; Watkins, 1997; Watkins & Callahan, 2019).

Such positive impacts on helpers notwithstanding, the relationship between the outcome of psychotherapy and practitioner participation in supervision is less clear. It is worth noting that, despite being a prerequisite for licensure in most countries and a requirement of many jobs, few actual studies of its effectiveness have been published (Caldwell, 2015). A recent review and meta-analysis by Keum and Wang (2020) found only four, with the effects being small and ranging from negative to positive. Meanwhile, two, large real-world studies found supervisors accounted for a negligible, if any, amount (0.0 to .04%) of the variance in client care outcomes (Rousmaniere et al. 2014; Whipple et al. 2020).

While the previous results may come as a surprise to many practitioners, the failure to establish a clear connection between supervision and improved client outcomes was predicted more than two decades ago. At that time, researchers Wampold and Holloway (1997) argued the complex interactions between the supervisor, practitioner, and clients made it difficult, if not impossible, to determine the true impact of supervision on outcome. From a FIT perspective, such findings are understood as resulting from the lack of direct focus on the client's experience of treatment (e.g., process and outcome) in traditional supervision.

According to the official guidelines of the American Psychological Association (2018), supervision is defined as:

> ... a distinct professional practice employing a collaborative relationship that has both facilitative and evaluative components, that extends over time, which has the goals of enhancing the professional competence and science-informed practice of the supervisee, monitoring the quality of services provided, protecting the public, and providing a gatekeeping function for entry into the profession. (p. 2)

A framework adopted by many government agencies, professional organizations, and regulatory bodies cites three functions of ongoing, clinical supervision:

1. **Formative (Educative):** relates to supervisee learning, skills development and professional identity development.

2. **Normative (Managerial):** refers to accountability, developing best practice principles, ethical and legal considerations, compliance with agency and organizational procedures and professional standards for the well-being of clients.

3. **Restorative (Supportive):** considers the impact of the work on the supervisee and the necessary psychological support and scaffolding required to offer professional support to the supervisee. This function can help mitigate the stresses and impacts of the work and promote practical well-being. (pp. 7-8, Creaner, 2014)

As can be seen, while perhaps assumed, neither definition mentions actively taking steps to help clients most at risk for dropping out or experiencing a negative or null outcome from care, much less an approach for identifying such clients independent of the interpretations of the practitioner and supervisor. Indeed, in most supervision, helpers choose both "what" and "who" to discuss. The process that follows, including any judgements regarding competence, quality, and gatekeeping, are based on the supervisor's evaluation of what the practitioner reports. Absent is any clear and unfiltered report from the client about: (1) their experience of the help being offered; or (2) the impact of the supervision their therapist receives.

The consequence of such an arrangement for clients is far from hypothetical. First, consider research showing that supervisees who rate their supervisor as "interpersonally attractive" are, in turn, rated by supervisors as effective, despite neither being related to outcome (Wampold & Holloway, 1997). Next, recall data cited in Chapter 1 showing that, "even when an evidence-based treatment is offered to carefully screened individuals who have the same disorder and see helpers who have been carefully selected, monitored, and supervised, 30-50% of patients fail to respond" (p. 81, Lambert, 2017). Among these, between 20 and 30% are not only not better, but actually worse than they were when treatment started (Lambert, 2013; Warren et al. 2009). And yet, as reported in Chapter 2, studies show helpers frequently fail to identify, much less make substantive changes in services for clients at risk for a negative outcome or dropout from treatment (Hannan et al. 2005; Hatfield et al. 2009; Lutz, 2014; Zilcha-Mano et al. 2015). In sum, even when the relationship between supervisor and supervisee is rated highly by both participants, failing to organize the process around the client's experience of their engagement in and outcome of care, undermines the potential helpfulness of treatment and supervision.

2. WHY FIT CONSULTATION VERSUS FIT SUPERVISION?

The first edition of the *ICCE Manuals on Feedback Informed Treatment* devoted an entire volume to what was then referred to as, "FIT Supervision." As stated in the manuals, the primary objective of the approach was, "to ensure services being delivered engage the client and are effective in each case" (p. 5; Bertolino & Miller, 2012). While the purpose has remained unchanged in the time since the publication of the series, the process has been renamed and refined. The specific changes in the approach will be described in the next section. As will be seen, most relate to the broader array of activities the FIT consultant will engage in beyond a focus on clinical case discussion; in the particular, supporting the adoption and implementation of FIT practice at both the practitioner and agency level.

The main reason for renaming the process, "FIT consultation," is to make a clear distinction between the approach described in this chapter and traditional supervision activities (e.g., learning particular techniques, providing psychological support for the helper, discussing cases based solely on practitioner and supervisor judgements and interpretations). Experience from FIT implementations around the world revealed the term "supervision" invited significant confusion among participants and agency managers. For example, believing staff were receiving the support they desired and valued, some managers replaced access to traditional supervision—recall, an activity, research shows, helpers value deeply—with attendance at "FIT supervision" meetings. In other instances, practitioners felt shut down in their attempts to discuss topics they thought important but unrelated to the singular focus on clients' experiences of care characteristic of FIT (e.g., theoretical discussions about particular diagnoses or cases where no outcome data was available, personal reactions to clients and the work)—all of which may be of value, but never were a part of FIT. Finally, the significant differences in the role and responsibilities of a traditional and "FIT supervisor" left many in a difficult position. Unlike the former, the latter were not professionally responsible for the cases discussed, were expected to refrain, as well as stop others from providing advice or direction and, lacked the authority to make helpers adopt specific recommendations or change how they were working. As such, the term "FIT consultant" is believed to better represent their role in facilitating the collaborative, interactive, and non-hierarchical process to be described next.

3. THE FIT CONSULTATION APPROACH

The FIT consultation approach is detailed in Figures 3.1 and 3.2 (see Appendices C and D). As is illustrated in Figure 3.1, initial steps are focused on determining whether cases practitioners bring are appropriate for FIT "clinical" consultation. Several conditions require the FIT consultant devote time to what has been termed, "administrative consultation" versus reviewing specific cases (Maeschalck et al. 2012).

Administrative Consultation

This type of work involves teaching FIT principles and practices, correcting misunderstandings, and addressing individual and agency barriers to using feedback tools with clients. For example, in the early stages of implementation (see Chapter 5), it is not uncommon for practitioners to introduce measures into their work with established clients. However, as the TRTs and SPI are only valid when outcome measures are administered from the outset of care, it is not appropriate to use the resulting data to inform treatment decisions. In such instances, consistent with the guidance offered in Figure 3.1, the job of the FIT consultant would be to help practitioners: (1) understand why use of the measures should be limited to new clients; and (2) teach how to develop a culture of feedback to ensure client engagement in the feedback process (see section 2 of the prior chapter). At times, agency traditions or policies may conflict with FIT principles and practice. For example, administration of the ORS may be delayed because of an intake or pre-treatment diagnostic process lasting several visits. As will be described in chapter 5, the FIT consultant will need to communicate such barriers to management and the group overseeing implementation (known as the Transition Oversight Group) for action and resolution.

Figure 3.1: FIT Consultation Approach

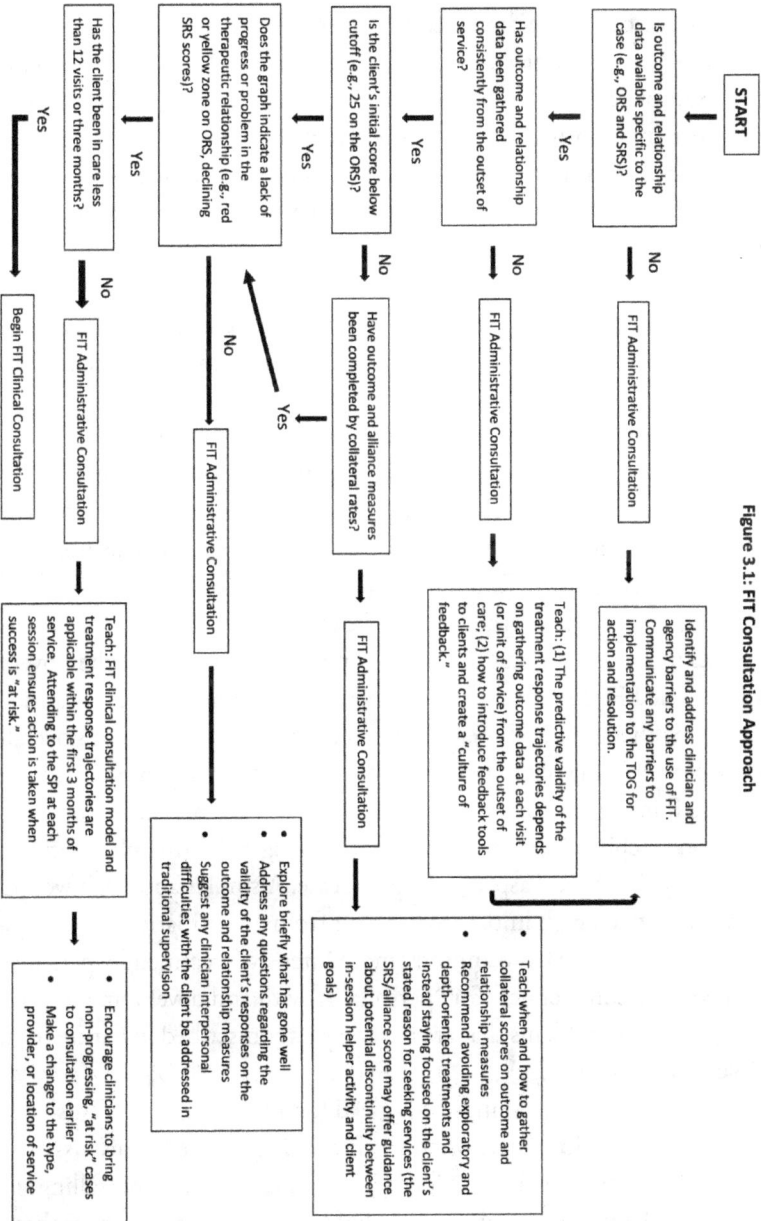

Figure 3.1: FIT Consultation Approach

Administrative consultation may also be called for when the intake score of the case to be discussed falls above the clinical cutoff (e.g., 25 on ORS). As reported in section 3 of Chapter 2, and illustrated in case example 2.7, such scores are often obtained from people who are in treatment because others are concerned about them (e.g., parents, school officials, the courts). From a FIT perspective, the best clinical practice is to gather internal and/or external collateral scores. In the absence of knowledge about or use of this fundamental FIT skill, consultation would be administrative in nature; that is, focused on teaching and practicing how to solicit and work clinically with such scores, as well as monitoring helper performance until proficiency is achieved (see Figure 3.1).

Another reason for intake scores falling above cutoff is that the client's concern or presenting problem does not impact their overall sense of well-being or level of functioning. Phobias are a good example. When not in contact with the feared situation, object, or creature, people are often highly functional. From a FIT perspective, the challenge in such cases is addressing the client's stated reason for seeking services in a manner that does not result in a deterioration of their overall scores. The FIT consultant would, therefore, recommend being cautious about any therapeutic strategy that could undermine the client's overall sense of well-being (e.g., confrontation, exploratory, depth-oriented). As suggested in Figure 3.1, consultation would be administrative, focused more on teaching, instructing, and role-playing FIT principles than discussing the clinical aspects of a given case. A similar approach would be advised when high initial scores result from: (1) initiation of services following discharge from another, more intensive treatment experience; (2) people seeking services for "personal growth and development"; and (3) presenting problems that are relatively circumscribed in nature (e.g., job change, test anxiety).

Two other situations indicate a need for administrative versus clinical consultation: first, when a helper brings a case for discussion where no concern or risk is evident in the graph (e.g., scores falling green zone); and second, when the client has been in care longer than 12 visits (or three months) without progress. Regarding the latter, given that a lack of improvement by the twelfth week is associated with a higher risk of a negative outcome at termination, consultation focused on the clinical aspects of the case (e.g., therapeutic relationship) would not be recommended. Instead, the FIT consultant would: (1) encourage helpers to bring non-progressing, "at risk" cases for consultation earlier in care (e.g., third visit); and, in the specific case (2) support the helper and manager to make more significant changes to the services being delivered (e.g., facilitating referral to a different provider, another type of help or outside agency or specialist for in-depth medical or psychological evaluation).

When helpers bring "green" cases to consultation, three administrative actions are possible. In the early phases of implementation, for example, experience shows allowing time for briefly exploring and celebrating what has gone well in an episode of care can be productive. Hearing about the successes of colleagues can be inspiring to practitioners who are struggling with their application of FIT while also offering some relief from the singular focus on "at risk" cases in the FIT consultation process.

In some situations, a helper may bring a "green" case for discussion because they have concerns about the validity of the data represented on the graph (see section 8, Chapter 2). As the client's perspective is central to FIT practice, the consultant would teach and model taking client scores on the outcome and relationship measures at face value. For example, instead of interpreting high SRS scores as, "people pleasing," the FIT consultant could: (1) remind the helper high scores on relationship scales are common; (2) recommend the helper thank the client for completing the measure and express openness to feedback in future sessions; (3) demonstrate how the helper can explore and utilize small variations on subscales to reveal more nuanced feedback; and (4) recommend reaching out after the session whenever the helper is concerned the client may not return.

Finally, although infrequent, helpers may cite "interpersonal difficulties" (e.g., inability to relate to the client, lack of fit, personal dislike, anger, sexual attraction) as the reason for wanting to discuss a "green" case. In a now classic study, Pope and Tabachnick (1993) found nearly a third of helpers reported feeling intense dislike for at least one of their clients. From a FIT perspective, unless such issues are putting the client "at risk" for a negative or null outcome or drop out from treatment (as evidenced by declining relationship or progress scores), they are better addressed in traditional supervision or the helper's own personal therapy.

Clinical Consultation

Having ensured the specific case is suited for FIT clinical consultation, the process proceeds in a series of four steps: (1) identifying patterns of concern: (2) case presentation; (3) exploring the helping relationship; and (4) consultant/team reflections. While each is discussed below, it is important to note that consultation continues only through as many steps as it takes for the helper to indicate they feel confident about how to proceed differently in future sessions.

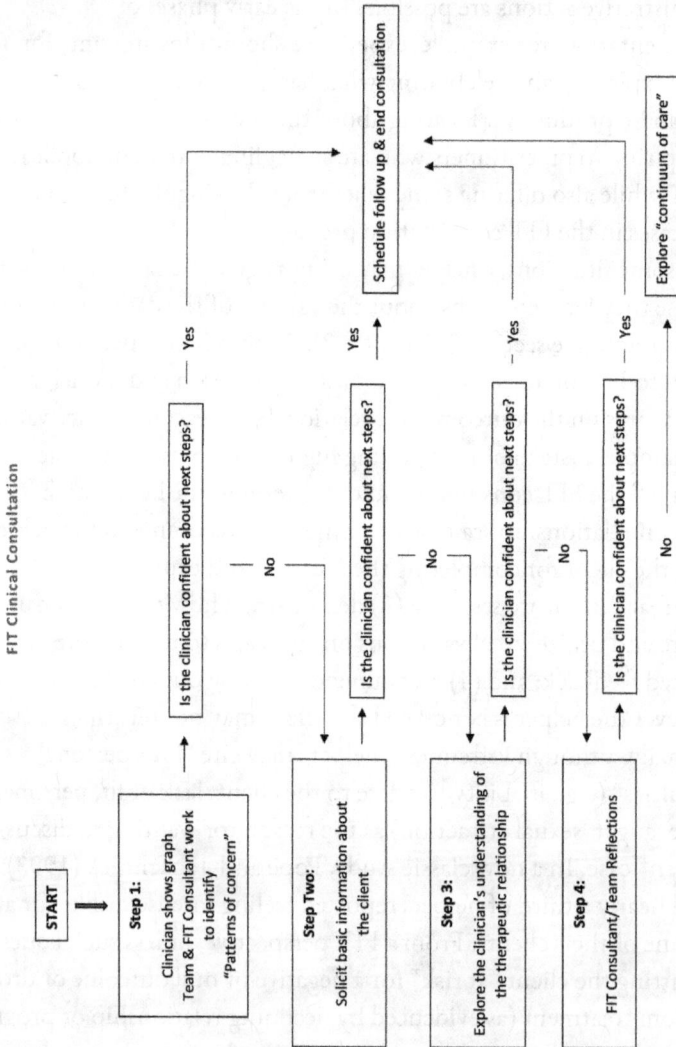

Figure 3.2: FIT Clinical Consultation

Identifying patterns of concern: As seen in Figure 3.2, first the client's graph is presented. At this point, no identifying information is shared (e.g., demographics, diagnosis, treatment approach) rather effort is directed toward identifying "patterns of concern" related to the client's progress and level of engagement. When conducted in a group context, the consultee listens without commenting as the FIT consultant leads a discussion focused on describing what is visible in the graph. Theory-driven interpretations or offering diagnostic formulations are actively discouraged. Typically lasting no more than 5 minutes, the FIT consultant then checks in with the helper, soliciting their perceptions.

Initially, identifying patterns of concern may prove challenging. After all, the course of change for individual clients can unfold in a near infinite number of ways (see Figure 3.3).

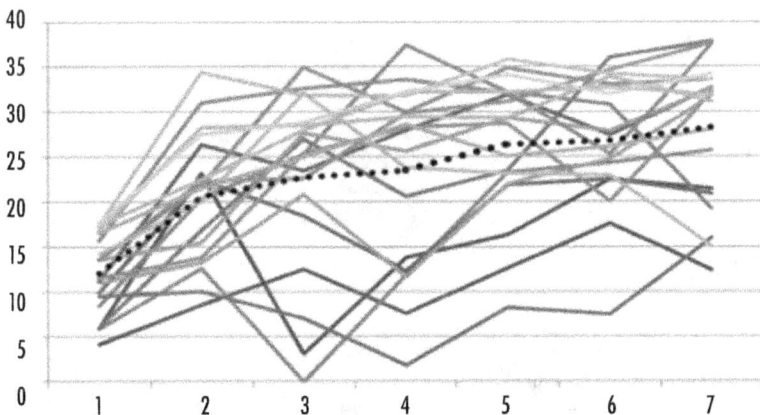

Figure 3.3: Individual client ORS scores recorded in one helper's practice. (The various lines represent different individual client ORS scores. The dotted line represents an average of all client ORS scores)

Fortunately, despite individual client variation, several patterns of scores are commonly seen when tracking client progress. Each of these patterns has different implications for understanding challenges associated with engagement in and the outcome of care. Three questions have proven useful for identifying these patterns:

- *Do outcome scores reflect improvement (at or above the green TRT line)?*

- *What do the relationship scores indicate regarding client engagement?*
- *What do the outcome and relationship scores, in combination with the Success Probability Index (SPI) suggest about the likelihood of care leading to sustainable change?*

With these questions in mind, consider the following graph (see Figure 3.4):

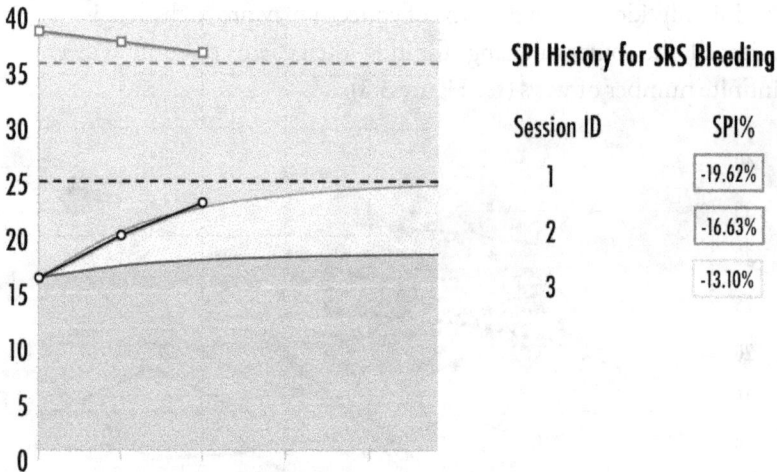

SPI History for SRS Bleeding	
Session ID	SPI%
1	-19.62%
2	-16.63%
3	-13.10%

Figure 3.4: Example 1 "Bleeding"

Question one is, "Do the outcome scores reflect improvement?" And, in fact, the black line representing the ORS is moving up. Additionally, the score at session 3 is in the "green zone." As noted in Chapter 2, scores falling in this area are indicative of clients who are on track for a positive outcome at the conclusion of treatment. Given this pattern of results, the answer to this first question is, yes, progress is being made. At the same time, the TRT (i.e., green line) indicates more improvement is possible if the client continues in care.

The answer to the second question—"What do the relationship scores indicate regarding client engagement?"—reveals a concern. As can be seen, the SRS is slowly deteriorating over time. This pattern of scores is termed, "bleeding" (Maeschalck et al. 2012). Recall, research has established that such a decline—even of a single point—is associated with a heightened risk of dropout or deterioration in future visits (Miller, Duncan et al. 2004; Owen et al. 2016).

Taken together, the outcome and relationship scores, and the session-to-session SPI, (in Figure 3.4, the first two SPI's are coded red, the third yellow) provide an answer to question three. Specifically, the declining SRS scores and negative SPI's indicate that both the client's gains and their engagement in care are at risk. The clinical implications of this pattern of results are obvious. At the next visit, the helper should directly address problems in the relationship. More, as dropout is a very real possibility, the helper should consider reaching out to the client prior to the next visit. The contact need not be long or involved. The point is to demonstrate awareness of potential client concerns, an openness to their feedback, and willingness to adjust service to achieve a better fit (de Jong et al. 2012).

A second example of a graph can be seen in Figure 3.5. Once again, consider the three questions. First, do the scores reflect improvement? As the ORS is increasing and falls in the "green zone" at the second session, it is clear the client is reporting progress. Regarding question #2, SRS scores are on the rise, a pattern associated with higher levels of client engagement and better outcomes at termination (Miller et al. 2004; Owen et al. 2016). So, does this example represent a "pattern of concern?" The answer can be found in question three, "what do the scores, in combination with the SPI, (first SPI coded red, second green) indicate about the sustainability of change?"

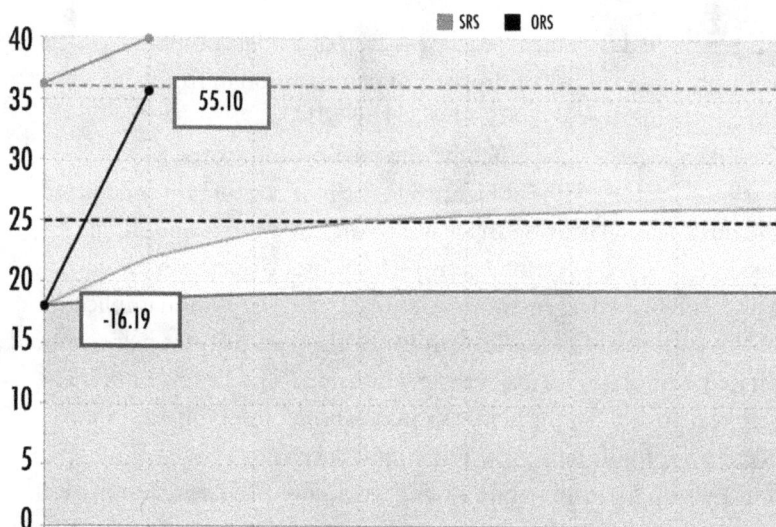

Figure 3.5: Example 2 "Surge"

The reader may already have noticed the size of the improvement in outcome scores between the first and second session, from 18 to 36. Such large changes relative to the TRT for successful treatment (i.e., green line), and reflected in the SPI (the first negative SPI is coded red, the second positive value is coded in green), are often explained by events external to care (e.g., getting or losing a job, the beginning or end of a romantic relationship, birth or death of a loved one, involvement in or resolution of a legal proceeding). Not surprisingly, these "surges," and their opposite—often referred to as "ditches" by FIT practitioners —typically return to pre-external event levels in a visit or two. With the former, the risk is that if unprepared, the subsequent downturn can result in the client concluding care is not helpful. As seen in the Figure 3.6, this is often reflected in a decline of SRS scores and lower SPI (a negative score coded red) in the sessions immediately following a surge. Predicting and normalizing a drop in ORS scores can be a helpful strategy for securing client engagement as outcome scores drop. Additionally, actively exploring how the client might maintain some of the gains associated with the surge can be effective in minimizing both the emotional impact and magnitude of the downturn.

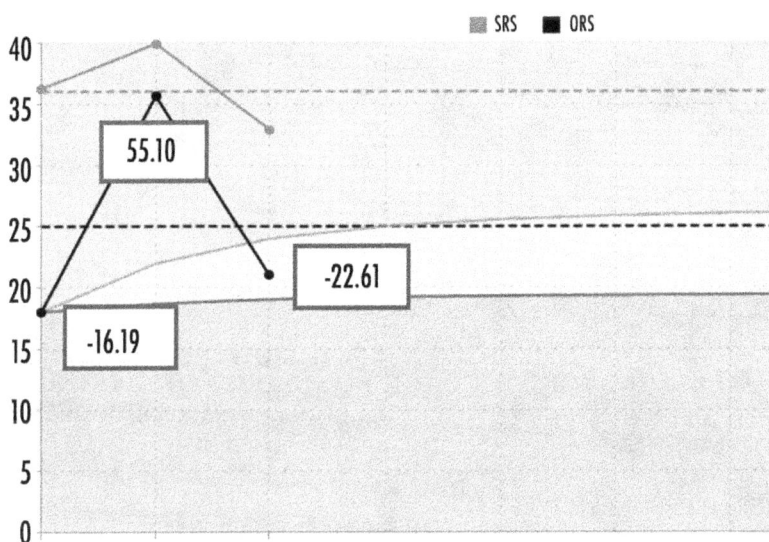

Figure 3.6: Example 2 at session 3

Clinical experience indicates helpers will encounter more "ditches" than "surges" when using FIT with clients. The reasons for this are unknown. It could simply be that downturns are seen as more critical subjects of conversation in therapy. Simply put, when a client has a painful and disruptive shift in their well-being, helpers may feel compelled to intervene. Consider the graph in Figure 3.7. With a bit of reflection, any number of situations could be represented by the pattern in the scores. For example, the client may have received bad news (e.g., an illness, death, loss of job, financial or legal difficulties) or experienced an interpersonal conflict (fight with partner, friendship, child). In contrast to surges, which pose a risk to client engagement when scores subsequently decline, ditches typically return to pre-external event levels without intervention within one or two visits (see Figure 3.8). As such, patience is warranted. Best practice is to provide support rather than immediately changing the type, frequency, nature or focus of care.

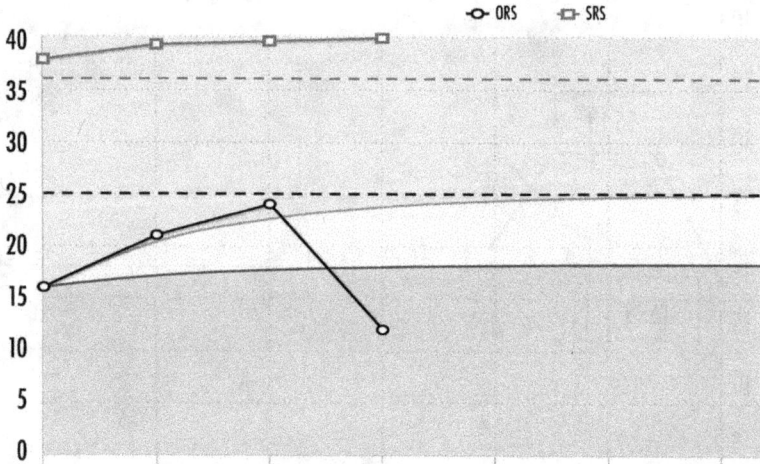

Figure 3.7: Example 3 "Ditching"

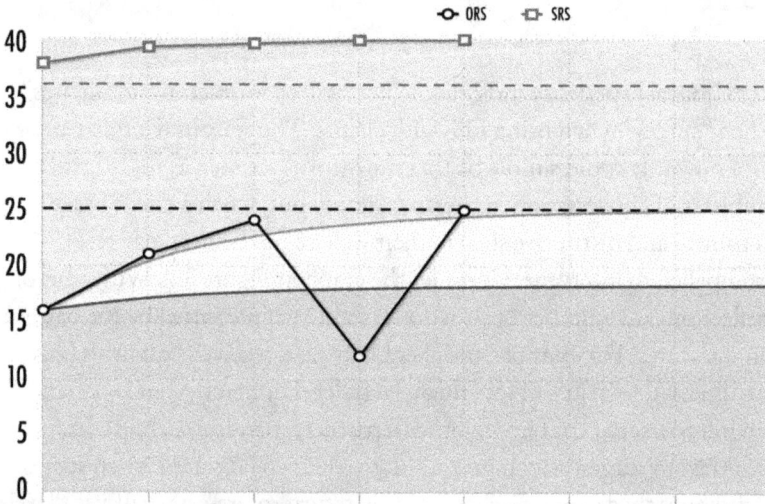

Figure 3.8: Example 3 the session following a ditch

A third example of a pattern of concern can be found in Figure 3.9. Returning to the three questions, the outcome scores at the last recorded visit are up and in the "green zone" (Q1). Relationship scores are also on the rise (Q2). However, when it comes to sustainability (Q3), a concern becomes apparent. Referred to as a "see saw," the outcome scores can be seen to ditch and surge from session to session. Regardless of the overall slope (i.e., increasing or decreasing), or number of scores in the green versus red or yellow zones, progress is unstable, putting the client at risk for continuing, but ineffective care (note: the same pattern is reflected in SPI scores which shift from yellow to green, then red, green, red and green).

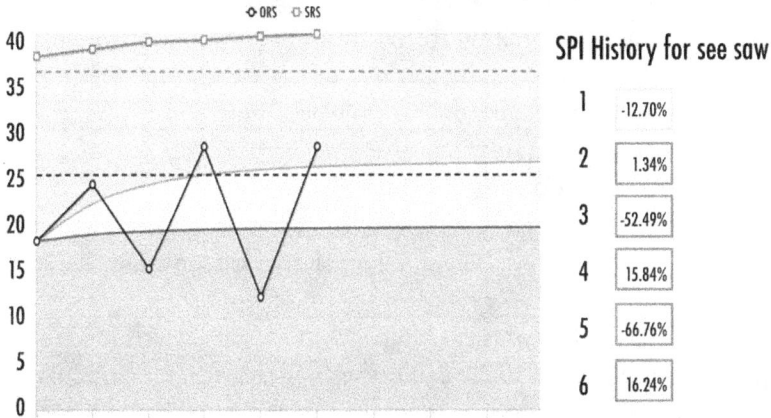

Figure 3.9: Example 4 "See Saw"

One of the chief causes of the "see saw" pattern is improper completion of the outcome measure. With the ORS, for example, clients are asked to, "think back over the last week, or since your last visit" when answering the four questions. Despite this instruction, it is not uncommon for clients—children and adolescents in particular—to respond based on how they feel at the moment. Instead of outcome, the graph merely reflects the impact of external events or transitory emotional states of the client at the time of measurement. As such, a useful first step when encountering this pattern is ensuring directions for completing the measure have been followed.

Beyond simple reminders, some clients may need more support to move beyond a focus on the "here and now." As introduced in Chapter 2, "process recall" has proven helpful in this regard. As the following example shows, it involves engaging in a bit of small talk related to events occurring between visits and prior to administering the ORS.

CASE EXAMPLE 3.1: PROCESS RECALL

David was a 22-year-old male living in state supported housing. It was his fourth apartment since entering the program three years earlier, and following multiple, unsuccessful foster care placements. He had a lengthy history of involvement with the mental health and legal systems beginning in his mid-teen years, including multiple hospitalizations and brief incarcerations. In addition to frequent emotional outbursts, he had been violent toward himself, program staff and other participants on multiple occasions. Psychological testing revealed significant cognitive/intellectual disability (e.g., IQ = 60, dyslexia, and autism). Multiple psychiatric diagnoses had been given over the years including alcohol and drug abuse and dependence, attention deficit and hyperactivity, depression, anxiety and psychosis.

Given David's history and challenges, the helper questioned the appropriateness of routinely administering the ORS. Of particular concern was David's capacity to recall and reflect on his experience, especially given that he reported "remembering nothing" about the prior week when asked to complete the measure during the initial visit. After seeing a video of another helper engaging in "process recall," the following dialogue ensued:

"So, David, today is Thursday and our last appointment was scheduled for a week ago."

David nodded in agreement and the helper continued, "But you canceled. Do you remember what was happening? What was going on that day that you decided to cancel our meeting?"

"Yeah," David began, "there were a lot of things going on in my head and I decided I just couldn't take in anymore."

Affirming his decision, the helper said, "Sounds like it was a good idea that we didn't meet, that you canceled," and then continued with a question about David's sense of well-being at the time.

"Do you remember how you were feeling?"

"Overwhelmed," he responded, "but not depressed. I just had a lot, too much, to think about. That's all."

Focused on helping David connect with events and feelings of the past week, the helper moved on to the next day. "And, how about Friday? What did you do then?"

Looking blankly, he quickly answered, "I don't know. I really have no idea."

Having prepared for their visit, the helper knew David had in fact met with other professionals during the week and used that information to foster further recollection. "Didn't you have a meeting with your social worker, Annie? The one who has been helping you with your finances?"

David immediately sat up straight. With a look of recognition, "Oh yeah! That's right. I went there after my girlfriend came over and we had lunch together."

Seeking details and nuance, the helper inquired, "And, how did that go, was it a good meeting?" To which David responded, "It was fine, nothing special." Then, following a brief pause, added, "After though, my girlfriend and I went to the park. That was fun."

Turning to his sense of well-being, the helper asked, "And do you remember how you were feeling that day?" He did. In particular, being less overwhelmed, calmer, and able to have a good time with his "sweetheart" without experiencing cravings for drugs or alcohol.

The same pattern continued for another 4 minutes reviewing each day of the week leading up to the present meeting. With each iteration, David's participation increased, and his recollection of events became more spontaneous. When asked to complete the ORS for the week just reviewed, he did so immediately and without difficulty. The same process was employed in subsequent sessions. Over time, David's scores improved consistent with the TRT. Importantly, collateral scoring completed by Annie, his employer and the apartment manager confirmed the reported progress.

In addition to the example above, it is possible "see-sawing" scores are due to ineffective care. Simply put, the ups and downs indicate that the client's life outside of therapy is having a greater impact on their functioning than the work occurring in treatment. Therefore, once improper completion of the outcome measure has been ruled out, this pattern would indicate changes need to be made in the help being offered.

Three additional "patterns of concern" are presented in Figures 3.10, 3.11, and 3.12. Review each example, taking time to answer the three questions:

- *Do outcome scores reflect improvement?*
- *What do the relationship scores indicate regarding client engagement?*
- *What do the outcome and relationship scores, in combination with the SPI, suggest about the likelihood of care leading to sustainable change?*

In each instance, also consider what steps the helper should take at the time of the last recorded visit to improve engagement and/or outcome.

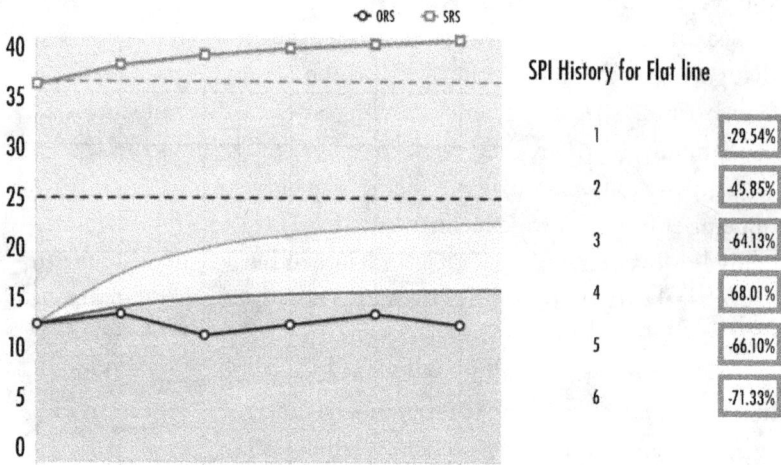

Figure 3.10: Example 5 "Flat Line"

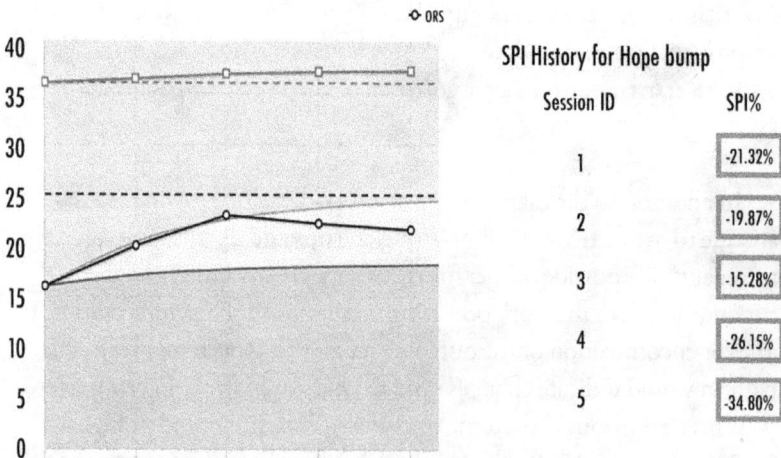

Figure 3.11: Example 6 "Hope Bump"

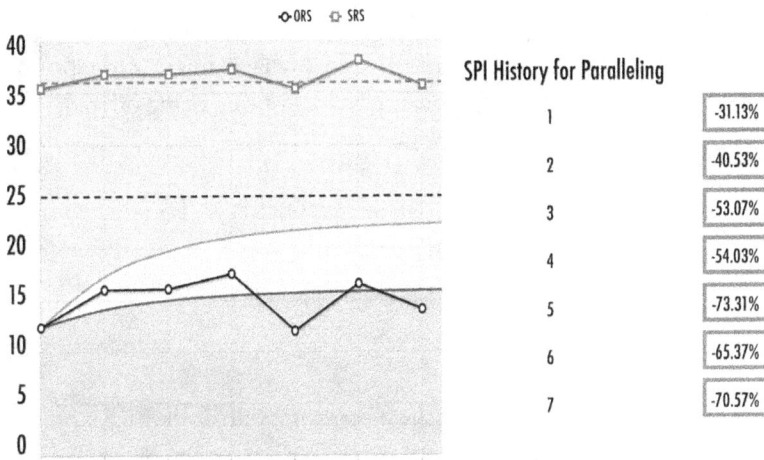

Figure 3.12: Example 7 "Paralleling"

Starting with example 5, referred to as "flat line" (Figure 3.10):

- *Question 1:* ORS shows no progress.

- *Question 2:* SRS scores are improving.

- *Question 3:* Continued engagement without progress and declining SPI (beginning and ending in red).

- *Next steps:* The client is "at risk" for coming to depend on the helper for ongoing support without therapeutic benefit (declining SPI). Check the client's understanding of the "culture of feedback"; specifically, what actions will be taken in the absence of progress (see page 31, Chapter 2).

Moving on to example 6, labelled "hope bump" (Figure 3.11):

- *Question 1:* ORS scores slowly decreasing following barely "on track" improvement (reflected in the TRT).

- *Question 2:* SRS scores are improving.

- *Question 3:* Progress is not being sustained. After a period of below average progress, the SPI (coded red throughout) drops significantly (beginning and ending in red).

- *Next steps:* The progress reported in the early visits is slowly dissipating. Sometimes referred to as a "hope bump," it reflects the impact of positive expectations versus actual change in the client's life or circumstances. The helper (and consultant) would want to explore what is missing in terms of the focus, amount, type or provider of care being offered.

Finally, example 7, or "paralleling" (Figure 3.12):

- *Question 1:* At the last session, the ORS score is in the red and close to the score recorded at the first visit.

- *Question 2:* The last SRS score falls below the clinical "cutoff" (i.e., 36). Beginning in the fourth visit, SRS scores have become variable.

- *Question 3:* Note how the ORS scores mirror the SRS scores, moving up and down in unison. Taken together, the outcome and relationship scores and SPI (coded red throughout) indicate both engagement in care and the potential for sustainable progress are at risk.

- *Next steps:* Similar to "see sawing," this pattern known as "paralleling," indicates that the client's ratings are disconnected from the care being offered. Thus, on a "good day," both well-being and the quality of the relationship are rated highly, and vice versa. After ensuring the client is completing the measures as instructed, the helper (and consultant) would need to move beyond exploring to making substantive changes in terms of amount, type or provider of services being offered.

It is worth pointing out that linking an individual client's graph to a "pattern of concern" often provides information sufficient for the helper to know and feel confident about the changes they must make in their way of working to improve the chances of success. In such instances, consistent with the guidance offered in Figure 3.2, a follow up would be scheduled and the consultation ended. Whether consultation is conducted individually or in a group format, should the helper remain uncertain about how to proceed, the process would move on to step 2, the brief "case presentation."

Case presentation: In contrast to traditional supervision, the case presentation in FIT consultation provides only the most basic information about the client and their care-to-date (see Figure 3.13). In total, this should take no more than 5 minutes, but most often is completed in 2 to 3. The purpose of this truncated format is to prevent the introduction of narratives about the client that may prematurely limit the ideas and approaches explored by the therapist, consultant, and team. It is worth pointing out that experienced FIT teams often skip the case presentation, allowing the information necessary for understanding client progress and engagement to emerge organically in the next step.

BASIC CLIENT INFORMATION
First Name:
Gender:
Age: (Child, adolescent, adult)
Family/relationships:
Work/education:
Referral source: (Who is concerned?)
Services start date:
Current services: (Type [including pharmacy], frequency, intensity)
Substance use: (Yes/no)
Client's stated reason for seeking treatment:

Figure 3.13: Basic Client Information

Although rare, it is possible a helper might develop ideas about how to proceed differently in future sessions during the presentation of basic client information. In such instances, except for scheduling a follow-up, no further discussion would be necessary. Together, the FIT consultant and group would move on to the next case. However, should nothing new emerge, the process proceeds to step three, "exploring the helping relationship."

Exploring the helping relationship: Recall from Chapter 1, research shows the client's experience of the relationship is one of the best predictors of their engagement and progress in care. As such, when the outcome and alliance data indicate a case is "at risk" for a negative or null outcome, or drop out, it makes sense to explore the helper's understanding of the client's expectations regarding their working relationship. The objective is to identify where the helper might improve alignment with the client so that the work can proceed in a more engaging and effective manner.

In chapter 1, the elements comprising the therapeutic relationship were depicted in the form of a three-legged stool (see Figure 3.14). In a typical FIT case consultation, the "relationship stool" is drawn (i.e., white board, flip chart) and the consultant explores the practitioner's understanding of each component. Starting with client goals (represented by the left most leg of the stool) and working through each component:

- *What does the client want from care?*

- *Is the client in agreement about the means and methods being applied?*

- *How does the client want to be understood and seen by the helper?*

- *What role does the client want the helper to play in reaching their specific objectives?*

Put more succinctly, "what does the client want, in what way, consistent with what values, beliefs, and preferences, and what role do they want the helper to play in the process?" It is important to note that the stool, central to the FIT consultation approach, is a tool for reflecting on and adjusting services for non-progressing cases. Although some practitioners and agencies have made it part of the treatment planning process, it was never intended to be used to plan, organize or conduct treatment with every client. More, doing so is not associated with better engagement or outcomes.

WITH "WHOM?"
Client preferences, values, identity, culture/worldview

THE "WHAT?"
Goals, meaning and purpose

THE "HOW?"
Means or methods

BY "WHOM?"
Client view of the bond and role of the helper

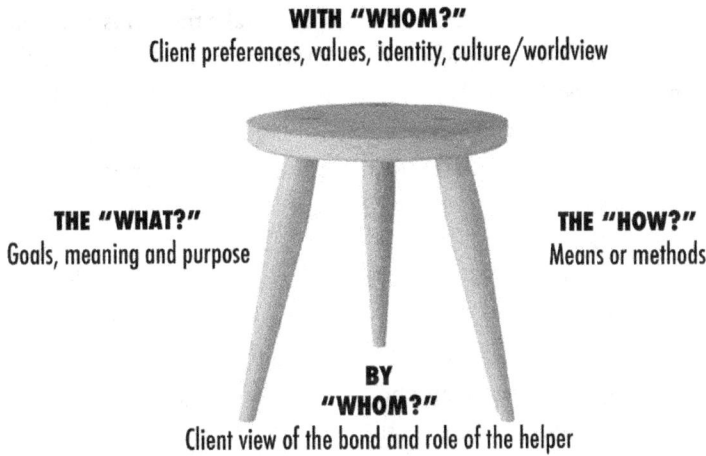

Figure 3.14: The Helping Relationship

As is true of FIT consultation in general, exploration of the various elements comprising the relationship continues only for as long as it takes the helper to develop ideas for how to proceed differently in future visits. Experience shows, for example, in as many as 70% of consultations, simply exploring what the helper believes the client wants is sufficient. Typical misalignments in this area include:

- Organizing services around what the referral source rather than client wants

- Equating the client's goal with their diagnosis/presenting problem, or helper's theory-driven objectives; and finally

- Inferring, guessing, or assuming rather than explicitly negotiating the client's desires, objective(s), and expectations for care

Beginning with the last, assumptions, inferences, and uncertainty regarding the client's goals is visible during consultation in several ways. For example, the helper responding, "I think … ," or "that's complicated" or silence and a blank stare when asked, "what does the client want?" Any answer beginning with, "They need … " or "The client is struggling with … " is a good indication of the first two types of misalignments. Thus, "The client is working on [regulating their emotions, resolving a past traumatic experience, depression, etc.]" or "They need to work on their parenting skills since the state is about to take their kids away" are instances demonstrating a lack of connection between the focus of the work and the client's stated hopes and desires. Simply asking the helper, "Is that what the client said they wanted?" can be helpful in learning what adjustments need to be made to ensure better alignment or, in the absence of a clear answer, that the helper needs to return to the client and ask directly.

While a lack of clarity about or misunderstanding of what the client wants is the most frequent, misalignments occur on the other three components of the relationship as well. It is not uncommon, for example, for helpers to conflate the "what" (client's goals, meaning or purpose) for seeking care with the "how" (it's means, methods, or process). Here, the issue is not uncertainty about, or an incorrect understanding of the client's objectives, but rather an overly narrow definition of the "what" constituting success.

To illustrate, return to graph represented in Figure 3.10. Having identified the pattern of concern (i.e., flat lining), determined that the client is "at risk" (i.e., dependency), and even solicited a brief case presentation, the FIT consultant would begin exploring the helper's understanding of the components of the therapeutic alliance. Now, imagine that when asked, "what is it that your client wants?" the helper quickly and confidently replies, "to stop drinking." From a FIT perspective, this is a perfectly reasonable objective at the outset of care. However, after 6 visits with no progress, and an emerging risk of dependency, it becomes questionable.

What can the FIT consultant do? Treating that initial, narrowly defined goal as a "means to an end," rather than an end in-and-of-itself, has proven helpful. Doing so achieves several objectives. First, it expands the focus beyond the binary, success-fail, nature of the present objective (i.e., stopping drinking), thereby increasing the number of indicators of a successful result. Second, it often serves to connect the work and helper to the client's deepest motivations.

Known as the "means-ends strategy," it involves exploring what would be different if the initial, yet failed, treatment objective was achieved. To wit, "And what would your client say would be different in their life (personally, relationally, and socially) after drinking was no longer a problem?" Most of the time, as the following dialogue shows, the process ends with a greater number of achievable objectives and the helper needing to return to their client for clarification or confirmation:

FIT Consultant (FC): *So, what is it that your client wants?*

Helper (H): *To stop drinking.*

FC: *Is that what your client actually said?*

H: *Yes. It's ruining their life.*

FC: (employing the means-end strategy) *And so, what would your client say will be different in their life after they stop drinking?*

H: *I'm not sure. He's been drinking so long. It's impacted almost everything in his life.*

FC: (persisting) *Take your time and think about it. What would your client say will be different in their life when drinking is no longer a problem for them?*

H: (after a pause) *Well, he hasn't worked in a while now, and I know how important working was to him. A lot of what he ruminates about, his low sense of self-worth, is tied up with that.*

FC: *So ... ?*

H: *I think he'd be back at work ... or, at least, preparing to go back.*

FC: (seeking to expand the number of indicators of success) *What would that look like?*

H: (after a pause) *I'm not sure ...* (with a laugh) *He'd have to get up before Noon!*

FC: *If he started getting back to routines, like getting up and going in the morning, things that are typical for people with a regular job, that would be a sign he is on track? Could this, and other changes, be topics you explore with him?*

The means-end strategy has no defined end point. In the dialogue above, for example, "getting a job" could also be treated as a "means," with the consultant exploring what would be different in the client's life once they had returned to work. The purpose is to generate options and connect the helper to what matters most to their client.

Moving on, the bond (represented by the middle leg of the "helping relationship stool") can also be a source of misalignment. Research has long shown, for example, that helpers and clients view the relational bond (including empathy, respect, genuineness) differently, with the client's perception being more highly correlated with engagement and outcome (Bachelor & Horvath, 1999; Bachelor, 2013; Norcross, 2002). Exploring the client's ratings on the SRS—in particular, any single item scored lower than others—can point the FIT consultant to aspects of the relational bond in need of repair or realignment. Inquiring about the helper's understanding of the role their client wants them to assume in the helping process can also be helpful in determining where a lack of clarity or mismatch exists. Does the client prefer a helper who accurately recognizes their innermost experience, appreciates, and understands how they think, or one who participates in their current feeling state, matching their affective experience? How about a helper who shares personal opinions, experiences and gives advice versus one who assumes a non-directive, exploratory, or reflective stance? In truth, all of the above have been shown to work. In each instance, the point of FIT consultation is facilitating better alignment between the client and helper.

The last component of the stool is the seat. Misalignments in this area occur when the helper's understandings or actions are incongruent with the client's preferences, beliefs, values, worldview, or identity (e.g., culture, gender, sexual orientation, ability, religion/spirituality, nationality, socioeconomic status). Occasionally, the helper has missed, or not responded to a direct request from the client regarding the provider or approach (e.g., meeting at a particular time of day, with a certain type of helper). Usually, however, the misalignment is more subtle. Simply put, the helper's actions, recommendations, characterization of or feelings about the client are at odds with the client's beliefs about who they are and what they value. For example, a helper who:

- Recommends parenting classes to a mother who sees herself as a "dedicated and responsible" parent mistreated by an unjust system
- Uses confrontation to "break through resistance" with a client who sees themself as "open, thoughtful, and cooperative"
- Initiates a course of individual treatment with an "acting out" youth who sees their parent/caretaker/school as the problem

As researchers Swift et al. (2023) note, even if "a 100% effective treatment delivered by an expert psychotherapist exist[ed], the chance of it making a difference for [a] particular client is zero ... if they are not willing to engage in it ... because of their culture, values, and beliefs" (p. 48). Meta-analytic studies show significantly larger gains in posttreatment outcomes and lower dropout rates for clients whose preferences, beliefs, values, and identity are accommodated compared with those whose are not.

One of the strongest clues that a mismatch exists in the "seat" of the alliance can be found in the language used by the helper to describe the client. Is it negative? Overly diagnostic? Do the words and concepts used, in effect, attribute the lack of progress or engagement to the client (e.g., poor motivation) rather than the help and helper? If so, asking, "Would the client agree with your description of them?" and "how does your client want to be viewed by you?" are two, time-tested ways FIT consultants can help initiate realignment.

As in the prior steps, should exploration of the elements comprising the relationship result in the helper developing ideas sufficient for proceeding differently in future visits, the consultation would be ended and a follow-up scheduled. If nothing new emerges, or the helper would like additional input, the process proceeds to step 4, "FIT Consultant/ Team reflections" (see Figure 3.2).

Consultant/team reflections: Up to this point, the consultant's role has been limited to soliciting information consistent with each step in the process. When conducted in the context of a group, except for actively helping to identify "patterns of concern" in step one, the team has been in observation mode, listening without commenting. Only in the fourth and final stage are the consultant and team members invited to share their personal reflections about the case. Advice-giving (e.g., "Have you tried ... ," "why don't you ... "), theorizing ("Maybe the client ... [insert professional lingo, e.g., can't mentalize, has an unresolved trauma, has an addictive personality]"), offering model-specific explanations ("This is clearly an example of ... [e.g., dysfunctional thoughts, needing to externalize the problem, countertransference reaction]") and diagnosing ("This person has ... [e.g., personality disorder, bipolar illness, dual diagnosis]") are discouraged. Instead, the helper is asked to listen without commenting while the consultant shares their own ideas or elicits thoughts from the team about elements in the relationship (i.e., goals, means, preferences, and role) or details in the graph that may have been missed, misunderstood, or are incongruent with the client's perspective.

Mindful that numerous, lengthy reflections risk overwhelming the helper, participants are encouraged to keep their comments and queries short and to the point, and to speak in tentative, appreciative and positive terms. Once done, the helper is asked which, if any, of the comments merit exploration with their client. The process is considered complete when the helper expresses confidence about what they will do differently in future visits to improve alignment with their client.

As an illustration, consider the following dialogue between a helper, consultant and team regarding a client who had been given an ultimatum to seek help for his problematic alcohol use or risk losing his family and job. Consistent with the FIT consultation process, a graph had been presented and "pattern of concern" (step 1) identified at the outset; in this instance, similar to the one depicted in Figure 3.10, "flat line" (see page 110). When the case presentation (step 2) and exploration of the helping relationship (step 3) failed to provide the helper with ideas sufficient for them to feel confident about how proceed differently, the consultant asked the team members to share their own reflections (step 4). As the team shared, the consultant added their comments to the FIT alliance stool initially drawn on a flip chart during step 3, and recreated in Figures 3.15 to 3.18.

The first team member (TM1) to speak noted the client's preference for being seen as a "good father, parent, and 'breadwinner'."

> **TM1:** *What stood out to me in both the discussion of the stool and case presentation was just how important family is to this client, and yet all the services being offered are focused exclusively on him. I was wondering what effect it might have were his family more involved, so they could interact regularly, see and encourage him. Even just integrating this core value into the individual work struck me as potentially quite motivating.*

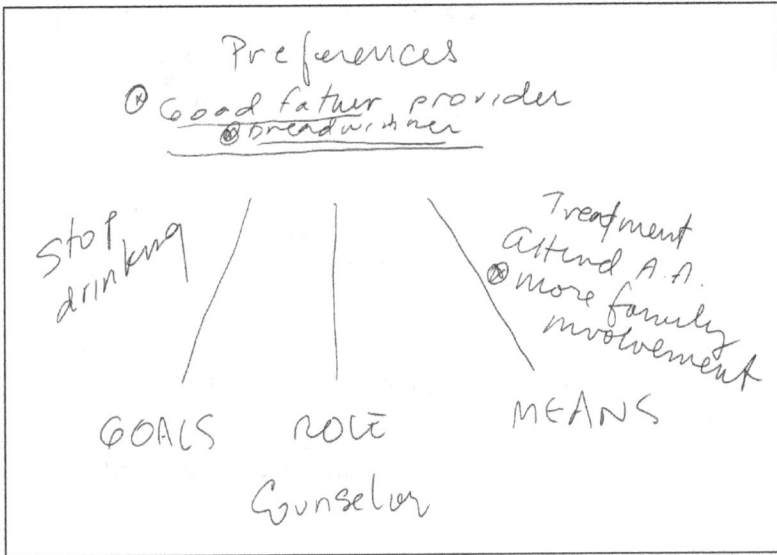

Figure 3.15: The Alliance Stool following Team Member 1 reflections

After underlining the words, "good father" and "breadwinner" above the alliance seat, and adding "family involvement" near the means and methods leg (additions denoted with a *), the FIT consultant asked whether other group members had reflections to share.

> **TM2:** *I first wanted to say that I appreciate your bringing this case to consultation today. Listening reminded me of several of my own clients—two in particular—where I think I may be missing what they want, you know, their goal. Actually, I think my focus has somehow been off. Not consciously, but (with a laugh) we work in a substance abuse treatment center, so of course, we talk, and we teach, and we work on skills and getting support for not using. It's literally drugs and alcohol 24/7! And that works for some people, a lot of people. But even though this client has been drinking for a long time, and has a positive family history, I'm beginning to think that not drinking is not his goal. It can be kind of confusing because the graph shows the relationship improving from session to session. But, at the same time, he's not getting better. So, clearly, something needs to be changed. And this discussion points to his preferences. What's important to him is independence, being a*

self-starter, a leader ... and what (TM1) pointed out, taking care of others, like his family and coworkers—all of which is a bit ironic, or kind of sad really, given that he's in here, in a very dependent and needy position.

FIT Consultant (FC): And so, would you put independence, and helping/taking- care-of-others here (pointing to the goals/meaning/purpose leg of the alliance stool)?

TM2: I do wonder what he'd say would be different, or maybe what his family and employer would notice was different if he took the lead right now, in this treatment and with his family.

FC: (Writing TM2's comments to the goals on the flip chart [i.e., independence, taking care of others]). Others have something?

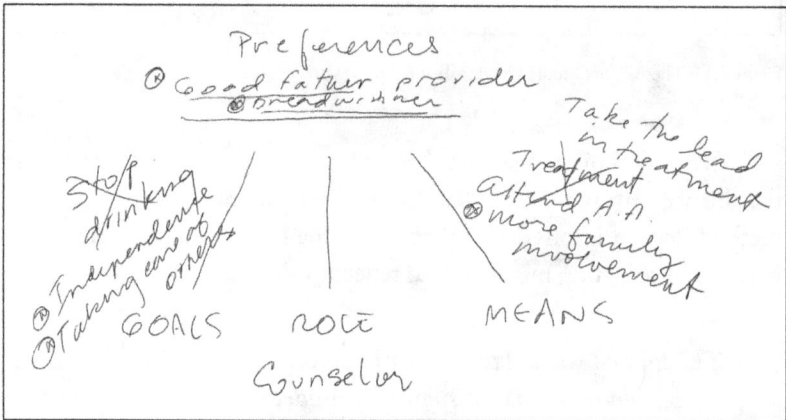

Figure 3.16: The Alliance Stool following Team Member 2 reflections

TM3: I'm kind of stuck on that middle leg. The role. If what everyone else is saying is true, I'm curious about what he wants (the helper) to do. What is he expecting and hoping for? How does he want (the helper) to act? Right now, you're his alcohol counselor. But maybe he wants, I don't know ... an intermediary, someone to "carry water" for him with his family and boss. (Pauses). Maybe less of a drug and alcohol counselor or teacher, and more of a (with a laugh) social worker, hostage negotiator or diplomat! I can even see, coach, since he's quite an accomplished and proud person, despite his struggles, who might value tips, cheerleading, and "fine tuning" more than an "overhaul" of his life and personality.

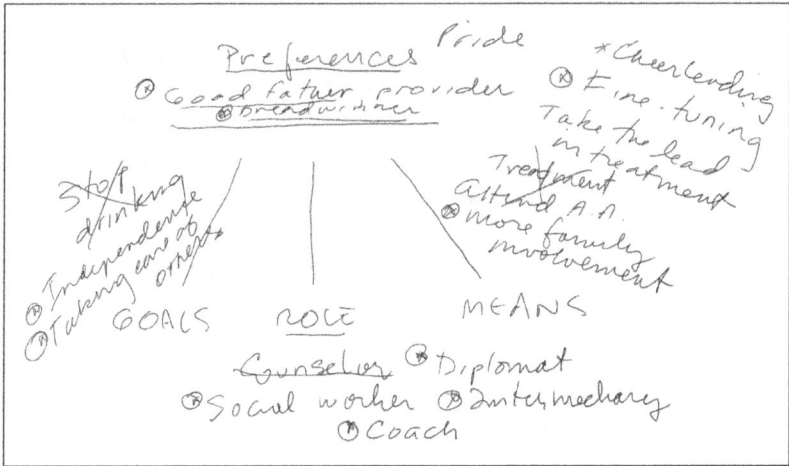

Figure 3.17: The Alliance Stool following Team Member 3 reflections

After recording TM 3's comments to the seat (i.e., pride), means (i.e., cheerleading, fine tuning), the middle leg of the alliance stool (i.e., diplomat, social worker, coach, intermediary), the FIT consultant asked the remaining team members if they had any further reflections to share. When nothing was forthcoming, attention was turned back to the helper.

> **FC:** *OK, you've had a chance to hear everyone's thoughts. Anything that stands out to you? Offers a path for approaching the coming sessions differently?*
>
> **Helper:** (Speaking slowly and thoughtfully). *Yeah ... I don't think I've truly appreciated the difficult position my client is in, being told to "get help or else." It's not that he is difficult to work or empathize with. He's a genuinely thoughtful person and hard worker. But, listening to the group, I think I've missed the parts of him, the preferences, he'd really value having esteemed, heard. That he is a capable, independent, self-made kind of guy. (Pausing) And with that in mind, I think I need to go back and explore what he wants me to do. What my role would be given who he is? Like (TM3) said, am I a social worker, diplomat, (with a laugh) personal consultant?*

Using a different colored pen, the FIT consultant highlighted the elements in the stool the helper would address in the next visit (see circled and newly underlined items (see Figure 3.18). At this juncture, the team and consultant (and perhaps reader) may feel the helper is missing an important element in the consultant's and team's reflections about the alliance stool (e.g., the shift in goals from "stopping drinking" to "independence" and helping others"). However, consistent with the goal of FIT consultation, the helper felt confident about next steps, so the consultation was ended, and a follow-up scheduled.

The best way to determine when to discuss a case again is simply asking the helper, "how many times do you need to meet with the client to know whether the ideas discussed today are helping?" Most often, the consultant and helper will agree to follow-up in two to three weeks, or after 2 or 3 sessions. Should the helper suggest a longer interval (e.g., more than a month or 5 visits), the consultant would want to encourage an earlier meeting as the possibility for improvement steadily declines as time in care without positive change lengthens.

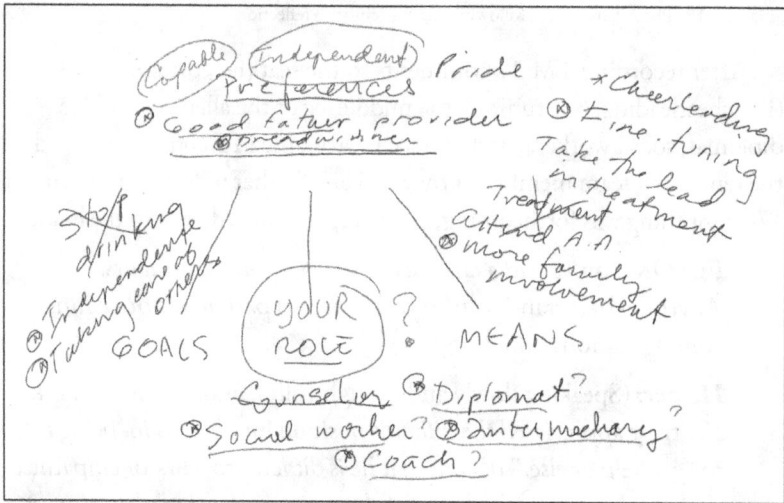

Figure 3.18: The Alliance Stool following Helper's comments

Although no studies exist at present, experience suggests a relatively high percentage of helpers (~ 70 to 80%) conclude an initial FIT consultation meeting with ideas for working differently in future visits with their "at risk" client. In the event nothing new emerges, the process becomes administrative in nature. Consistent with earlier recommendations for non-progressing cases, the FIT consultant would support the helper and manager meeting to determine what to change in the services being delivered (e.g., facilitating referral to a different provider, another type of help or outside agency or specialist for in-depth medical or psychological evaluation).

From start to finish, a FIT consultation inclusive of all four steps should take no more than 15 to 20 minutes. It can take a bit longer when first implementing the approach. Experience shows the leading causes for running longer are: (1) spending too much time reporting the history of the client and their treatment; (2) extracting details about the elements in the alliance stool beyond what is necessary to offer the helper new understandings about the client and their care; and (3) allowing team members to comment at length in step 4. At such moments, the FIT consultant will need to be prepared to intervene to keep the process on track. As limiting, interrupting, and redirecting the focus of sharing contrasts sharply with traditional, open-ended and supportive supervision practices and can be experienced as rude, hurtful, or offensive, it is important at the outset of FIT consultation to secure the groups' explicit permission for the consultant's active management of the process.

SUMMARY

Supervision has a long history in the field of mental health. Evidence shows regular participation improves helper self-awareness, treatment knowledge, skill acquisition and use, and sense of self-efficacy. Unfortunately, the same body of research fails to document any connection between the amount of supervision received and improved client engagement or outcomes. In this chapter, the FIT consultation approach was introduced. In contrast to "formative, normative, and restorative" objectives of traditional supervision, FIT consultation is either administrative or clinical in nature. The former involves teaching FIT principles and practices, correcting misunderstandings, and addressing individual and agency barriers to using feedback tools with clients. The latter is focused exclusively on ensuring services being delivered are effective in each case. It occurs in a series of four steps: (1) identifying patterns of concern; (2) brief case presentation; (3) exploring the helping relationship; and (4) consultant/team reflections. Research and real-world experience in diverse clinical settings around the world indicate the process leads to improved client outcomes (Goldberg, Babins-Wagner et al. 2016; Bargmann, 2017).

QUIZ

1. Which of the following characteristics are typical of the FIT consultation model:

    a. Supports helpers dealing with the impact of their work on their personal well being

    b. Providing a structure for helping practitioners process client feedback

    c. Involves theorizing about causes for client problems

    d. Supports helpers with their use of specific models

2. Traditional supervision has been shown to improve which of the following:

    a. Client outcomes

    b. Practitoner outcomes

    c. Helper's ability to form strong working relationships with clients

    d. Skill acquisition and treatment knowledge

3. What percentage of clients fail to improve despite being matched with helpers who are screened, monitored and supervised?

    a. 0-30%

    b. 30-50%

    c. 50-80%

    d. 20%

4. Administrative FIT consultation involves which of the following tasks?

    a. Teaching helpers when and how to administer outcome and alliance measures

    b. Identifying agency or helper barriers to using FIT

    c. Teaching which cases should be brought for FIT case consultation

    d. All of the above

5. Which of the following would indicate that a case was appropriate for a FIT clinical consultation:

    a. The helper wants help determining the client's diagnosis

    b. The client has been seen for 20 visits and is in the red zone

    c. The client has been seen 3 times and their scores on the ORS fall in the "red zone"

    d. The helper is experiencing "interpersonal difficulties" with the client even though outcome scores are in the "green" zone

6. Which of the following 4 steps of a FIT clinical consultation might be considered unnecessary by experienced FIT practitioners:

    a. Identifying patterns of concern

    b. Case presentation

    c. Exploring the helping relationship

    d. Consultant/team reflections

7. Which of the following questions is not used to identify cases of concern for a FIT clinical consultation?

    a. Do outcome scores reflect improvement?

    b. Are the client's scores trustworthy?

    c. What do the relationship scores indicate regarding client engagement?

    d. What do the outcome and relationship scores, in combination with the SPI, suggest about the likelihood of care leading to sustainable change

8. What are the clinical implications of a see saw pattern?

    a. The client may not understand how they are supposed to complete the measure

    b. The client's life outside therapy may be having a bigger influence than the therapy

    c. Progress is unstable

    d. All of the above

9. A paralleling pattern of scores may indicate:

    a. The client may not understand how to complete the measure

    b. Progress is unstable

    c. The helper and care are not having an impact on the client

    d. None of the above

10. Why is exploration of the elements of the therapeutic alliance central to FIT clinical consultation?

    a. Because misalignment on one or more elements of the alliance is common in non-progressing cases

    b. Because outcome scores are not as important as alliance scores

    c. Because the alliance is a strong predictor of outcomes

    d. A and C above

Answers: *1. B, 2. D, 3. B, 4. D, 5. C, 6. B, 7. B, 8. D, 9. C, 10. D.*

CHAPTER 4

COLLECTING AND UNDERSTANDING AGGREGATE OUTCOME AND RELATIONSHIP DATA

THIS CHAPTER EXPLAINS HOW to measure the effectiveness of mental health services. Guidelines are provided for: (1) ensuring the quality of the data collected; and (2) calculating, understanding, and reporting a variety of statistical indices related to outcome and engagement. Consistent with previous chapters, the examples provided are based on the Session Rating Scale (SRS) and Outcome Rating Scale (ORS). As will be seen, however, the principles and practices described are applicable regardless of the specific scales a practitioner, agency or healthcare system employs. The information provided is divided into three sections, including:

1. Ensuring the quality of outcome and relationship data

2. Common statistical indices/performance metrics

3. Authorized FIT electronic outcome management/feedback systems

1. ENSURING THE QUALITY OF OUTCOME AND RELATIONSHIP DATA

Although the idea had been around for some time, George Fuechsel, a computer programmer during the early days at IBM, is generally credited with coining the expression, "garbage in, garbage out" (Tech Contributor, 2008). Known by the acronym GIGO, it meant that the quality of any output was determined by the quality of the information one put into the system. As sloppy programing inevitably led to erroneous results, users were counseled to exercise considerable care upfront during the coding and data input process.

Nowadays, GIGO is an operating principle in many fields (e.g., audiology, navigation, accident investigations, sound and video engineering), including feedback-informed treatment (FIT). Simply put, faulty, incomplete, inconsistent, or imprecise data (inputs) increase the risk of errors in interpreting results and failures in clinical decision-making (outputs). Two practices help feedback-informed practitioners ensure the quality of the outcome and therapeutic relationship information they solicit from clients: (1) using standardized measurement tools; and (2) adopting a systematic data collection process.

Standardized measurement tools: Questionnaires are a part of everyday life. One promises to reveal how long you can be expected to live, another your "home decorating personality." A few years ago, a 36-item quiz published in the *New York Times* claimed to help people fall in love (Jones, 2015). Meanwhile, after paying for groceries or purchasing a big-ticket item in a retail outlet, it's not uncommon to be asked to provide feedback. "Please use this QR code to answer 3 brief questions," the salesclerk enthusiastically recommends, "and you will be entered into our monthly drawing for a $100 gift card!"

How about questions asked in a live, interview format? Doing so is a standard practice among many employers and graduate school programs, even though decades of research shows the process is time-consuming and expensive, but relatively poor at predicting future performance—a fact that holds true regardless of an interview's duration, and even when the questions are specific and relevant to the domain supposedly being assessed (Edwards et al. 1990; Kreiter et al. 2004; Tuff et al. 2022; Thorsteinson, 2015). Turns out, judgements based on unstructured interview questions, while deeply influential in the selection process, are often based on factors not predictive of success (i.e., participants sharing similar personal qualities, the interviewee's question-answering ability) and prone to confirmation bias (Bohnet, 2016). Such findings are particularly relevant for mental health professionals, most of whom rely on observation, and informal and unstructured feedback, in their day-to-day clinical decision-making. Indeed, it likely explains, in part, research cited in Chapter 1 documenting that helpers do not improve with time and experience in the field.

Standardized measurement scales have several advantages over informally gathered feedback and the brief questionnaires routinely encountered in daily life. First, they have been tested psychometrically to establish validity and reliability. The former refers to an instrument's documented ability to measure what it claims to measure (e. g. outcome or the quality of the therapeutic relationship). The latter, as the term implies, is an indication of a scale's consistency and dependability. Said another way, all things being equal, a reliable scale returns the same result every time its administered. Regarding the ORS and SRS, since first being developed, scores of studies have been published examining the two measures (Schuckard et al. 2017; Seidel & Miller, 2012). Reviews of such research not only show the scales to be valid and reliable, but also capable of assessing factors relevant to effective psychological care (e.g., changes in client engagement and well-being/distress due to treatment versus the influence of extratherapeutic events).

Another advantage of standardized scales is that developers have typically established "cutoffs," and other norms relevant for interpreting the scores produced. As discussed in Chapter 2, the cutoff on the ORS indicates whether a person is scoring more like people who are in treatment (the "clinical range") or those who are not in treatment (the "nonclinical range"). Similarly, on the SRS, a score of 36 represents the dividing line between typical scores (i.e., 36 to 40) and those indicating a potential problem in the helping relationship (i.e., 35.9 and lower). For both scales, knowing the cutoff can provide the helper with information critical to clinical decision making. The way a helper would handle the end of a first visit with a client who scored 32 on the SRS would be markedly different, for example, from someone falling at the top of the scale (e.g., 37-40)—in particular, with scores below cutoff, the typical expression of thanks and openness to feedback in future visits would give way to a more detailed inquiry about the status of the relationship, including an exploration of any specific items scored a point or more lower relative to others (see Chapter 2 for a detailed discussion).

In a similar way, the TRTs and SPI—based as they are on millions of completed episodes of care delivered by thousands of helpers working in diverse settings around the world—provide highly accurate and representative norms for identifying clients "at risk" for a negative or null outcome or dropout from care. As illustrated in Chapter 3, seeing that a particular client's score on the ORS falls in the "red zone" of the TRT enables the helper to make changes in real time to the services being provided, while the SPI provides a numerical indication of when more substantial action will be needed to secure a successful result (e.g., changing the treatment location or provider).

Systematic data collection: One of the most important, and easiest ways to ensure the quality of outcome and relationship data central to FIT is being systematic in the collection process. Seemingly insignificant variations in how, when, and who administers and completes measurement scales can have significant impacts on the results obtained. Imagine the difficulty of making sense of data gathered by a large agency where each helper introduces the ORS in a different way or at different times during the treatment process. Waiting until the first official "treatment" session versus administering the scale at intake, for example, is known to make services appear less effective overall. The same result, plus higher dropout rates, are likely when helpers wait to solicit feedback until after an "assessment phase" is completed (e.g., 1 or more visits dedicated to history gathering and/or diagnostic interviews or testing). Alternately, leaving little time for discussion at the end of a visit, combined with a hurried introduction of the SRS, can have the opposite effect, leading to artificially inflated relationship ratings. In sum, to ensure quality and consistency, outcome and relationship measures should be administered in the same way to all clients beginning with their first contact and continuing at each visit over the entire course of care. Specific recommendations regarding frequency of administration for circumstances where completing the scales at each point of contact may be uninformative or excessive were provided in Chapter 2 (e.g., residential/inpatient, ongoing supportive or statutory services).

Beyond training, practice, and supervisory oversight, two decades of experience implementing FIT in solo practices, public and private agencies, and large healthcare systems has established the value of having a formal, well-defined, written plan and policy regarding data collection. Figure 4.1 provides a portion of the FIT data collection policy developed for a large, public community mental health outpatient agency. As is hopefully apparent, specifying in detail when, how, from and by whom feedback is to be sought not only ensures the quality and consistency of the data collected, but also provides practitioners, supervisors and managers with a protocol for identifying and correcting problematic sources of variation.

FEEDBACK INFORMED TREATMENT DATA COLLECTION POLICY & PLAN

When?	How?	Who?
ORS is administered at every visit (maximum of once a week), beginning when the first appointment is scheduled.	At the initial contact, the "culture of feedback" is introduced using a prepared script that includes: (1) a description of the process of routinely asking for feedback regarding progress and quality of the relationship; (2) introduction of the measures; and (3) explanation of how scores are used to guide and inform decision-making. At each visit, the client is briefly reminded of the "culture of feedback" and instructions for completing the ORS. When meeting multiple providers, or several sessions per week, ORS administration is completed at the first meeting to take place. The ORS is completed via the web-based FIT system. When a helper has cases that predate FIT implementation, the measures are not administered or entered into the system. When a case is transferred to another provider or program due to lack of progress or unplanned staffing change, "outcome data follow the client." Specifically, the new program or helper continues to administer the measure on the same graph. Whenever a period of two or more months elapse without contact, the client's scores are plotted as a new episode of care (e.g., graph) unless the interval was planned in which case scores would continue on the same graph.	The helper providing services administers the measure to all clients at the outset of the session (within the first 10 minutes).

Collateral ratings on the ORS are sought whenever initial client outcome scores fall above the clinical cutoff (i.e., 25 for adults, 28 for adolescents, 32 for children) and/or when the client is in care at the request of someone else (e.g., parent, employer, courts).	"Internal collateral ratings" (the client completes the measure as if they were the person who sent them to treatment [e.g., parent, employer, courts]). "External collateral ratings" (stakeholders rate the client). Whenever possible, collateral scores are gathered via the web-based FIT system. Scores derived from oral, or paper-and-pencil administrations are entered into the electronic system in a timely manner.	The helper providing services asks the client to consider how others might rate them or solicits ratings from relevant external stakeholders.
The SRS is administered at the end of each visit beginning with the first outpatient session (maximum once a week, ~10 minutes before the end of the visit), including intake and assessment sessions.	At the conclusion of the initial contact, the SRS is introduced using a prepared script emphasizing: (1) the critical role the relationship plays in successful care; (2) the helper's interest in and openness to any and all feedback; (3) an explanation of how scores will be used to guide and inform decision-making; and (4) instructions for completing the measure. At the end of each visit, the client is briefly reminded of the "culture of feedback" and instructions for completing the SRS. When meeting multiple providers, or several sessions per week, SRS administration takes place at the last meeting held. In such instances, the practitioner instructs the client to consider all interactions occurring during the week when completing the scales. The SRS is completed via the web-based FIT system.	The helper providing services administers the scale to all clients prior to ending the session.

Figure 4.1: Sample Feedback Informed Treatment Data Collection Policy & Plan

2. COMMON STATISTICAL INDICES/PERFORMANCE METRICS

Over time, as measures are administered at every session with all clients, data accumulates sufficient to begin calculating metrics indicative of the quality and effectiveness of mental health services. In this section, definitions and formulas are provided for twelve common performance indices. As will be seen, some are easily computed using a calculator and basic math. Others require the use of sophisticated analyses that, for most, will necessitate using a statistical consultant or accessing an online, outcome management system (see section 3, this chapter). It is important to note that no single metric is more important or revealing than any other. Rather, each provides valuable information (i.e., feedback) regarding a specific aspect of the services being provided. When used in combination, a more complete and nuanced picture of the strengths and weaknesses of a helper or agency emerges—the latter which, of course, may be useful in identifying when, where, with, and by whom any performance improvement efforts should be undertaken.

Average intake outcome score: Calculated by adding together all first session scores and dividing the sum by the total number of clients, the average intake outcome score provides general information about the nature and level of functioning of a helper or agency's cases at the outset of care. On the ORS, for example, lower initial scores are associated with higher levels of distress indicating a need for and ability to benefit from services. The lower the score, the earlier, more frequent, and intense services are warranted. Conversely, an average intake ORS score above the clinical cutoff could be, as discussed in section 3 of Chapter 2, an indication of a caseload made up of many mandated clients or people who are relatively well-functioning but seeking help for a specific issue or concern. For clients whose initial score falls below the cutoff, data gathered from millions of clients seen in diverse settings around the world shows an average ORS score of 16 for adults, 20 for adolescents, and 23.5 for children.

Average intake relationship score: Helping relationships that improve, studies show, are associated with better outcomes than those that start and stay strong or deteriorate over the course of care (Owen et al. 2016; Miller et al. 2007). Not surprisingly, therefore, the most effective helpers work to create an atmosphere where negative feedback (i.e., lower/poor relationship scores at intake) is not only permitted but actively encouraged. One indicator of having created a "feedback friendly" culture is a lower average initial intake relationship score, calculated by adding together all first session scores and dividing the sum by the total number of clients. On the SRS, for example, scores falling at or near 36—the 25th percentile—versus the top end of the measure, are considered optimal.

Average number of sessions/duration of care: Data regarding the average number of sessions and length of time people engage in psychological care has remained consistent over the years. In 1978, Garfield summarized results from a "representative number of investigations carried out in several types of clinics" and found a "clustering around 6 interviews" (p. 195). Thirty-seven years later, using a sample of more than 20,000 clients, Erekson et al. (2015) reported a mean of 5.8 sessions, delivered over an average of 9.1 weeks of contact. Roughly similar results have been reported in other studies with large and diverse samples (Baldwin et al. 2009; Stiles et al. 2015).

To calculate the average treatment duration and number of sessions, use data from all clients who have ended treatment (single session, terminated formally or dropped out, as well as those without contact for at least two months). Next, count the number of weeks and sessions each client attended. Finally, divide each figure by the total number of clients. It is important to note that treatment length is affected by a variety factors, including age, gender, socioeconomic status, race, and practice setting (i.e., private or public [Swift & Greenberg, 2015]). Without access to large samples, and fairly advanced statistical skill, determining if and how such factors may be influencing the average length of time and number of sessions clients remain in treatment can be very challenging. Despite the ease of calculating these figures by hand, using a computerized outcome management system provides access to more precise, normed comparisons and performance feedback.

Modal number of sessions: Over the last four decades, data regarding the modal number of visits—that is, the value that appears most often in a distribution—has also been remarkably consistent. About 30% of clients attend only a single session (Chow, 2018; Garfield, 1978; Hansen et al. 2002; Connolly-Gibbons et al. 2011). While some have argued that "most ... who quit ... do so because they have accomplished what they intended" (p. xi, Talmon, 1990), available evidence indicates otherwise. While the follow-up research is admittedly limited, what it does show is that a sizeable number of people who discontinue (~50% or more) leave feeling dissatisfied, unchanged, or worse off (Miller et al. 2023; Swift & Greenberg, 2015).

Effect size: Put simply, effect size (ES) refers to the degree of impact treatment has on the well-being or functioning of clients. It is one of the most commonly reported indices of therapeutic effectiveness. On the graphs produced by the computerized FIT systems, it is how far on average a helper's (or agency's) clients extend into the green zone. The further into the zone a given client (or group of clients) lands at their last visit, the higher the effect size (see line B in Figure 4.2).

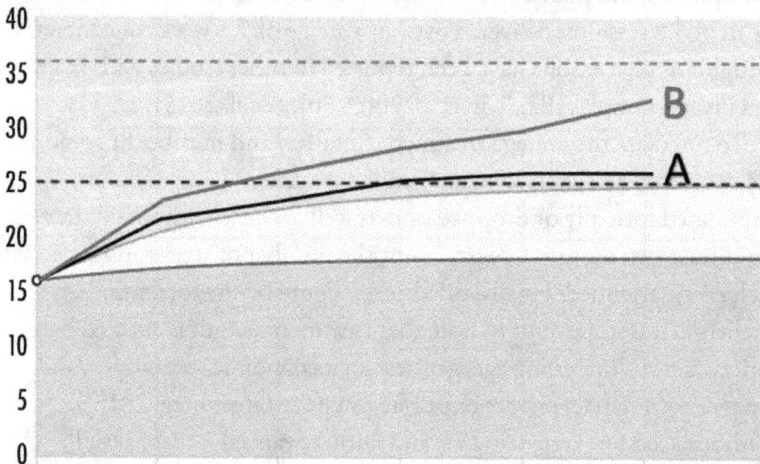

Figure 4.2: Two individual client ORS scores representing higher and lower ES

Numerically, ES is reported in standard deviation units (σ) from a mean of zero representing the well-being of a similar, untreated comparison group. Decades of research conducted in laboratory and real-world settings shows outpatient psychological care has an ES of .8 σ (Smith & Glass, 1977; Wampold & Imel, 2015). By adding the numbers falling to the left of the downward arrow line displayed in

Figure 4.3 (.14, 2.14, 13.59, 34.13, and ~30.0), an ES of .8 σ indicates that the average person receiving mental health care is better off than 80% of people with similar concerns (or problems) that do not get help. As the ES for the latter group (e.g., waitlist controls, placebo groups) typically falls between .0 and .2 σ, any number greater than .2 σ indicates people are improving as a result of the services offered, while a figure at or near .8 σ indicates results are on par with outcomes typical for the field.

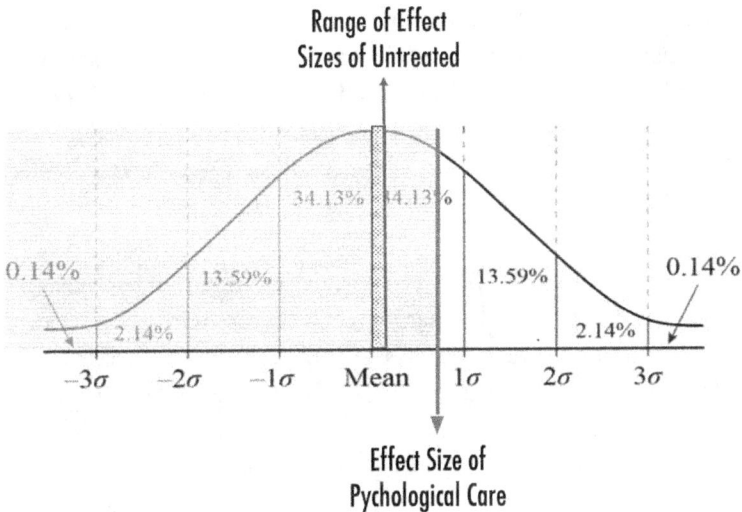

Figure 4.3: Effect size of psychological care compared to the mean and range of the untreated sample

Many different methods exist for calculating effect size (Seidel et al. 2013). One commonly used formula involves subtracting the mean of clients' post-treatment scores on whatever outcome tool is being used (e.g., ORS) from the mean of their pre-treatment scores, and then dividing the resulting number by the standard deviation of the entire sample (a brief description of, and formula for calculating the standard deviation can be found in Appendix E). The complete equation:

$$\frac{[\text{Post-treatment Mean}] - [\text{Pre-treatment Mean}]}{\textit{Standard Deviation of the Clinical Sample}}$$

While it is possible to compute ES using a calculator or spreadsheet in the manner described above, doing so has significant drawbacks outside of small, solo practice settings. First, as is hopefully obvious, calculating the ES of each practitioner and program in an agency or group practice is time consuming and error prone. Second, and most important, a variety of factors other than the actual effectiveness of the treatment provided can affect the validity of the index. Without correcting for severity of distress at intake, for example, the calculated ES may say more about the ease or difficulty of a helper or agency's caseload than the effectiveness of the treatment provided. In section 3 of this chapter, three computerized systems utilizing the ORS and SRS are described. All automate data collection and analysis, and rely on large, international samples, and sophisticated statistical procedures for generating accurate—known as, "severity adjusted"—estimates of effect size (Miller, Hubble, & Chow 2020; Prescott et al. 2017).

Relative effect size: Whereas ES measures treatment impact, relative effect size (RES) shows how that impact compares to the effectiveness of other practitioners/agencies. As with ES, RES is reported on a standardized scale, with a zero ($\bar{x} = 0$) indicating results are on par with the normative sample, and deviations above or below ($+$ or $-\sigma$) better or worse performance, respectively. While the mathematical skills needed to determine RES are not complicated, two obstacles will prevent most from doing the necessary computations: (1) gaining access to a comparison group (i.e., data generated by other practitioners/agencies); and (2) proficiency with the statistical procedures needed to ensure results are being compared to a population of clients with similar problems or levels of functioning (a process known as "case-mix adjustment" [Sibert et al. 2021]). For this reason, most practitioners and agencies will choose to use an online, outcome management system. The RES calculated by the three authorized systems using the ORS and SRS, for example, is based on a sample of thousands of practitioners, and millions of clients, treated in diverse settings, around the world (Miller, 2011).

Reliable, clinically significant change, and percentage of clients reaching service targets: When a client's scores on an outcome measure improve, it is essential to know whether it's because of the care being provided or the consequence of some other, unrelated influence or factor. The passage of time, occurrence of chance, change-producing events, and imprecision in the measurement process can affect outcome scores. In 1984, researchers Jacobsen et al. recognized this problem and proposed formulas for determining when changes in therapy could confidently be attributed to the treatment. The "reliable change index" (RCI), as Jacobsen and Truax (1991) later called it, can be found in the administration and scoring manual of most commonly used outcome tools.

With regard to the ORS, Bertolino & Miller (2012) reported an RCI of 5. In application, any difference in the total score exceeding 5 points, either from the first to the last session, or between visits, could be said to meet the benchmark for reliable change. When positive, it could be inferred clients are improving as a result of treatment. Negative scores, on the other hand, indicate care is making the client worse.

According to Jacobsen and Truax (1991), clinically significant change (CSCI) is, "the extent to which therapy moves someone outside the range of the dysfunctional population or within the range of the functional population" (p. 12). Briefly, change is deemed clinically significant when: (1) it exceeds the RCI; and (2) falls above the clinical cutoff established for the outcome measure used. As reported in Chapter 2, research has determined the cutoff on the ORS—the dividing line between a clinical and non-clinical level of distress or functioning—is 25 for adults, 28 for adolescents, and 32 for children.

A simple tool for quickly determining which clients have achieved either reliable or clinically significant change can be found in Figure 4.4 (see Appendix F). Known as the "Reliable Change Chart," it works by crossing the client's pre-treatment score (along on the horizontal axis) with their current or post-treatment score (the vertical axis). The titles in the area where the lines intersect instantly show whether a reliable improvement or worsening has occurred. Should the lines meet in the area labeled "no reliable change" (representing the RCI), then it can be inferred change is insufficient to be attributed to therapy ($\leq \pm 5$ points). A difference in scores falling in the area labeled, "clinically significant change," indicates an improvement that is both reliable (> +5 points) and within the range of the functional population (> +5 points and above the clinical cutoff of 25).

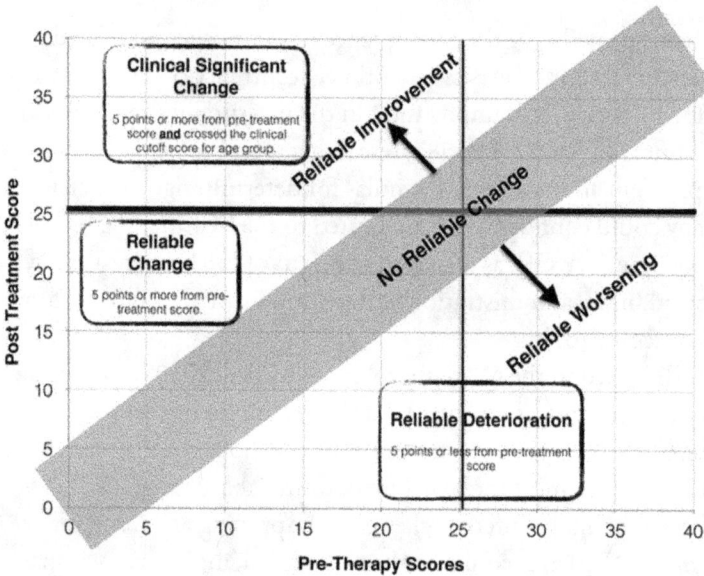

Figure 4.4: Reliable and Clinically Significant Change Chart for the Outcome Rating Scale

What the RCI and CSCI offer in ease and simplicity of identifying who is benefiting from treatment, they lose in terms of accuracy, precision, and efficiency. Given that the RCI is an average, not specific to the individual client, it overestimates the amount of change required to be reliable for some (i.e., those who are more functional, less distressed at intake) and underestimates it for others (i.e., clients who are less functional, and more distressed at the outset of services). The TRTs discussed in Chapter 2 represent a significant advance over the static RCI, instantly showing whether a client's improvement from session-to-session is "on track" for a successful outcome relative to their initial level of distress or functioning (e.g., green zone). In the three systems using the ORS and SRS (described in section 3 below), the overall percentage of a practitioner or agency's clients "on track" are reported as, "the percentage of clients reaching service targets" or "percentage of clients in the green zone."

Deterioration rate: Research shows between 5 and 10% of adults, and 12 to 24% of children and adolescents end care worse off than they were at the beginning (Cuipers et al. 2021; Cuipers et al. 2018; de Jong et al. 2024; Flor, 2016; Lambert, 2010; Lazar, 2017). A simple way to calculate the rate of deterioration is to divide the number of clients whose scores at termination fall below the RCI on whatever outcome scale is being used, by the total number of people who have completed therapy. In the three electronic systems using the ORS and SRS (described in section 3 below), the rate of deterioration is the percentage of clients whose scores at the conclusion of care fall in the "red zone" of the TRT. Such a figure, based on progress estimates for each individual client rather than an average applied to all, offers a far greater degree of accuracy and precision than the RCI.

Dropout rate: According to Swift et al. (2017), drop out occurs, "whenever a client begins an intervention, but then unilaterally terminates ... prior to recovering from the problems that led him or her to seek treatment in the first place" (p. 48). Their research documents 20-22% of people who initiate services stop attending, prior to benefiting from care. Calculating the dropout rate is simple and straightforward. First, identify the clients who terminated unilaterally (i.e., without consulting or planning with the helper). Next, count the number of those whose outcomes scores on whatever measure is being used did not exceed the RCI or, for systems using the ORS and SRS, did not end in the green zone. Third and finally, divide the resulting figure by the total number of clients who have finished treatment. Most electronic outcome management systems do this quickly and efficiently, helping users classify cases correctly as well as providing real time calculations.

Planned and unplanned termination: Research shows that therapies in which the client and helper jointly decide to end treatment have better outcomes (Chow, 2014; Saxon et al. 2010; Swift et al. 2017). To calculate the number of planned terminations, count the number of cases when both parties agreed to end treatment regardless of outcome. Likewise, for unplanned terminations, count the number of clients that did not return for therapy. Divide each of the two figures by the total number of cases seen to obtain the average rate of planned and unplanned termination cases.

A summary of these common statistical indices can be found in Figure 4.5.

COMMON STATISTICAL INDICES/PERFORMANCE METRICS

Index/Metric	Definition	Benchmark
Average intake ORS	The sum of all initial ORS scores divided by the total number of initial ORS administrations.	For clients scoring below cutoff at intake: 15-16 (adults), 20 (adolescents), 23.5 (children)
Average intake SRS	The sum of all initial SRS scores divided by total number of initial SRS administrations.	75% of clients score 36 or higher Improving scores associated with better outcomes
Average number of sessions	The sum of all sessions divided by the total number of clients (or episodes of care).	$\bar{x} = 5.8$ ($\sigma = 4.2$) 90% of outpatient clients attend 20 sessions or less
Modal number of sessions	The most frequent number of times clients attend outpatient therapy.	30% of clients attend only 1 session
Effect size (ES)	The magnitude of change resulting from treatment as compared to no treatment (also known as "absolute" ES).	.76
Relative effect size (RES)	The ES of a practitioner, agency, or system of care as compared to the average ES of other practitioners, agencies, and systems of care.	.00 The majority of ES's fall between -0.3 and + 0.3

Percent reaching service targets (Reliable change)	The percentage of clients who have experienced a reliable change (i.e., last score is in the green zone).	64–74%
Percent experiencing clinically significant change (CSC)	The percentage of clients in the green zone and over the clinical cutoff.	~25%
Deterioration rate	The percentage of clients who end treatment in the red zone.	5–10% (adults) 15–25% (children)
Dropout rate	The percentage of clients who unilaterally end services without experiencing a reliable change (i.e., green zone).	20–25%
Unplanned termination (UP)	The percentage of clients who end unilaterally and have experienced a reliable change (i.e., green zone).	~25%
Planned termination (PT)	The percentage of cases in which the helper and client mutually agree to end treatment.	~50%

Figure 4.5: Summary of common statistical indices/performance metrics

3. ELECTRONIC FIT OUTCOME SYSTEMS:

At present, three computerized outcome systems are authorized to administer, score, graph and compare client results to the TRTs, and report individual, agency, and healthcare system performance data. No other programs or applications are authorized or permitted. More, as stated explicitly in the licensing agreement (see Appendix G), any and all digitalization or electronic administration of the ORS or SRS via third-party software or web-based platforms (e.g., Google Forms, Survey Monkey, Excel) is prohibited. The three authorized systems are:

- Fit-outcomes.com
- Myoutcomes.com
- OpenFIT.com

Each is independently owned and operated, and solely and individually responsible for their own pricing and customer support. Slight differences do exist between the three systems in terms of user experience, similar in nature and scope to varying computer and mobile phone operating systems (e.g., Android versus Apple iOS, and MS phone OS). That said, all have been vetted and found to meet or exceed the strictest U. S. and European data use regulations (i.e., HIPPA, GDPR) as well as data management and reporting standards established by the International Centre for Clinical Excellence (see Appendix H). Additionally, and importantly, all three systems:

- Utilize the same ICCE-approved translations of the measures in various languages, and formulas for plotting the TRTs and computing the SPI and other statistical indices defined in section 2 of this chapter.

- Have an established track record of at least a decade of continuous operation.

- Offer a free trial period of full functionality designed to help users decide which offers the best fit in terms of form and functionality.

SUMMARY

Feedback informed treatment relies on gathering valid and reliable data regarding client engagement and progress. In this chapter, guidelines were provided for ensuring the quality and consistency of the data collected. Instructions were also offered for calculating and interpreting a variety of statistical indices related to outcome and engagement. While a number of the metrics can be computed using a calculator or spreadsheet, access to the normative databases and sophisticated statistical procedures available in computerized and web-based outcome management systems simplifies the process and offers greater precision. Presently, three such systems are authorized to administer, score, compare client progress to treatment response trajectories, and compute and report an array of evidence-based performance indices for individuals, agencies, and healthcare systems using the ORS and SRS.

QUIZ

1. The quality of feedback data is dependent on:

    a. How truthful clients are when they complete feedback surveys

    b. The correct interpretation of the data by the practitioner

    c. Using standardized measurement tools to gather the data

    d. All of the above

2. The clinical cutoff on the Outcome Rating Scale is used to determine:

    a. If a client needs services based on their level of distress at intake

    b. Is the same for all clients seeking services

    c. If the client's distress is in the "clinical" or "non-clinical" range at intake

    d. When services should be terminated

3. With regard to initial scores on the Session Rating Scale, a score of 32 out of 40:

    a. Would be considered high and would not warrant any follow up

    b. Would be considered low and warrants follow up with the client

    c. Indicates the client feels uncomfortable providing feedback

    d. Indicates that transfer to another service provider is needed

4. Minor differences in how service providers introduce outcome measures to clients:

    a. Have little impact on the quality of the data

    b. Are normal given the diversity of clients

    c. Have a significant impact on the quality of data

    d. A and B above

5. A policy for collecting client feedback data should specify:

    a. When outcome and relationship measures should be administered

    b. How outcome and relationship measures should be administered

    c. By whom and to whom outcome and alliance measures should be administered

    d. All of the above

6. Several metrics can be calculated using outcome and relationship feedback data. Of these:

    a. Certain metrics are more important than others in determining effectiveness of services

    b. No single metric is more important or revealing than any other

    c. Each provides valuable information regarding a specific aspect of the services being provided

    d. B and C above

7. The average intake ORS score for adults seeking behavioral health services is:

    a. 16

    b. 18

    c. 20

    d. 25

8. The most effective helpers

    a. Have the highest initial relationship scores

    b. Have the lowest initial relationship scores

    c. Have high initial and ongoing relationship scores

    d. Have low relationship scores that improve over time

9. Which of the following statements is false?

    a. The average number of sessions and length of time people engage in psychological care is about 6 sessions over 9 weeks and has remained consistent over the years

    b. About 30% of clients attend only a single session

    c. An ES of .8 σ indicates that the helper is successful with 80% of their clients

    d. Between 5 and 10% of adults end care worse off than they were at the beginning

10. Which of the following are advantages of using one of the three approved computerized outcome systems (Fit-Outcomes, MyOutcomes and Open FIT)?

    a. They allow clients to complete the measures electronically and then score and graph the results automatically

    b. They compare client progress to a large and diverse normative sample to determine if progress is off or on track for successful outcomes

    c. They report individual, agency, and healthcare system performance data.

    d. All of the above

Answers: *1. C, 2. C, 3. B, 4. C, 5. D, 6. D, 7. A, 8. D, 9. C, 10. D*

CHAPTER 5

IMPLEMENTING FEEDBACK INFORMED TREATMENT IN AGENCIES AND SYSTEMS OF CARE

THIS CHAPTER DESCRIBES THE steps for implementing feedback-informed treatment (FIT) in agencies and healthcare systems. Both research and experience show the process requires far more than providing practitioners with research, theory, and skills training. As will be discussed, a significant investment of time, planning, and leadership is needed for making the changes in organizational structure, culture, and capacity necessary for long-term, sustainable success. A flowchart will be presented outlining the timeline, key questions, objectives/tasks, supportive tools, and the parties responsible for each stage of implementation. Finally, concrete suggestions are provided for addressing the most frequent causes of setbacks and failure. The specific tools mentioned throughout this chapter can be found in the appendix section at the end of the volume. Information is divided into two sections:

1. Introduction to FIT implementation
2. The stages of implementation

1. INTRODUCTION TO FIT IMPLEMENTATION

In 2009, Anker et al. published the first randomized clinical trial (RCT) on FIT. Reportedly "the largest RCT of couple therapy ever done" (p. 26, Duncan, 2010), the results were nothing short of extraordinary. Clients of helpers using feedback "reached clinically significant change nearly *four times* more than non-feedback couples" (emphasis added; p. 26, Duncan, 2010). Moreover, couples in the feedback condition maintained therapeutic gains and separated or divorced half as often, when assessed 6-months post-treatment. An effect size of .5 was reported—noted by the researchers to be, "at least twice as large as the upper bound of the difference between psychological therapies intended to be therapeutic" (p. 699; Anker et al. 2009). Such results notwithstanding, perhaps the most impressive finding was that FIT was, "more easily transportable to community settings" (p. 701; Anker et al. 2009), requiring seventy-five percent less time to implement than specific treatment approaches (e.g., emotionally focused therapy [EFT], cognitive behavioral therapy [CBT], acceptance and commitment therapy [ACT], EMDR, trauma informed treatment).

Within a few short years, a different picture began to emerge. In quick succession, multiple studies appeared showing FIT did not improve outcome:

- Van Oenen et al. (2016) reported FIT not only did not help but was actually associated with less improvement compared to treatment-as-usual, in people with acute and severe psychosocial or psychiatric problems referred in the middle of a crisis and seen in a hospital setting.

- In a study published by Rise and colleagues (2016) conducted in a hospital setting, practitioners using FIT achieved no better results in terms of mental health symptoms or patient activation than another group of practitioners providing treatment-as-usual.

- Among outpatients in group psychotherapy for eating disorders, Davidsen et al. (2017) found FIT neither reduced dropouts nor improved treatment results.

- de Jong and colleagues (2018) reported providing feedback to the practitioner and client resulted in a dramatic deterioration in scores in people diagnosed with cluster B and personality disorder not otherwise specified (PD-NOS) during the first 6 months of treatment.

- Rint de Jong et al. (2018) found helpers using FIT produced no better results in terms of symptom severity of autistic children than practitioners providing treatment-as-usual.

- Pejtersen et al. (2022) reported findings from a study of "support workers" (e.g., social workers, occupational therapists, physiotherapists) providing "floating" in-home services to people identified as having longstanding mental health challenges. Across multiple measures (including well-being, reasons for terminating, length of treatment, housing stability, or employment status), staff using FIT had no better results than those engaged in care-as-usual.

The contrast in results between Anker et al. (2009), and the studies noted above, could not be starker. Various explanations were proffered for the difference, largely attributing the lack of impact to population variables (e.g., patient/client capacity for reflection, motivational level, diagnosis, degree of distress/functioning). Van Oenen et al. (2016), for example, suggested FIT might be inappropriate for "patients ... unable or reluctant to think about the treatment process" owing to their "low level of functioning" (p. 11). In a meta-analysis of feedback studies using the ORS and SRS, Østergård et al. (2018) drew similar conclusions, attributing "the lack of ... effects ... to factors related to patient and treatment characteristics." After indicating FIT might be effective with less distressed people seen, for example, in a counseling setting, Østergård and colleagues continued, "Psychiatric patients ... may have little motivation ... lack the capacity to reflect on feedback. In psychiatric settings, also, more patients with therapy-resistant symptoms and lack of early progress can be expected" (p. 11).

Mental health professionals are trained to think in terms of diagnosis, treatment approach and service delivery setting. As a result, the explanations cited above have a certain common-sense appeal. Indeed, a layperson would likely draw similar conclusions. A less obvious explanation perhaps is the degree to which FIT was actually implemented. Most helpers can think of an example of an agency change initiative that was not given adequate resources, time, planning or follow-through (e.g., implementation of a new electronic health record system, documentation practice, equity work, trauma informed practices, etc.), the result of which was poor quality or total failure of the initiative. A number of aforementioned studies were similarly limited. Consider one example. Recall, de Jong et al. (2018) reported deterioration in people diagnosed with certain personality disorders. Diverging sharply from the FIT principles and practices described in this volume, however, progress feedback was delayed a week rather than being delivered in real time (de Jong et al. 2021; Slade et al. 2008). Additionally, the helper and client did not process the feedback together when it was made available—a fact the same researchers had found, in a prior study, mitigated the impact of FIT (de Jong et al. 2012). Instead, clients received a note delivered in a closed envelope in the context of a group therapy session indicating whether or not they were making progress. According to the researchers, "it was up to the patient to decide to discuss the feedback" and helpers were free to "decide for themselves if they wanted to actively use the feedback" during care (p. 7).

Given that de Jong et al. (2018) did not control how, or even if, "feedback was integrated into therapy" (p. 17), it is hard to know what to conclude from their study. Does using FIT make people diagnosed with certain personality disorders worse? Or do practitioners behave differently when receiving feedback about clients with certain diagnoses? The evidence shows, for example, people with a "Cluster B" diagnosis are particularly prone to stigmatization by society and mental health providers—in particular, being treated in a more distancing, less empathic and hopeful manner (Black et al. 2011; Bodner et al. 2015; Klein et al. 2022).

Additional questions regarding the impact of the degree of implementation emerge when one considers the limited amount of training and support helpers received prior to and during the trials mentioned above. All appear to have taken Anker et al.'s (2009) promise of "easy transportability" seriously. de Jong et al. (2018), for example, only states "staff received a training session" (p. 7). While inconsistently reported, the aforementioned meta-analysis by Østergård et al. (2018) reveals an average of 4.2 and mode of 1 hour of training in FIT. Regarding the amount of ongoing support (e.g., consultation, supervision) helpers received while participating in the studies, reports are even less clear, ranging from "zero" to "regularly." No information regarding agency financial investment in FIT or level of management support/buy-in (both key factors in successful implementation) was provided in Østergård et al. (2018) nor typically reported in individual studies of FIT.

Brattland et al. (2018) was the first to highlight the importance of a robust and long-term implementation strategy, documenting that implementing FIT took far more effort than was reported by Anker et al. 2009. In the first years of their four-year study, for example, the researchers found FIT had no impact on outcome. Instead, confirming what research from the field of implementation science has long indicated, success increased with time and dedication, with the best results obtained after four years of ongoing training and support, including staff supervision, consultation with experts, agency financial investment, and management buy-in. By contrast, the duration of most randomized clinical trials on FIT has only been as long as is needed to recruit the number of participants necessary for statistical analysis.

Thanks to Brattland et al. (2018), and the other studies cited above, understanding what is required to successfully implement FIT has evolved considerably since the publication of the original *FIT Treatment and Training Manuals* more than a decade ago (Bertolino & Miller, 2012). In the section that follows, the timeline is divided into four stages using terminology borrowed from the broader field of implementation science (Bertram, Blase et al. 2014; Fixsen, Blase, Naoom et al. 2013). For each stage, the key questions, core tasks, supportive tools, and leaders/groups responsible for support, execution and monitoring are identified and discussed.

2. THE STAGES OF IMPLEMENTATION

The four stages of implementation include: (1) exploration; (2) installation; (3) initial implementation; and (4) full implementation. While each of the four builds on prior stages, research and experience show progress does not necessarily occur in a stepwise, linear fashion (Duda, 2008). No matter how well-planned, few implementations can anticipate all the potential challenges within each stage, much less those imposed from without (e.g., policy, funding and staff changes, organizational mergers). For this reason, revisiting prior stages is best viewed as natural and helpful—a sign *feedback* about the process is being received and addressed.

Exploration: As can be seen in Figure 5.1, the first stage is exploration (the complete document including all stages can be found in Appendix I). Experience with FIT implementations over the last two decades shows this to be the most overlooked and commonly missed step. Instead of taking the time to explore whether to adopt FIT (e.g., reasons for and against, potential benefits and likely barriers), someone, somewhere, somehow decides to immediately jump into action.

Most commonly, a manager, supervisor or influential staff member hears about FIT (e.g., at a workshop, meeting with other leaders). Helpers are then sent to one and two-day workshops, software licenses are purchased, and manuals and measures are distributed to staff. In many other instances, practitioners are simply told to begin administering the ORS and SRS to all clients on a regular basis to comply with mandates to "measure outcomes" issued by professional or regulatory bodies (e.g., Joint Commission, n. d. ; Social-og-Boligstyrelsen, n. d.).

More troubling than the premature expenditure of scarce financial resources (e.g., training, licenses, software), is the impact failing to engage staff in a collaborative, exploratory process can have on perceptions of FIT and agency morale. Suspicions may develop about the "true" purpose of implementation (e.g., limiting services, reducing staff, cutting costs). Instead of being viewed as a way of informing practice, the measures come to be seen as just "more paperwork"— burdensome, disruptive, even countertherapeutic. Not surprisingly, in time, use of FIT becomes perfunctory, a standard to comply with rather than a meaningful contributor to care. Once in place, such perceptions are very difficult to change, frequently resulting in the staff becoming passive, waiting for organizational interest in FIT to wane and the next "change initiative" to come along.

EXPLORATION

TIMELINE MONTHS: 0 — 6 to 12

Questions	Tasks	Tools	Who
• What is the mission of the agency or system? • How would FIT be an improvement over the current way of working? • How has FIT worked in similar agencies/systems? • How ready is the agency/system to adopt a FIT culture?	• Organize an initial implementation team (IIT) responsible for answering this stage's key questions • Become knowledgeable about FIT principles and practice • Consult with FIT experts • Visit other agencies/systems which have implemented FIT	• FIT manual • ICCE certification courses, list of certified trainers and e-learning platform • ICCE discussion forum • The Feedback Informed Gap Assessment Tool (FITGAP)	• Small group whose members have an interest in and passion for FIT

DECISION POINT — Will FIT benefit our agency?

- YES → Is management committed to at least three years of support for implementation?
  - YES → Begin Installation
  - NO → STOP
- NO → Is further EXPLORATION likely to alter this decision?
  - YES → (return)
  - NO → STOP

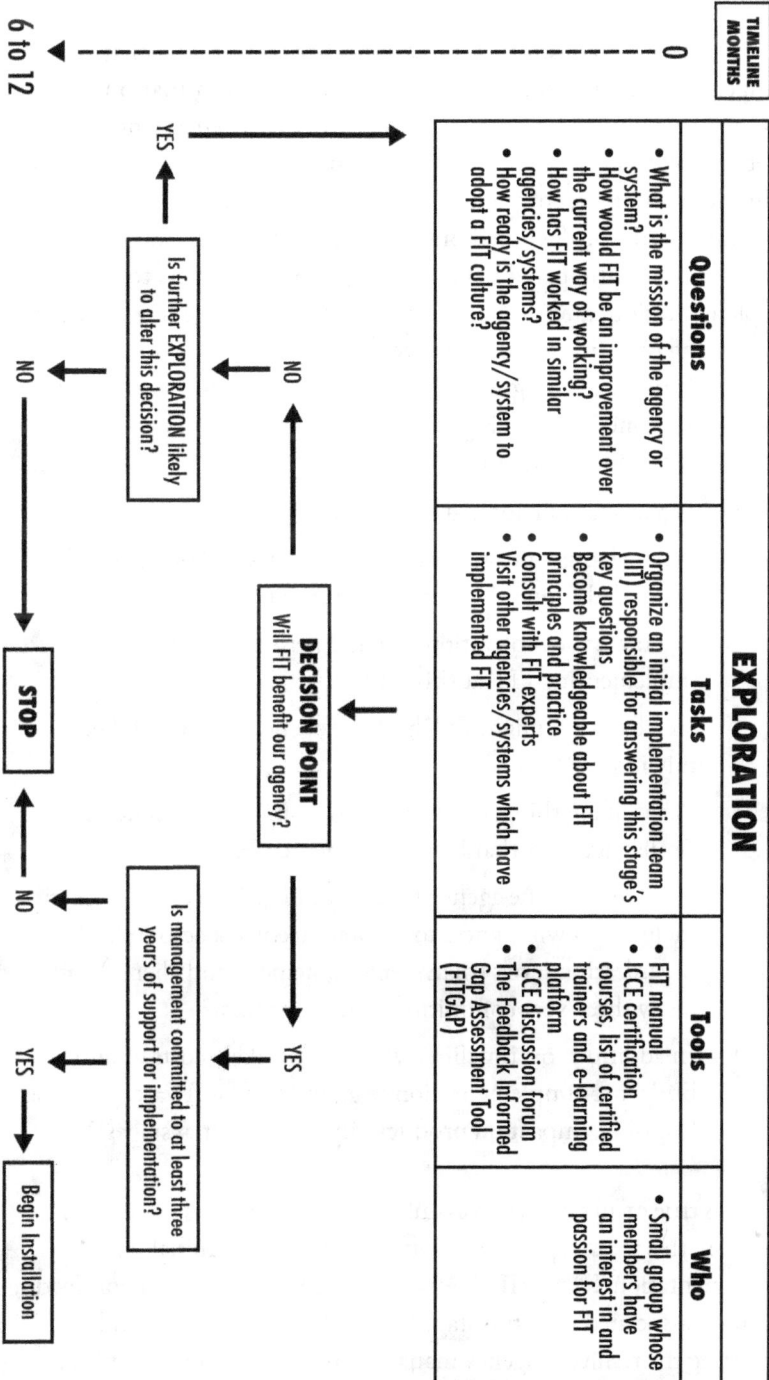

Figure 5.1: FIT Implementation Flow Chart: Exploration Stage

Successful exploration involves actively considering a change in agency practice and culture. It is a time when information about FIT should be gathered, shared, and discussed at length in meetings with management and staff—in particular, the reasons for considering implementation of FIT (e.g., community/client needs, program needs, professional practice needs, resources, stakeholder support), the anticipated benefits and potential barriers to implementation, and the agency's capacity for change (e.g., budget, competing organizational initiatives, time). Depending on the size of organization, the length of time involved can vary between a few months and one year (see Figure 5.1). During that time, important questions to address, include:

- What does FIT look like in actual practice?

- What changes in agency culture, policies and practices would be needed should FIT be implemented?

- What are the motivations for and reasons against implementing FIT at this time?

- In what ways might FIT help the agency better fulfill its mission?

- What, if anything, can be learned from the experience of similar agencies that have implemented FIT?

- How ready is the agency to adopt FIT principles and practice, including a willingness to embrace feedback across all organization levels (management, helpers, and clients) and likely three-year commitment to the process?

- In addition to a timeline, what are the likely costs of and budget for implementation (e.g., training, software/measures licensing, impact on productivity during initial stages)?

As is true of all stages, successful exploration requires leadership. Early on, this means forming a group, known as the "Initial Implementation Team" (IIT), who assume responsibility for completing the tasks associated with this stage (see "tasks" in Figure 5.1) and reporting the results to agency management and personnel. Typically, membership is made up of a handful of people who share a keen interest in (or knowledge of) FIT as well as agency history and operations.

Resources available to IIT members to complete their work include:

1. The five chapters of the revised *FIT Treatment and Training Manual*. The information contained within is the most current and specific regarding FIT principles and practices. The manual is provided to all participants who attend ICCE-sponsored trainings. Additional copies may be purchased directly from ICCE at a discounted rate.

2. The four certification courses offered by the ICCE. Briefly, the *FIT Intensive* provides a thorough grounding in FIT principles and practices; the *FIT Consultation* training teaches a model for using graphs and data to improve client engagement and outcomes; the *FIT Implementation Intensive* outlines the evidence-based steps of implementation and helps participants prepare a plan for success; and the *Training of Trainers*, an entirely experiential course aimed at helping participants develop and improve presentation and training skills. The most up-to-date information about dates, times, and costs can be found at: https://www.eventbrite.ie/o/the-international-centre-for-clinical-excellence-298540255.

3. *The ICCE Discussion Forum*, a private, no-cost, ad-free group hosted on Facebook and monitored by ICCE leadership and certified trainers. Members working in diverse locations around the world share their experiences and post questions. To join, go to: https://www.facebook.com/groups/122558661308.

4. *The Feedback-Informed Treatment Gap Assessment Tool* (FITGAP) is a checklist designed to help identify and address gaps between FIT principles and practices and current organizational policy, practice, and structure. It replaces and should be used instead of the *Feedback Readiness Index and Fidelity Measure* (FRIFM) published in the original *Feedback-Informed Treatment and Training Manuals* (Bertolino & Miller, 2012). Briefly, the tool assesses agency compatibility with FIT across four organizational realms (clinical, administrative, documentation/information technology, and stakeholders) with few or no gaps representing an agency in stage 4, or "full implementation." Completing the tool during the exploration stage is helpful

in providing management and IIT members with a clear sense of changes required for a sustainable implementation of FIT. Administering and then comparing the responses of staff, supervisors, and managers can also help identify critical differences in perception that could impede success. A copy of the tool can be found in Appendix J at the end of this volume.

5.   Consultation with a FIT expert (training@ centerforclinicalexcellence.com) or ICCE Certified Trainer (CT [see https://centerforclinicalexcellence.com/fancy-list-of-fit-certified-trainers/). The amount of information, and number of decisions to be made during the exploration stage, can be overwhelming. Over the years, IIT members consistently report that scheduling a couple of hours of consultation with a FIT expert, prior to expending resources (staff time, money), improves effectiveness and efficiency.

While the exploration stage begins with a commitment to investigate agency adoption of FIT, it ends with a decision either to abandon implementation or proceed to the next step, installation. While by no means exhaustive, several signs indicate agency readiness to move on to stage 2:

• A thorough exploration of the plusses and minuses and potential changes to agency culture and practice involved in adopting FIT has taken place.

• Following discussions with staff across all programs, consensus has been reached between the IIT and management that adopting FIT will help the agency better achieve its mission.

• The IIT has developed an initial budget and implementation timeline which has been approved by management.

• In many instances, a FIT expert has consulted with management and the IIT, and agrees the agency is ready to move forward.

Installation: Once the decision has been made to move forward with FIT, the second stage of implementation begins. Where exploration was focused on the possibility of change, installation is devoted to building the infrastructure necessary to sustain the shift in agency culture and practice supportive of FIT. For this reason, the installation stage is cost-intensive, accounting for a significant portion of the total expenses associated with implementation.

As can be seen in Fig. 5.2 below, one of the first tasks of installation is forming the "Transition Oversight Group" (TOG). The purpose of the TOG is to oversee and manage the remaining stages of implementation. As such, its composition is purposefully different from the IIT. Representativeness—in terms of programs, professional disciplines, supervisors, leaders, and member enthusiasm for FIT—is essential. In contrast to the IIT, whose members often share a keen interest in the approach, it is also important to involve at least one critical/skeptical person. Depending on the size of the agency, the TOG can also include a representative from the quality assurance department, manager with executive decision-making power (including "power of the purse"), and any relevant external stakeholders (funders, donors, politicians, community leaders, consumer representatives). Experience shows the most effective TOGs contain enough members to reflect the diverse people and programs within the agency while being small enough in number to meet regularly and come to agreement about implementation challenges and plans.

INSTALLATION

Questions	Tasks	Tools	Who
• How does FIT work in this setting? • What changes in agency identity, workflow, culture and practice are required to support FIT?	1. Form a Transition Oversight Group (TOG) responsible for implementing this stage's core tasks: a. Development of a detailed implementation plan b. Securing resources c. Aligning agency policies and procedures with FIT d. Conducting in-house training 2. Run small pilot projects to test the application of FIT in various programs within the agency: a. Participants commit to fully implement FIT for the duration of the pilot b. Feedback is provided to the TOG about struggles and successes c. Use learnings to create a template for agency-wide implementation	• FIT manual • FIT Core Competencies • Project description and plan • Communication plan • Formal policy regarding use of FIT • Formal policy regarding access to and use of data generated by FIT • The Feedback Informed Gap Assessment Tool (FITGAP)	• Transition oversight group in relationship with a manager who has "power of the purse" • Leaders of the program tasked with piloting FIT • External FIT expert consultant and/or trainer

DECISION POINT
Was FIT successfully implemented in the pilot projects?

NO → STOP

YES → Begin initial implementation

TIMELINE MONTHS	
6 to 12	18 to 24

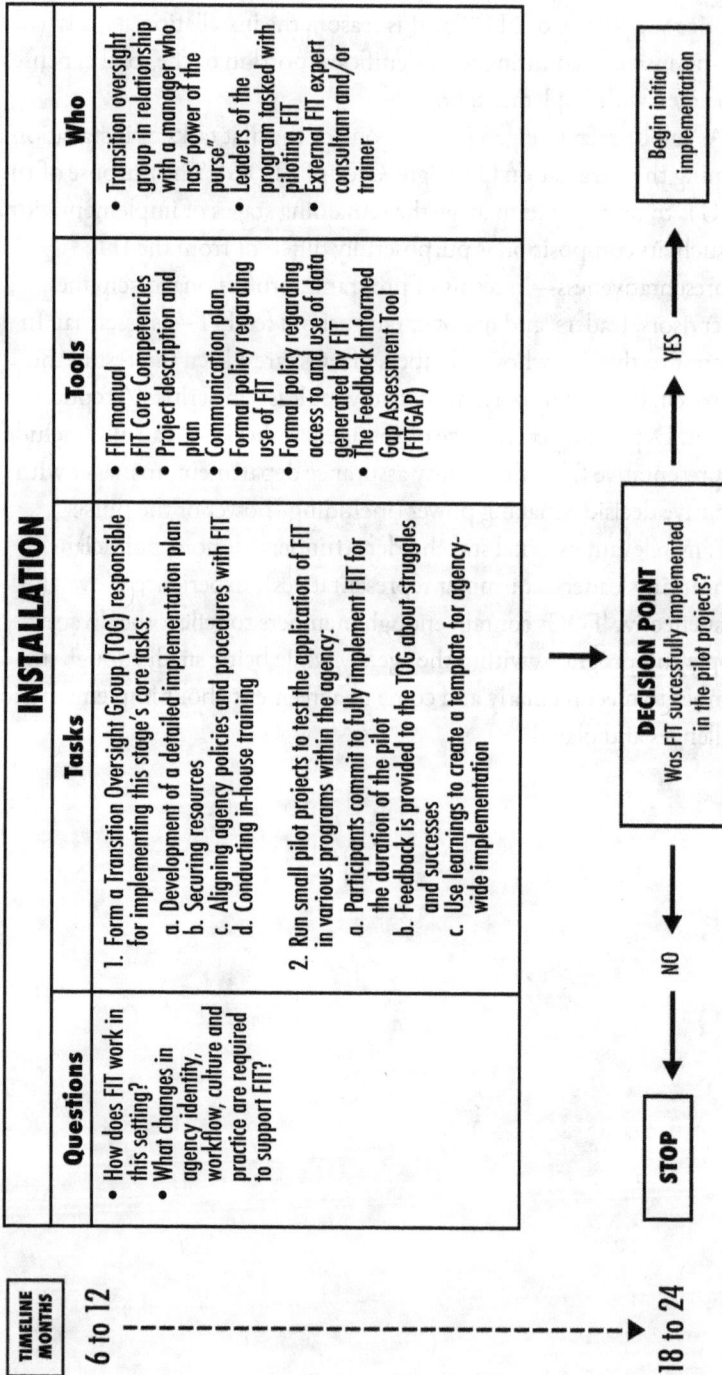

Figure 5.2: FIT implementation Flowchart: Installation Stage

During installation, the TOG engages in activities designed to establish the aforementioned infrastructure supportive of FIT, including:

- Development of a detailed implementation plan (including objectives, tasks, timelines, budget, framework for communication, reporting and accountability [examples can be found in Appendix K]).

- Securing the resources necessary for implementation (e.g., time, funding, personnel, leadership, and access to data and software systems).

- Working to align agency policies, procedures, and workflow (e.g., access to regular FIT consultation, integration of feedback into service planning and delivery) with FIT principles and practices (see Appendix L for an example).

- Assigning responsibility for the various implementation tasks to specific TOG members (e.g., communication regarding implementation, scheduling of TOG meetings, development of the in-house training program, compiling feedback from pilot projects for review by TOG, monitoring/reporting FIT developments and collaboration with external FIT consultants).

- In-house training on FIT with staff, supervisors, and management.

- Securing staff access to and time for FIT consultation.

- Running pilot projects to test the application of FIT in different programs at the agency.

Piloting FIT in different programs, client groups, and service settings within the agency is a critical part of installation. Regarding the amount of time required, the piloting period should be long enough to cover the course of care typical for the agency or program (e.g., intake, treatment, discharge, follow up). The purpose is to identify problems, deficiencies, and barriers that might impede future, agency-wide implementation, or reveal an overall lack of viability of FIT at the agency. In the latter case, a decision would be made by the TOG to end implementation of FIT. More often, however, the feedback provided via pilot testing enables the TOG to address hinderances and make changes in policy and practice necessary for sustainable implementation. Two examples serve as useful illustrations.

CASE EXAMPLE 5.1: FIT IN STATUTORY SERVICES

A few years ago, a large social service agency in Scandinavia began piloting FIT in their child protective services division (Miller, 2021). Agency policy and government statutes mandated "an actual, individual assessment as to whether [a] child needs support, [dictating] when and how one can and must intervene" (p. 28; Mackrill et al. 2020). During initial "in-house" FIT training sessions, statutory social workers expressed uncertainty about how they could be open and responsive to family members' feedback and preferences while simultaneously meeting their statutory obligations regarding the protection of children at risk. Traditionally, initial visits were devoted to completing a standardized risk assessment (involving direct interviews with parents, child or children, school officials, and other stake holders) and then making referrals to the professionals and agencies believed to have the requisite expertise to address the problems identified. It was not uncommon for this phase of service delivery to take 3 to 6 months to complete.

Staff concerns were relayed to the TOG which, following exploration and discussion, made two crucial decisions. First, and most immediate, they proposed a series of trainings be developed to provide line staff with opportunities to practice and refine core therapeutic skills (e.g., empathy, acceptance, emotional engagement, relational responsiveness). While most had been exposed to the concepts before, little if any training had been offered on their utilization in statutory work. Second, and slightly longer-term, agency leaders agreed to seek clarification and, if necessary, variances in legal mandates perceived to limit initial contacts between the agency, families, and stakeholders to assessment and referral (see p. 9, Mackrill et al. 2020).

Ultimately, the TOG's efforts paid off. Ongoing training provided by in-house FIT experts helped workers bridge the gap between therapeutic and statutory work. Permission granted by the authorities to deviate from the standard way of working ensured fidelity to FIT principles and practices rather than simply adding the ORS and SRS to the already lengthy "standardized assessment" battery. The adoption of FIT had a dramatic effect. As the agency neared full implementation after several years of effort, the number of children forcibly removed from the home decreased by 50%, and complaints filed by families against the agency and staff all but disappeared. At the same time, worker job satisfaction improved, as indicated by a significant reduction in workdays missed due to illness (~50%) and complete elimination of staff turnover over a two-year period.

CASE EXAMPLE 5.2: FIT AND SESSION LIMITS

A second example comes from a medium size, publicly funded community mental health center in North America. Like similar agencies, funding and capacity were an ongoing challenge. To meet government guidelines regarding access to care—10 days or less between initial contact and first appointment—management had introduced a policy limiting the number of sessions helpers could offer before having to undergo an extensive review and permissions process. While intended to make more staff time available for intake appointments, the policy was clearly incongruent with the principles of FIT. As introduced and illustrated in Chapters 2 and 3, both duration and intensity of care should be determined by the individual client's outcome score rather than psychiatric diagnosis, program length, or pre-established session limits.

Wanting to move forward with the implementation of FIT, while simultaneously recognizing management concerns, the TOG arranged a consultation with an external FIT expert. The consultant first presented research showing how FIT improves efficiency without the need for session limits (i.e., overall reduction in costs and number of sessions for clients making progress [de Jong et al. 2021; Delgadillo et al. 2017; Kendrick et al. 2016]). Next, they recommended conducting a small pilot project limited to a single program within the agency thereby allowing for a test of FIT while simultaneously minimizing any risks to capacity believed possible with an agency-wide removal of session limits. At the end of one year, an analysis of program data by the TOG showed implementation of FIT (including the removal of session limits) had no impact on the average number of sessions helpers met with clients. That said, because the use of FIT resulted in a significant decline in the percentage of long-term, non-progressing clients, an increase in the number of planned terminations, and fewer clients reinitiating services following a brief hiatus (e.g., dropout, no show, program graduation), capacity nonetheless improved. This result continued when FIT was rolled out to the entire agency.

Experience with FIT implementations around the world shows the most effective pilot projects contain all of the following:

- A leader/manager who understands, supports, and actively enforces the use of FIT in the pilot group.

- A pilot group that works together in the same program/service (versus a group made up of individual staff representing different programs within the agency), whose staff and leadership are stable, and clients and service type seem most compatible with FIT principles and practices.

- Tools and resources necessary for working with FIT (training consistent with the FIT Core Competencies [see Appendix M], time, personnel, hardware and software, external expert support).

- Participants (helpers, supervisors, program leaders) who are committed to using FIT in their work with all new clients (assessment, treatment planning, supervision).

- Ongoing, seamless flow of and responsiveness to feedback between the pilot members and TOG.

The last point in the list above is important but can be challenging to achieve in practice. Ultimately, the point is to create an atmosphere within the agency that mirrors the "culture of feedback" FIT demands helpers establish with their clients—one in which, as described in Chapter 2, they feel safe sharing their experience and trust their feedback will be taken seriously. Consider the example below.

CASE EXAMPLE 5.3: POST-IT IN THE LUNCHROOM

The TOG at an outpatient public behavioral health agency had a problem. One of their programs had been piloting FIT for 6 months and a review of data from the outcome management system showed use of the measures remained inconsistent. While helpers administered the scales to some clients at each visit, most of the time measurement was a one-off event. Despite repeated requests for feedback from the helpers regarding challenges associated with using the scales, little was provided. Several meetings of the TOG were devoted to understanding why. Two hypotheses emerged. First, although helpers had been encouraged to offer critical feedback, it was believed fears about potential repercussions might still exist. Second, the process for providing feedback to the TOG was seen as a potential barrier. With regard to the latter, helpers either needed to find a member of the TOG or wait until their next monthly FIT consultation session to report any concerns.

Following extensive discussions, the TOG designed a solution they believed could address both hypotheses. A large flipchart and black, felt-tip marker were placed in the agency lunchroom. Titled, "Questions and Feedback about FIT," its purpose was to enable staff to communicate easily and freely, whether by name or anonymously, with the TOG. Comments were carefully reviewed each time the TOG met. A record of the team's responses was then shared via email with pilot project members as well as being posted next to the flipchart in the lunchroom.

The impact was immediate. In the first month, the number of comments and questions filled several pages. Most were offered anonymously, seemingly confirming the TOG's first hypothesis. "This isn't about helping clients," wrote one person, "it's really about figuring out who to fire so management can save money." "FIT is old wine in new bottles," noted another, "who is actually profiting from us chasing this latest fad?" Others complained about very practical matters (e.g., technology and software problems, knowledge and skill deficits, insufficient time and support for integrating FIT into their clinical work). Regardless, all were taken seriously.

To begin, the TOG prioritized open discussions of helpers' concerns during their regularly scheduled FIT consultation meetings. They ensured management was actively involved in this process, being present at meetings to clarify agency intentions, answer questions, and address any fears. A plan was developed for each practical problem reported via the flipchart that was, in turn, shared with staff. When not immediately resolvable, the team was transparent about the steps and timeline for addressing the particular concern.

Over the next several months, the number of critical and anonymous comments shared via the flipchart declined. A noticeable shift began to take place in the climate, or culture, of the pilot project. Participants became less skeptical and suspicious, more collaborative and trusting of one another. At the same time, as practical barriers to implementation were identified and resolved by the TOG, utilization of FIT by staff increased.

As can be seen in Figure 5.2, the installation stage typically takes between 6 and 18 months to complete. When deciding whether to move forward to the next state of implementation, key questions to consider include:

- Was FIT successfully implemented in the pilot project(s)?

- Was the organization able/willing to make the adjustments in policy, practice (e.g., routine administration of FIT measures and discussion of graphs with clients) and workflow (e.g., access to regular FIT consultation, integration of feedback into service planning and delivery) necessary to sustain FIT?

- What value, if any, did helpers report FIT added to their clinical work and quality of work life?

- What impact, if any, did the use of FIT in the pilot project(s) have on the outcome and efficiency of treatment, rates of client satisfaction, and interactions with stakeholders involved in client care?

- Did the pilot result in a template for rolling out FIT in the larger organization (e.g., management's role, the type of training and support required, time and financing)?

Should the answers to the questions above be positive, a decision would be made to move on to stage 3, "initial implementation." For large and diverse agencies, additional pilots conducted with different groups and in other service settings may be necessary (e.g., outpatient, inpatient, statutory, residential, specialty programming). In many instances, instead of starting to do FIT, it has proven helpful for new pilot groups to start at stage 1 (i.e., discussing the questions and completing the tasks associated with exploration [see Figure 5.1]). Meanwhile, programs that have successfully piloted would continue working with FIT. Installation would end when the TOG decides sufficient information has been gathered from enough programs/services to establish the applicability of FIT across the entire organization.

Prior to moving to the next stage, mention should be made of a resource that often emerges when piloting. Known as "practice champions," the term refers to staff members (supervisors, practitioners) who develop a deep interest in and desire to know more about FIT (e.g., the technology, software, philosophy, data analysis) or the FIT community (e.g., like-minded peers, knowledge experts [Bertolino & Miller, 2012]). In implementations around the world, such individuals have proven critical to providing support (e.g., training, consultation, mentoring) as FIT is rolled out to additional programs within the agency. Identifying and facilitating the development of these individuals addresses one of the key threats to successful implementation; namely, outsourcing training (e.g., attending workshops, reading articles, watching demonstration videos) rather than using internal staff resources to provide live, on-the-job teaching, practice, and coaching (Fixsen et al. 2009). At the same time, it is critical that practice champions be protected by management. For example, careful consideration should be given to whether or not they serve as members of the TOG. Neither should they be put in a position of working to either convince staff to use FIT or enforce compliance. Doing so, experience shows, not only risks alienating champions from their colleagues but may also lead to their burning out. Some strategies for protecting champions include connecting with other champions, making time available to consult with external FIT experts, and funding attendance at advanced training courses (e.g., the 4 FIT intensives offered by ICCE).

Initial implementation: Stage 3 is what most people think of when asked to define implementation. Unfortunately, it is also where many groups begin, forgoing exploration and installation, and jumping directly into action. Over the years, many different justifications have been offered by managers and leaders for skipping the first two stages:

- "We can start because our staff is motivated to learn FIT."
- "We have always gathered feedback, just informally. This isn't a huge step for us."
- "FIT is so simple; our staff will have no problem learning it."
- "This isn't our first implementation; we've adopted many new approaches."

All justifications aside, experience shows shortcutting the process significantly increases the risk of implementation failure. Indeed, while it may sound bold, no implementations of FIT are known to have worked when the initial stages are skipped. By contrast, when FIT has been thoroughly explored and successfully piloted, the decision to implement across the larger organization is a logical and, most importantly, credible next step. Staff have been engaged in a collaborative process. Questions about the practice have been answered. FIT has been tested and found to work in enough programs/services to establish its applicability across the entire organization and a formal decision to move forward has been made by management, the TOG, and pilot project participants.

At this point in the implementation, it is no longer a question of "whether and if" FIT will be adopted, but "how and when." The exploration and evaluation characteristic of the two prior stages give way to doing. Leadership at each level of the organization—from senior managers to program directors—plays a critical role, both in communicating the decision to proceed and setting and enforcing expectations regarding the use of FIT in all parts of the organization.

As shown in Figure 5.3, the time required to complete initial implementation can vary significantly depending on a variety of factors, including: (1) the size and heterogeneity of the organization; (2) resources available (e.g., time, funding, staffing); and (3) the success and thoroughness of prior stages. For this reason, it is helpful to think of this stage as an iterative process where progress is both gradual and cyclical, involving constant refining and tweaking. During that time, it is essential the TOG continues in its role of overseeing and managing the process through monitoring, revising, and executing, including:

- The agency implementation plan (e.g., the order, pace, time, funding, persons responsible for execution)
- Program-specific FIT practice guidelines
- In-house training program and FIT consultation
- Agency policies and procedures supportive of FIT culture and practice
- Compliance and fidelity standards

TIMELINE MONTHS

18 to 24

36 to 60

INITIAL IMPLEMENTATION

Questions	Tasks	Tools	Who

• How should implementation proceed?
• What are the expectations of staff in terms of FIT practice?
• What resources are needed to support the learning of and use of FIT across the agency?
• How does agency policy need to be revised to support use of FIT across the organisation?
• How will fidelity to FIT principles and practice be assessed and maintained?
	1. Revise the implementation plan in light of pilot project findings and experience:
	  a. Stepwise or the entire organisation at once
	  b. Develop a plan for ongoing, in-house training and consultation
	  c. Ensure the availability of time and funding
	2. Develop practice guidelines
	3. Consider modifications of agency policy needed to support FIT
	4. Monitor individual and organisational fidelity
		• Project description & plan of FIT
		• Formal policy regarding use of FIT
		• Practice guidelines
		• Training plan
		• FIT web-based data system
		• Formal policy regarding access to and use of data generated by FIT
		• Implementation Star
		• The Feedback Informed Gap Assessment Tool (FITGAP)
			• Transition oversight group, agency manager with "power of the purse," and program leaders
			• External FIT Experts
			• Practice champions

TOG and management uses the FITGAP, implementation star, and implementation structures (e.g. experts, champions, internal consultants, data systems) to identify problems and take remedial action.

NO

DECISION POINT
Is FIT being used with 85-95% of clients seen at the agency?

YES →

Move to Full Implementation

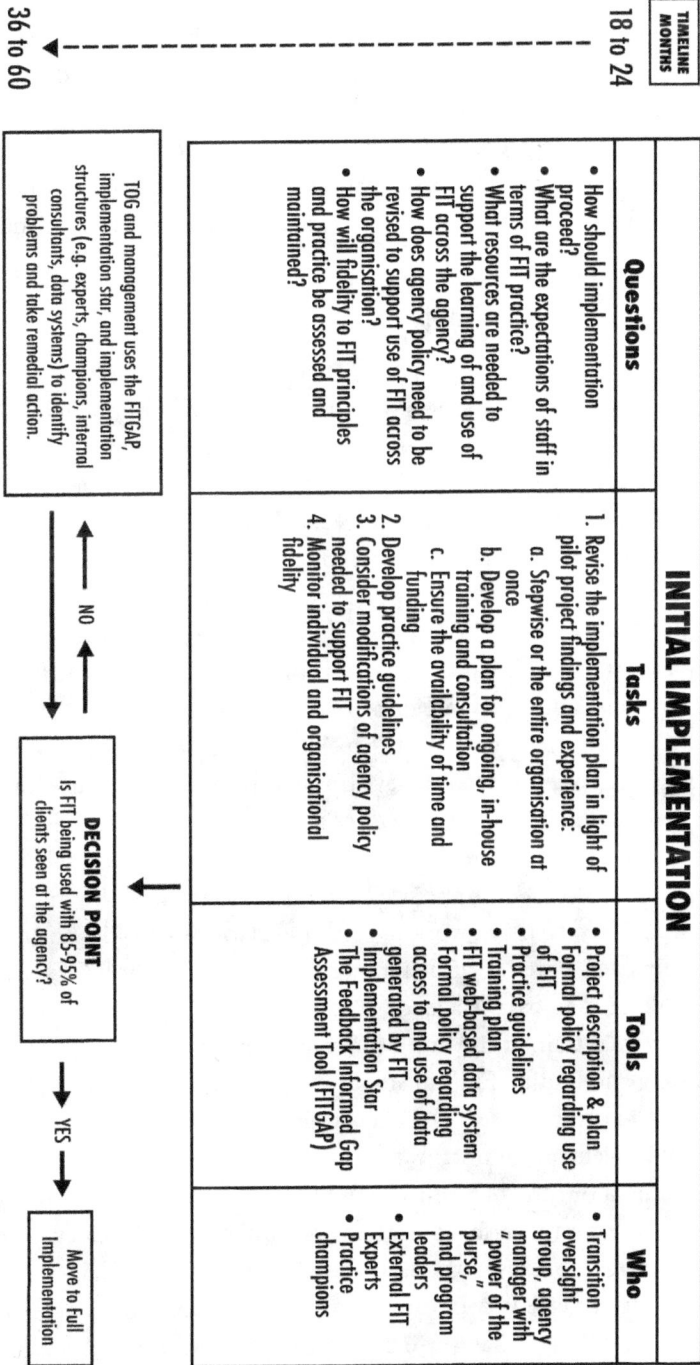

Figure 5.3: Implementation Flow Chart: Initial Implementation Stage

Two tools are useful in achieving these objectives: the FITGAP and the Implementation Star. The former—first administered during the exploration stage—can be readministered at regular intervals to determine the degree to which changes necessary for a sustainable implementation are being made. Specific items or realms with lower scores can then be targeted for remediation by the TOG (see Appendix J).

CASE EXAMPLE 5.3: MIXED MESSAGES

Leadership and practitioners working at a publicly funded mental health agency were in their fourth year of implementing FIT. The process was a textbook example of putting the steps outlined in this chapter to work in an organized and systematic way. As recommended, in the first year, they thoroughly explored FIT, both consulting with external experts and visiting agencies where the practice was in use. After securing a commitment from management to support implementation, they moved on to the installation stage. Consistent with the tasks outlined in Figure 5.2, a TOG was formed and piloting of FIT in different programs began. By the end of the second year, enough had been learned to develop a template and structure for implementing FIT across the entire agency. At this point, a decision was made by management and the TOG to move on to initial implementation. Given the size of the organization, all programs were expected to begin working with FIT. Consistent with the tasks for this stage, practice guidelines were developed by the TOG and disseminated across the agency. Additionally, a team of in-house "FIT experts" was trained and given the responsibility for conducting staff training and leading FIT consultations.

At a meeting of the TOG occurring about a year-and-a-half into the initial implementation stage, the in-house FIT experts began voicing concerns about the FIT consultations. Staff dutifully attended and brought non-progressing cases (e.g., red and yellow) for discussion. Suggestions for cases in the early stages of treatment (e.g., changing the focus, type or intensity of care) were met with interest and agreement. By contrast, larger changes (e.g., changing the provider, level of care, or agency/treatment setting) for clients in care for longer periods (i.e., more than 3 months) without improvement were rarely, if ever, made. In such instances, the atmosphere of the consultation sessions became stilted and uncomfortable, with time being spent offering reasons for continuing with "more of the same" rather than following the "FIT Consultation Approach" guidelines (see Figures 3.1 and 3.2). Increasingly, non-progressing cases were labelled "exceptions" based on the severity, diagnosis, problem or treatment history, quality of the therapeutic alliance, client's explicit request not to change, or the helper's treatment method. Administrative efforts focused on reviewing the research and guidelines, and teaching FIT skills (e.g., culture of feedback) had not had any impact.

In response to the report from the FIT consultants, the TOG decided to readminister the FITGAP to staff and management. While several items were scored lower, a significant divergence between management, the FIT consultants, and clinical staff was observed on items 23 and 25. The two items read:

23. *Leadership and managers actively lead the implementation of FIT (e.g., attending the Transition Oversight Group [TOG], establishing an implementation plan and budget, addressing barriers, and establishing an accountability framework*
25. *Leadership and managers ensure client feedback regarding progress and quality of the relationship is included in all clinical discussions*

Two members of the TOG were assigned to follow up on the results, interviewing a handful of staff and senior managers as well as the FIT consultants. "Powerless" is the word the latter used to describe their experience dealing with non-progressing cases in their meetings with staff. Beyond teaching and making recommendations, they had no authority to enforce the guidelines regarding making larger adjustments to service delivery (e.g., adding new, different or more help, changing the provider, referring the client to another agency or setting, stopping services). For their part, managers reported few conversations on the subject with staff, relying on the FIT consultants to address the issue. In the few instances where a discussion with leaders had taken place, staff reported the manager typically did not consult the graph and usually advised "relying on their own clinical judgement."

When the results of the FITGAP and follow-up interviews were reviewed by the TOG, it became clear that managers and leadership had to make two critical changes in their interactions with staff around non-progressing cases. First, to keep the focus on the well-being and outcome of the client, all such discussions needed to include a review of FIT data and graphs. Second, and more importantly, instead of deferring to the helper, leaders needed to hold them accountable for making the larger changes necessary for increasing the likelihood of successful care.

While seemingly straightforward, the solutions agreed upon by the TOG represented a significant departure from agency culture and practice. Up to this point, leaders were minimally involved in matters related to treatment decisions. Within a few months, however, the impact of their more "hands on" approach became noticeable. Management support of the guidelines led to a change in the atmosphere of the FIT consultation meetings. Instead of asking permission to continue with non-progressing cases, staff became more collaborative, energetic, and creative in resolving barriers to making larger changes.

The second tool for identifying implementation problems and challenges, is the "Implementation Star" (see Figure 5.4; Appendix N). It is based on the pioneering research of Everett Rogers (2003) who identified five factors influencing the adoption of new ideas and practices. These include:

1. *Relative advantage*, or the degree to which a new idea/practice is perceived to be better than what it is replacing;

2. *Compatibility*, or the congruence of the new idea/practice with current organizational and individual values and perceived needs;

3. *Complexity*, or how difficult the new idea/practice is to understand and execute;

4. *Trialability*, the ease with which the new idea/practice can be experimented with or "tried out"; and

5. *Observability*, how visible the use and utility of the new idea/practice are to self and others.

Simply put, new ideas or practices are more likely to be implemented when they are seen and experienced as advantageous, compatible, simple, easy to try out, and observable. Presenting the factors in the shape of a star is purposeful as doing so emphasizes how each of the five is connected to and impacts the others influencing adoption. Thus, not seeing FIT as an improvement over the usual way of working (relative advantage) is likely to decrease the chances of trying FIT (trialability). Similarly, no matter how convinced a helper might be that FIT represents an improvement (relative advantage), utilization rates are bound to remain low if the approach is experienced as incompatible with their preferred treatment method (compatibility) or too difficult to understand or put into practice (complexity).

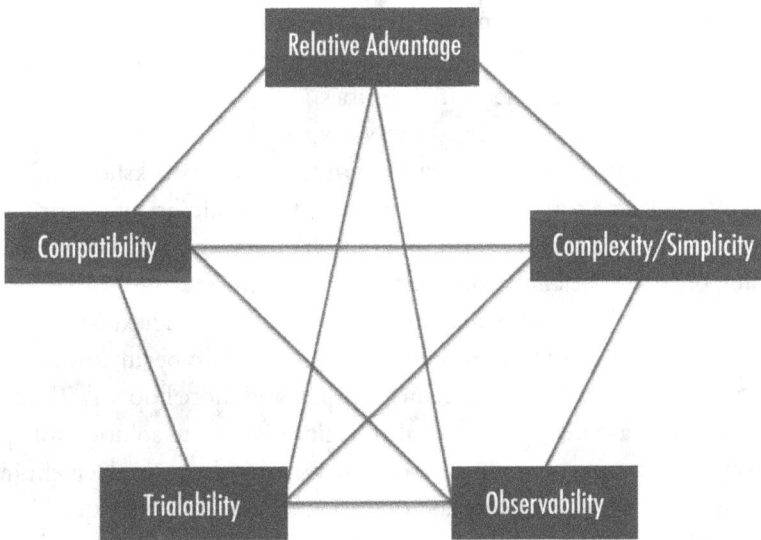

Figure 5.4: The Implementation Star

While it can be useful to consider the five factors during the exploration and installation stages, the implementation star has proven particularly helpful in identifying and troubleshooting difficulties encountered during initial implementation. For example, despite having made a formal decision to adopt FIT agencywide, and the presence of supportive infrastructure (i.e., management buy-in, access to training, consultation, and technology), it is not uncommon for utilization by specific staff members and within certain programs to remain uneven, selective, and even nonexistent. As the following example illustrates, FIT consultants, TOG members and managers can use the tool as a framework for discussion and problem-solving.

CASE EXAMPLE 5.4: FIT "ON THE STREETS"

In a large, metropolitan area located in Europe, a program designed and funded for working with the city's "most vulnerable" was implementing FIT. Available 24-hours-a-day, 7-days-a-week, every-day-of-the-year, dedicated practitioners met people living on the streets, in abandoned buildings, shelters, the jail or emergency room. Most of those served had long histories with the public healthcare system, hospitals, police and other public entities.

Implementation had started two years ago. A small group of practitioners attended a large, two-day, introductory workshop on FIT led by an international trainer. Inspired by the possibility of offering clients more "voice and choice" in their care, they immediately began using the outcome and alliance measures on their return to work. Excitement among this pioneering group grew over the next 6 months, eventually catching the attention of management. To begin, leaders noticed these staff members seemed happier and more hopeful. They also saw FIT as offering a practical and clinically-sound solution for meeting new government regulations mandating client involvement in all aspects of service delivery and decision making. Relatively quickly, agency leadership decided to implement across the entire organization, developing a detailed plan and installing structures supportive of FIT (e.g., organizing a TOG, developing an in-house training program, scheduling regular FIT consultation sessions, and ensuring ongoing support and encouragement from management).

While members of the TOG were planning the budget for the third year of the project, a discussion began about the progress of the agency's implementation efforts. Many were concerned about the slow pace. Use of the scales remained inconsistent. Time during training sessions was spent revisiting the same questions, doubts, and critiques expressed at the outset of implementation (e.g., "Do I use the ORS or SRS first?" "What button do I press in the software program to administer the scales?" "Do I have to use the scales every time I meet the client?" "Our clients can't read, so this won't work." "FIT may be fine in an office setting, but not with people living on the streets in need of immediate help." "Has FIT been researched in our setting?"). In FIT consultation meetings, most helpers did not participate and, despite attendance being mandatory, prioritized other work. Finally, complaints about the person conducting the monthly FIT consultations were constant and increasing (e. g, too boring, academic, abstract, rigid). With the viability of the implementation in serious question, the TOG decided to bring in an external consultant.

At the request of the consultant, a special meeting was arranged for the staff and leaders. Consistent with the principles of FIT when applied in clinical work, the objective was twofold. First, to foster an open and transparent discussion regarding the staff's experience of using FIT in their work. Second, to engage the staff in a collaborative problem-solving process. Aware the implementation had stalled, the consultant began the meeting with a brief presentation of the "implementation star." Each of the five factors was defined and illustrated with concrete examples. Next, staff, supervisors and managers were put into small groups and asked to share their personal experiences with FIT in relationship to the five factors. Specifically, they were asked to discuss:

- What are the relative advantages of using FIT in your work?

- How compatible is FIT with the way you work in your setting with your clients?

- How complex is learning and integrating FIT in your work?

- How easy has FIT been to try out?

- How observable is FIT in your own and others' work at the agency?

Once back in the larger group, the consultant recorded responses from each of the groups on posters. While the experiences varied widely—i.e., some seeing no advantage of using FIT, while others reported improved client engagement—two patterns emerged. The most obvious was a lack of "observability." As agency staff largely worked solo, no one had ever actually witnessed a colleague applying FIT. Even the regularly scheduled

FIT consultation sessions—organized in part to make FIT visible—had proven ineffective as discussions were rarely practical or focused on work with specific clients. It was also clear that the lack of observability had impacted staff perceptions of the "compatibility" of FIT in services delivered outside a formal office setting. Indeed, several times during the meeting, staff expressed surprise on hearing how others at the agency had successfully applied FIT in their work.

Having identified the factors of the "implementation star" posing the greatest threat to implementation, staff were asked to return to their groups to discuss potential solutions. As they did, the energy in the room slowly began to shift. Frustration gave way to a lively and energetic consideration of the changes needed to make FIT more observable, including:

- Identifying staff members with greater knowledge and expertise about FIT that could mentor and train others (e.g., practice champions)

- Holding regular skill building sessions where staff reviewed and shared personal experiences of applying core FIT practices in their work with clients (e.g., establishing a "culture of feedback," introducing and administering the ORS and SRS, reviewing graphs)

- Following the FIT consultation decision trees rather than using the time to pose questions, express doubts, and deliver critiques

- Development of a series of brief, "how to" videos featuring staff role-playing specific skills and practice applications

- Creating a feedback portal where practice-related questions and challenging scenarios could be posted and responded to anonymously

Although not directly related to observability and compatibility, one additional theme emerged from the group discussions: exposure to and guidance from a different FIT consultant. Combined with the feedback received previously, it was clear staff had lost confidence in the person currently leading the biweekly consultation meetings. This, and the other suggestions, were reported to the agency TOG for action. One-by-one, the ideas generated by the staff, including the hiring of a new FIT consultant, were implemented.

Prior to moving on to the last stage, mention should be made of a vulnerable period falling at or near the end of initial implementation. By this time, the level of management participation, staff energy, and resource allocation has been at high levels for two to three years. Those working in agency settings—especially in the public sector— know new initiatives requiring time and attention to implement are inevitable (e.g., record keeping, legal mandates, adoption of different treatment approaches, idiosyncratic grant funding requirements). The problem is not the initiatives per se, but rather their occurrence at a time when the implementation of FIT seems complete to everyone involved. On the cusp of full implementation, with FIT being employed across agency programs, and the measures used in 85 to 95% of cases, turning attention to other projects can telegraph the message, "It is now possible for FIT to run on its own." As will be seen, more is required when moving from "initial" to the fourth and final stage known as, "full implementation."

Full Implementation: If exploration addresses the question, "should we?", installation, "can we?", and initial implementation, "did we?", full implementation centers around, "how do we keep FIT going?" (see Figure 5.5)

FULL IMPLEMENTATION

Questions	Tasks	Tools	Who

• What structures are necessary to sustain FIT culture and practice?
• How does the agency use FIT data for program and professional development?
• What, if any, adaptations or innovations in FIT practice would improve all clients' ability to impact and improve service delivery and outcome?
	1. FIT is integrated into the agency mission statement, hiring decisions, and program development process.
	2. Review program and agency outcome data:
	  a. Identifying performance deficits
	  b. Set performance improvement goals
	  c. Develop and execute a professional development plan
	3. Replace the TOG with the FOG
		• Service Delivery Agreement (SDA) & Progress Note (PN)
		• Ongoing FIT training program
		• The Feedback Informed Gap Assessment Tool (FITGAP)
		• Realtime data system
		• Leadership/management succession plan
			• Feedback Oversight Group
			• Internal/local FIT experts
			• Practice champions

TIMELINE MONTHS: 36 to 60 ------------------------------▶ ?

Figure 5.5: FIT Implementation Flowchart: Full Implementation Stage

At this juncture, research and experience clearly show implementations can and do fail, even when years of time and effort have been invested and prior stages completed successfully (Moss & Mousavizadeh, 2017). New ideas come along, managers and staff take new jobs, practice champions leave the agency, and clinical attention is directed to new projects. All are threats to sustaining a fully implemented FIT culture and practice.

In truth, the question of "how to keep the process going" is a challenge at each stage. During exploration, heavy workloads and competing agendas can result in a loss of momentum. Since no formal decision to adopt FIT has been made at this point, meetings are easily canceled, and other responsibilities given priority. In stage two, the installation of crucial FIT practices and infrastructure can give way to existing policies and agency traditions. Consultation and TOG meetings may be scheduled, for example, but end up poorly attended, spent addressing non-FIT-related issues, or perceived by attendees as a waste of limited clinical time. Initial implementations are often derailed by overly ambitious plans and timelines. Simply put, the size and scope of agency wide rollouts make it impossible to provide staff and participating programs with the attention, support, and education necessary for success. Seldom do agencies abandon FIT altogether. Rather, it is far more common for implementation to drift. For example, bits and pieces of the process (e.g., administration of the ORS or SRS) may be adopted or utilization of FIT limited to a small number of practitioners and programs within the agency, ultimately resulting in little or no impact on the effectiveness of care provided.

CASE EXAMPLE 5.5: FIT LITE

A large, privately-owned mental health organization was in its fourth year providing "feedback-informed" treatment services. Early on, the staff—numbering in the hundreds—had attended a two-day training on FIT conducted by a well-known, international FIT trainer. Shortly thereafter, management had secured access to one of the authorized outcome management systems so that practitioners could easily administer the ORS and SRS and track individual client progress. In addition, several individuals within the organization with an interest in FIT had been sent to advanced training. In time, all completed the requirements for designation as a "FIT Certified Trainer."

At a regularly scheduled meeting of the TOG, discussion focused on continuing struggles with programs and practitioners acting on client feedback. Compliance with administering the measures was high as was attendance at biweekly FIT consultation meetings. However, the limited treatment options available and lack of connection to resources outside the agency left staff feeling powerless to make meaningful changes with their non-progressing cases. After much back and forth, the manager interrupted the conversation, stating, "We've reached the level of implementation possible for us. We have the data required for communicating with our funders. Not all agencies can fully implement FIT. For many, like us, 'FIT lite' is good enough."

Over the next two years, use of FIT at the agency continued to drift. The time once dedicated to FIT consultation meetings was redirected to other administrative and clinical activities (e.g., paperwork, quality assurance, case discussions). Additionally, utilization of the measures to guide and inform treatment services all but disappeared.

CASE EXAMPLE 5.6: MEET THE NEW BOSS (NOT THE SAME AS THE OLD BOSS)

Helen had a vision for improving the effectiveness of mental health services delivered to "at risk" children. Evidence from a large study spanning several decades showed the long-term, damaging effects of children placed in care outside the home. Given its emphasis on the clients' goals and experience, she believed FIT could improve parental engagement in the helping process, thereby enabling more families to stay together. Similar to other agencies, implementation at Helen's was not without challenges. Her steadfast leadership, combined with a well-functioning TOG and dedicated practice champions, allowed for the detection and resolution of problems as they arose (e.g., revisiting the tasks of prior stages of implementation, fine-tuning the in-house training program, use of outside FIT experts, adjusting the frequency of FIT consultations).

Under her leadership, the publicly funded agency reached full implementation after 5 years. Data gathered over that period showed FIT improved collaboration with and engagement of parents. During the initial implementation stage, both the "effect size" and percentage of families and collateral raters (e.g., school officials, family physicians, legal authorities) "reaching service targets" grew. At the same time, forceful removals of children from the home and formal complaints about the process (e.g., length, amount, type and provider of service) dropped significantly.

News of such successes spread, serving as an inspiration and model for other agencies. Then Helen was offered a new job. In terms of career advancement, it was a big step up. More responsibility. A chance to have a greater impact on children's services. Within a few months, a new leader took over management of the agency. When interviewed, this person expressed an interest in and willingness to support FIT but acknowledged having no direct experience with the approach.

Six months after assuming the position, the new leader introduced a different structure for service delivery, including thorough pre-treatment assessments and diagnostically driven, manualized treatments. The TOG members immediately expressed concerns about conflicts between the proposed changes and existing FIT culture and practice. Failing to see a problem, the leader ultimately instructed staff to "just do both." The impact on implementation of FIT was significant. By the end of the leader's first year, use of the scales had declined precipitously, and several key practice champions had left the agency.

Two decades of experience implementing FIT in diverse settings around the world reveal the key to sustainability is structure. Time and attention are finite resources. Like willpower, they are quickly depleted by the day-to-day demands of work in an agency setting. By contrast, in successful agencies, FIT becomes part of the "organizational DNA"—its mission, values, guiding principles, policies and practices—reflected in the items of the FITGAP. In particular:

- Client/service user outcomes are a central feature of the agency's "Mission Statement" and strategic plan (realm 2, item 19).

- Agency has policies and practice guidelines consistent with the principles and practice of FIT including, but not limited to:

    - How outcome and relationship data are collected, utilized, and shared with clients, staff, managers, and external stakeholders.

- Using individual client outcome data (i.e., SPI [Success Probability Index] and TRT) to guide care (e.g., intensity, type, provider) and discharge planning.
- Timing and process of ending services or transferring clients to different providers or service settings when outcome data indicate care is unhelpful.
- Using outcome data to guide the type and funding of professional development activities (realm 2, item 20 a-d).
- Access to FIT consultation is sufficient to address the number of cases identified as "at risk" for a negative or null outcome (realm 1, item 8).
- Knowledge about, attitude toward, and experience using FIT are essential qualifications in the hiring of new staff and leadership (realm 2, item 21).
- Training on FIT is available on an ongoing basis to both new and existing staff (i.e., helpers, managers, supervisors [realm 1, item 12]).
- Clinical documentation is consistent with and supportive of FIT principles and practice (i.e., FIT Service Delivery Agreement and Progress Note [realm 3, item 34]).

Two additional structures associated with sustainable implementations are: (1) the creation of a detailed "succession plan" for the support and continuation of FIT when changes in leadership occur; and (2) the formation of a group responsible for monitoring and updating FIT culture and practice at the agency (see "feedback oversight group" or FOG below). As was illustrated in case example 5.6, the departure of a manager can have a significant impact on sustainability. Indeed, in that example, and many other real-life instances, changes in leadership impact both fidelity and long-term utilization (Bertolino & Miller, 2012; Moss & Mousavizadeh, 2017; Woltmann et al. 2008).

Although rare in mental health settings, succession planning is a popular topic in the business literature. Still, as Quen (2024) has reported, most do not have a formal plan in place, "leaving them vulnerable to leadership gaps and business disruption." The impact, according to a step-by-step guide published by the U. S. National Institutes of Health (2021), includes:

- Loss of mission critical knowledge and focus
- Successors who lack personal drive and commitment as well as critical knowledge, training or skills
- Significant loss of time and money invested in implementation
- Disruption of established workplace processes and protocols

Of particular importance, the guide recommends "leveraging positions, not people" when developing a succession plan. The drift and eventual failure of the agency described in case example 5.6, for example, speaks to the danger of FIT being too closely associated with and driven by a person rather than the position they occupy. Therefore, an effective plan needs to include:

- A list of key competencies of the leadership position required for the continuity of FIT
- An interview process designed to assess job applicant knowledge of and commitment to FIT
- A training program for addressing newly hired leaders' FIT knowledge and skill deficits as well as fostering understanding of the role of FIT within the organizational structure and culture

The NIH guide includes three simple and easy-to-use tools for starting the succession planning process. First, the "Tracker Template," which helps identify key organizational positions in need of succession planning. Second, the "Profile Template," which specifies the competencies (education, experience, knowledge, skills, responsibilities, and duties) for each key organizational position. Third, and finally, the "Transition Planning Interview Guide," designed to document and preserve the knowledge and skills necessary to ensure continuity when individuals leave key positions. Links to each tool can be found in the guide (https://hr. nih. gov/sites/default/files/public/documents/2021-03/Succession_Planning_Step_by_Step_Guide.pdf).

In the original edition of the FIT manuals, it was noted that the TOG usually disbanded during the full implementation stage (see p. 23, Manual 6 [Bertolino & Miller, 2012]). While continued performance monitoring was recommended, no specific group, person, or structure was identified or assigned responsibility. The result was entirely predictable. Without a formal structure, no monitoring took place.

Invariably, FIT culture and practice began to drift (e.g., inconsistent administration of the measures, discussion of cases without client feedback, accumulation of non-progressing cases). Successful agencies, it was observed, replaced the TOG with a smaller group. Made up of a few members of the TOG and someone from the quality assurance department, this "Feedback Oversight Group" or FOG, was tasked with the responsibility for monitoring compliance (e.g., administering the FITGAP at regular intervals, reviewing agency data), operating the in-house training program, reviewing and updating agency and FIT policy and guidelines, and remaining up to date with innovations in FIT practice and research.

SUMMARY

Research and experience make clear that the successful implementation of FIT requires a significant investment of time, planning, and leadership involvement. In this chapter, the key questions, core tasks, supportive tools, persons responsible, and timeline were identified for each of the four, evidence-based stages of implementation. Potential pitfalls and challenges to sustainability were discussed and illustrated with real world case examples, including most notably, the temptation to skip steps (especially exploration), lack of management buy in/ support, linking of agency implementation efforts to specific individuals (managers, practice champions) versus agency structure and policy, and failure to anticipate and prepare for leadership changes and externally imposed organizational change mandates. No matter how well planned or tightly executed, few implementations occur in a stepwise, linear fashion. Thus, revisiting prior stages is likely and best viewed as an opportunity to reflect on implementation efforts, refine strategy, and assess the usefulness and applicability of FIT for specific programs and the agency.

QUIZ

1. Studies showing FIT has little or no positive impact on outcomes often result from:

    a. Low level of client functioning

    b. Severity of diagnosis

    c. Lack of client motivation

    d. Implementation deficiencies

2. What step(s) is/are most commonly missed when implementing FIT?

    a. Exploration

    b. Installation

    c. Exploration and installation

    d. Initial implementation

3. Successful Exploration involves:

    a. Determining if FIT is compatible with the services provided

    b. Identifying a transition oversight group

    c. Provision of training on how to do FIT

    d. Developing agency policies supportive of FIT

4. The Transition Oversight Group should:

    a. Be a reflection of the professionals and programs at the agency

    b. Include a mechanism for clinical staff to provide feedback on successes and challenges

    c. Develop plans to address implementation challenges

    d. All of the above

5. When piloting FIT:

  a. Leadership can take a backseat and let the pilot group try it out on their own

  b. A group of individual staff representing different programs within the agency should do the pilot

  c. Each pilot member should decide how much and with whom they want to use FIT

  d. It is essential to have mechanisms for a seamless flow of and responsiveness to feedback between the pilot members and TOG in place.

6. How long does the installation stage usually take?

  a. 0-6 months

  b. 6-18 months

  c. 18 -24 months

  d. 24-36 months

7. When implementing FIT, it is best to:

  a. Outsource training (e.g., attend workshops, read articles, watch demonstration videos)

  b. Use internal staff resources to provide live, on-the-job teaching, practice, and coaching

  c. Send all staff to a minimum of 2 days of training

  d. Read a book about FIT

8. The 5 factors influencing the adoption of FIT are:

  a. Leadership buy in, adequate resources, helper attitudes, client diagnosis, availability of FIT software

  b. Exploration, installation, implementation, full implementation, sustainability

  c. Relative advantage, compatibility, complexity, trialability, observability

  d. None of the above

9. The FIT Implementation Flow Chart:

    a. Is designed to assess the agencies stage of implementation

    b. Identifies who needs to be involved in an implementation

    c. Provides an overview of the considerations and resources for each stage of implementation

    d. None of the above

10. The FITGAP is designed to:

    a. Be used on an regular basis to identify strengths and deficiencies in the implementation process

    b. Be used a single time at the outset of implementation

    c. Provide evidence of a successful implementation

    d. Determine which programs and client populations are inappropriate for the application of FIT

Answers: *1. D, 2. A, 3. A, 4. D, 5. D, 6. B, 7. B, 8. C, 9. C, 10. A*

APPENDIX A: FIT Service Delivery Agreement

WITH "WHOM?"
Client preferences, values, identity, culture/worldview

THE "WHAT?"
Goals, meaning and purpose

THE "HOW?"
Means or methods

BY "WHOM?"
Client view of the bond and role of the helper

Name:	
Date:	
Client's stated reasons or motivation for seeking services:	
Agreed upon goals, meaning or purpose for services:	
Agreed upon means and methods (including type, frequency, provider):	
Feedback informed process explained (routine outcome and alliance measurement): Yes No	
Clinician signature	Client signature

APPENDIX B: FIT Progress Note

Feedback Informed Progress Note

Name:	Date:

ORS Administered: Yes No	Outcome: → ↑ ↓
Collateral Score: Yes No	

Outcome addressed in session by:

Between session plan (eg. maintain & consolidate gains/address deterioration/revise approach):

SRS Administered: Yes No	Score is: Above 36 Below 36
	Score is: Increasing Same Decreasing

SRS scores addressed directly before the end of the session: Yes   No

Client feedback (if any):

Clinician signature	Client signature

APPENDIX C: FIT Consultation Approach

Appendix C

Figure 3.1: FIT Consultation Approach

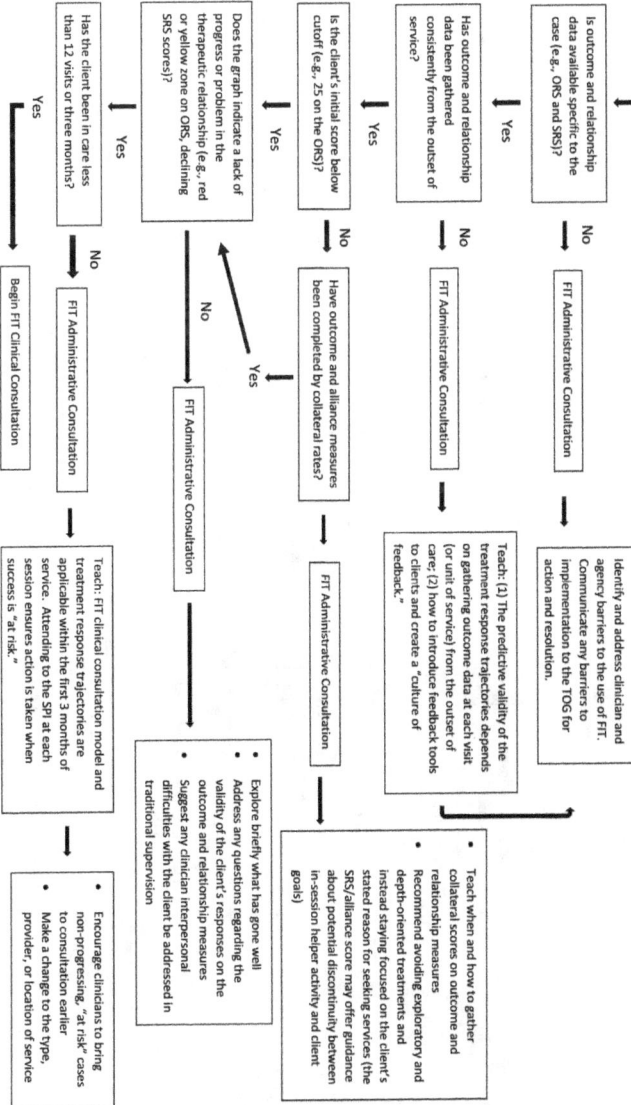

START

Is outcome and relationship data available specific to the case (e.g., ORS and SRS)?

— No → FIT Administrative Consultation
- Identify and address clinician and agency barriers to the use of FIT.
- Communicate any barriers to implementation to the TOQ for action and resolution.

— Yes →

Has outcome and relationship data been gathered consistently from the outset of service?

— No → FIT Administrative Consultation
- Teach: (1) The predictive validity of the treatment response trajectories depends on gathering outcome data at each visit (or unit of service) from the outset of care; (2) how to introduce feedback tools to clients and create a "culture of feedback."

— Yes →

Is the client's initial score below cutoff (e.g., 25 on the ORS)?

— No → Have outcome and alliance measures been completed by collateral rates?
  - No → FIT Administrative Consultation
    - Teach when and how to gather collateral scores on outcome and relationship measures
    - Recommend avoiding exploratory and depth-oriented treatments and instead staying focused on the client's stated reason for seeking services (the SRS/alliance score may offer guidance about potential discontinuity between in-session helper activity and client goals)
  - Yes →

— Yes →

Does the graph indicate a lack of progress or problem in the therapeutic relationship (e.g., red or yellow zone on ORS, declining SRS scores)?

— No → FIT Administrative Consultation
- Explore briefly what has gone well
- Address any questions regarding the validity of the client's responses on the outcome and relationship measures
- Suggest any clinician interpersonal difficulties with the client be addressed in traditional supervision

— Yes →

Has the client been in care less than 12 visits or three months?

— No → FIT Administrative Consultation
- Teach: FIT clinical consultation model and treatment response trajectories are applicable within the first 3 months of service. Attending to the SPI at each session ensures action is taken when success is "at risk."

— Yes → Begin FIT Clinical Consultation
- Encourage clinicians to bring non-progressing, "at risk" cases to consultation earlier
- Make a change to the type, provider, or location of service

APPENDIX D: FIT Clinical Consultation

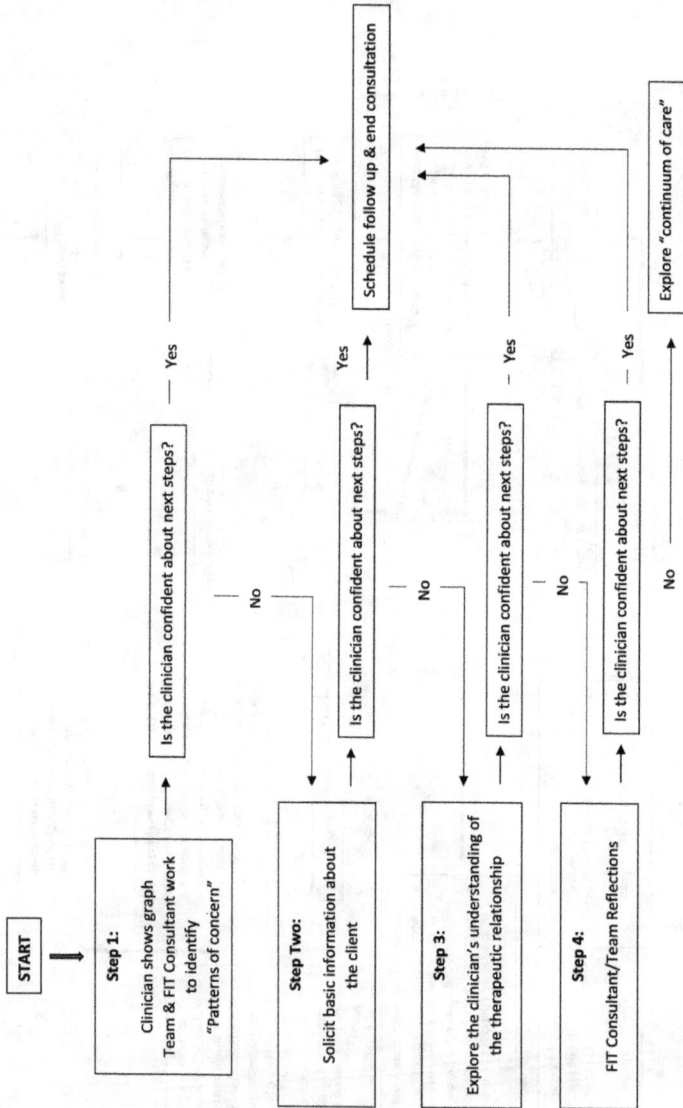

Appendix D

FIT Clinical Consultation

START

Step 1:
Clinician shows graph
Team & FIT Consultant work
to identify
"Patterns of concern"

Is the clinician confident about next steps? — Yes → Schedule follow up & end consultation

No

Step Two:
Solicit basic information about
the client

Is the clinician confident about next steps? — Yes → Schedule follow up & end consultation

No

Step 3:
Explore the clinician's understanding of
the therapeutic relationship

Is the clinician confident about next steps? — Yes → Schedule follow up & end consultation

No

Step 4:
FIT Consultant/Team Reflections

Is the clinician confident about next steps? — Yes → Schedule follow up & end consultation

No → Explore "continuum of care"

APPENDIX E: Calculating Standard Deviation

Given the widespread availability of online calculators, few would calculate a standard deviation by hand. That said, here is the formula for calculating standard deviation.

$$\sigma = \sqrt{\frac{\sum (x_i - \mu)^2}{N}}$$

N = The number of data points

$(x_i - \mu)$= Each of the values of the data

μ = The mean of Xi

The i=1 in the summation indicates the starting index. For example, suppose your outcome measure (Outcome Rating Scale, ORS) for the first sessions are 15, 16, 17, 18, 19, then i = 1 would be 15, and i = 2 would be 16, and so on. Hence, the summation notation simply means to take each of the first session ORS's, minus the mean, and then square it, i.e., $(x_i - \mu)^2$ on each value through N. In this example, N is 5 since there are 5 ORSs in this data set.

$$\mu = (15 + 16 + 17 + 18 + 19)/5 = 17$$

$$\sigma = \sqrt{((15-17)^2 + (16-17)^2 + (17-17)^2 + (18-17)^2 + (19+17)^2/5)}$$

$$\sigma = \sqrt{(4 + 1 + 0 + 1 + 4/5)} = 1.58$$

As simpler way to calculate standard deviation is to use a spreadsheet (Microsoft Excel or Google Sheets). Here are the steps:

1. Input all of your first session outcome measure scores (e.g., ORS) in a column (e.g., B2 to B65);

2. Go to the bottom of that column (keep a few rows blank so that if you use a filter to sort your data, it will not affect your computations at the bottom), and key in the following in the bottom cell:
   "= STDDEV(B2:B65)"

Alternatively, you can use an online calculator such as https://www.calculator.net/standard-deviation-calculator. html.

APPENDIX F: Reliable and Clinically Significant Change Chart for the Outcome Rating Scale

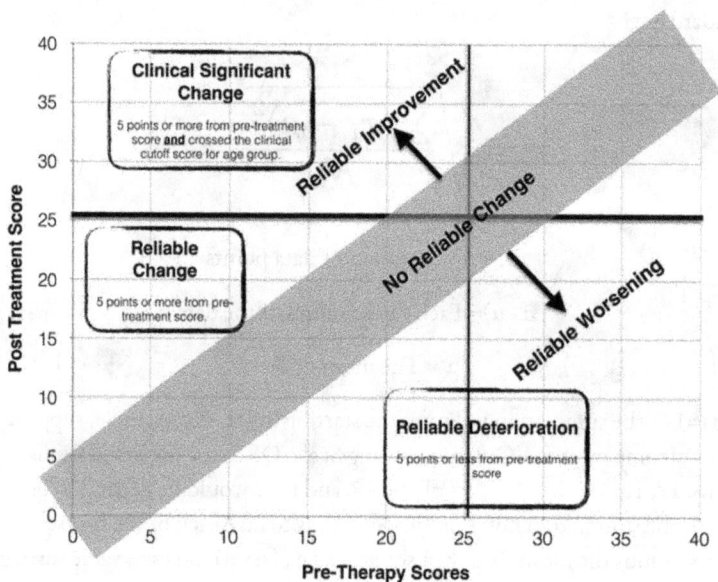

APPENDIX G: ORS and SRS Licensing Agreement

Licensee: By downloading or by any other means acquiring the measures, you or you and your constituents, are hereby licensed by Performance Metrics (hereafter PM) to use the ORS and SRS in paper and pencil format, and by virtue of downloading or otherwise acquiring, are the "licensee" under this agreement.

ORS and SRS: The ORS and SRS means any and all paper and pencil (no electronic use/digitalization of the measures is permitted by this license) versions of the outcome and process measures.

License: Subject to the terms and conditions of this agreement, PM grants to the licensee a license to use the ORS and the SRS in paper and pencil format in connection with the licensee's bona fide health care practice. The measures, administration and scoring manual, graph associated with the ORS and SRS may NOT be copied, transmitted, or distributed by the licensee. Paper and pencil versions of the ORS and SRS may be copied for use in connection with the licensee's bona fide health care practice.

Modifications: The licensee may NOT modify, translate into other languages, change the context, wording, or organization of the ORS and SRS or create any derivative work based on them. The licensee may put the ORS and SRS into other written, non-electronic, non-computerized, non-automated formats provided that the content, wording, or organization are not modified or changed.

Copies, Notices, and Credits: Any and all copies of the ORS and SRS made by the licensee must include the copyright notice, trademarks, and other notices and credits on the ORS and SRS. Such notices may not be deleted, omitted, obscured or changed by the licensee.

Use, distribution, and changes: The ORS and SRS may only be used and distributed by the licensee in connection with licensee's bona fide health care practice and may not be used or distributed for any other purpose.

Responsibility: Before using or relying on the ORS or SRS it is the responsibility of the licensee to ascertain the suitability of the ORS and SRS for any and all uses made by the licensee. The ORS and SRS are not diagnostic tools and should not be used as such. The ORS and SRS are not substitutes for an independent professional evaluation. Any and all reliance on the ORS and SRS by the licensee is at the licensee's sole risk and is the licensee's sole responsibility. Licensee indemnifies PM and it's officers, directors, employees, representatives, and authors of the ORS and SRS against, and hold them harmless from, any and all claims and law suits arising from or relating to any use of or reliance on the ORS and SRS and related products provided by PM. This obligation to indemnify and hold harmless includes a promise to pay any and all judgments, damages, attorney's fees, costs and expenses arising from any such claim or lawsuit.

Disclaimer: Licensee accepts the ORS and SRS and associated products "as is" without any warranty of any kind. PM disclaims any and all implied warranties, including implied warranties of merchantability, fitness for a particular purpose, and non-infringement. PM does not warrant that the ORS and SRS are without error or defect. PM shall not be liable for any consequential, indirect, special, incidental or punitive damages. The aggregate liability of PM for any and all causes of action (including those based on contract, warranty, tort, negligence, strict liability, fraud, malpractice, or otherwise) shall not exceed the fee paid by the licensee to PM. This license agreement, and sections 7 and 8 in particular, define a mutually agreed upon allocation of risk. The fee reflects such allocation of risk.

Construction: The language used in this agreement is the language chosen by the parties to express their mutual intent, and no rule of strict construction shall be applied against any party.

Entire agreement: This agreement is the entire agreement of the parties relating to the ORS and SRS.

Governing law: This agreement is made and entered into in the State of Florida and shall be governed by the laws of the State of Florida. In the event of any litigation or arbitration between the parties, such litigation or arbitration shall be conducted in Florida and the parties hereby agree and submit to such jurisdiction and venue.

Modification: This agreement may not be modified or amended.

Transferability: This agreement may not be transferred, bartered, loaned, assigned, leased, or sold by the licensee.

Violations: Violations of any provision or stipulation of this agreement will result in immediate revocation of this license. Punitive damages may be assessed.

APPENDIX H: List of ICCE Approved Statistical Indices

The items below identify the statistical indices that must be included in all authorized computer systems and API users employing the ORS and SRS family of measures (ORS, SRS, CORS, CSRS, GSRS) and associated formulas and trajectories developed by Scott D. Miller, Ph. D and licensed by Performance Metrics, LLC. No other statistical indices may be included in data reporting by any system without permission from Scott D. Miller, Ph.D. In cases where the measures are used as part of an API, the system developer has the responsibility to ensure that the user of the API defines and reports data according to the ICCE standard.

The following indices must be reported in a simple, easy-to-understand, side-by-side comparison of active (in treatment) and inactive (closed cases). The same indices must also be reported from both the client's and collateral rater's perspective (internal [e.g., client about others], and external [e.g., personal network and professional ratings]).

Number of Clients: The number of clients broken down by age (adult, adolescent, child).

Number of Treatment Episodes: Inclusive of all clients involved in a particular course of treatment.

Number of Collateral Raters: The number of raters for a particular client or episode of care.

Average Intake ORS: The mean score for all clients on ORS at first session broken down by age (adults, adolescents, and children).

Average Intake SRS: The mean score for all clients on SRS at first session.

Average Number of Sessions: Total of sessions divided by the total number of episodes. System operators are free to include the total number of sessions in reports.

Average Treatment Length: Total number of days from opening a case to the last session or closing divided by the number of episodes.

Effect Size (pre-post effect size): The effect of treatment compared to no treatment (when correcting for number of sessions, regression to the mean, severity at intake and bias).

Relative Effect Size: Comparing the effect size of the clinician or agency to the grand mean effect size of the normative sample (comparing to the mean of other treatments).

Percentage of Clients Reaching Target: The percentage of clients whose last ORS score falls in the green zone.

Dropout: Systems need to have a method in place for clinicians to categorize the end of treatment. Treatment can end either by: (1) mutual agreement; or (2) unilateral termination by client. If the treatment is terminated unilaterally by the client, a system must be in place that offers clinicians two choice: (1) outcomes falling outside the green zone (without effect); or (2) outcomes falling within the green zone (with effect). The percentage of clients who terminate unilaterally (2.1) without effect should be reported as "dropout."

Average Raw Change: (this index should no longer be included).

Clinically Significant Change: Defined as clients who begin treatment with an intake score starting below 25 and whose last score falls above the clinical cutoff (25) AND in the green zone.

Reliable Change Index: This index should no longer be included as reliable change is calculated for each individual based on their first session score and represented in the treatment response trajectory as the green line.

OTHER SYSTEM REQUIREMENTS

Treatment Response Trajectories: A client's treatment response trajectory (TRT) is based on their individual initial score on the ORS. The ORS trajectories should be displayed in a graph with a green, yellow, and red area (the calculation must follow the official formulas and algorithms developed by Scott D. Miller, Ph. D. and included as part of the licensing of authorized independent systems by Performance Metrics, LLC or via an API from an authorized vendor). The client's actual score from session to session should be displayed on a separate black line in the graph against the TRT. A score in the green area indicates a change similar to successful treatment (clients on track) and a score in the red area indicates a change less than expected (clients not on track). A score in the yellow area indicates an uncertain change tendency.

Success Probability Index: The SPI provides a prediction of the likelihood of success based on the pattern of SRS and ORS scores. Unlike the static TRT, the SPI is dynamic, updating at each session. The data used to generate the SPI at any given session varies depending on what most accurately predicts success at the end of care (e.g., the average of scores, their slope, and change in scores since the prior visit or across sessions). A positive SPI is coded in green indicating care is on track for a successful result. A negative SPI is coded in red and indicates the probability of success is below the average successful client.

SRS Scores: The client's SRS scores from session to session should be displayed on the same graph as the ORS, distinguished by a different color.

ORS and SRS Cutoff Scores: Age-related cut-off scores for ORS and SRS should also be included in the graph. On this score, the ORS cut-off for adults is 25, 28 for adolescents aged 13-18 years, and 32 for children aged 6-12. The SRS cut-off for all age groups is 36.

*Any metrics not included in this list need to be reviewed and approved by Scott D. Miller, Ph. D. prior to implementation.

APPENDIX I: FIT Implementation Flowchart

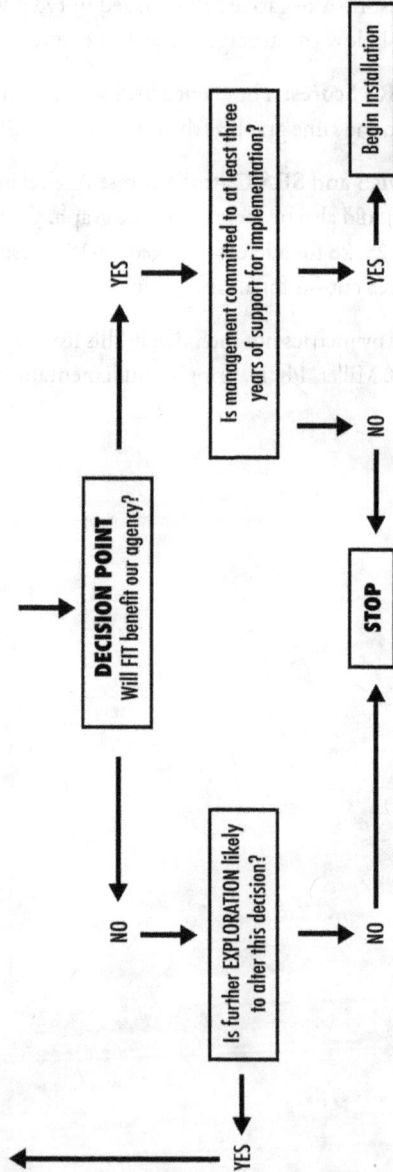

TIMELINE MONTHS	Questions	EXPLORATION — Tasks	Tools	Who
0	• What is the mission of the agency or system? • How would FIT be an improvement over the current way of working? • How has FIT worked in similar agencies/systems? • How ready is the agency/system to adopt a FIT culture?	• Organize an initial implementation team (IIT) responsible for answering this stage's key questions • Become knowledgeable about FIT principles and practice • Consult with FIT experts • Visit other agencies/systems which have implemented FIT	• FIT manual • ICCE certification courses, list of certified trainers and e-learning platform • ICCE discussion forum • The Feedback Informed Gap Assessment Tool (FITGAP)	• Small group whose members have an interest in and passion for FIT

DECISION POINT — Will FIT benefit our agency?

NO → Is further EXPLORATION likely to alter this decision?

YES

Is management committed to at least three years of support for implementation?

YES → Begin Installation

NO → STOP

NO

6 to 12

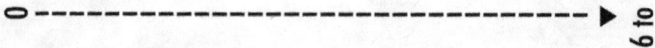

APPENDIX I: FIT Implementation Flowchart (cont)

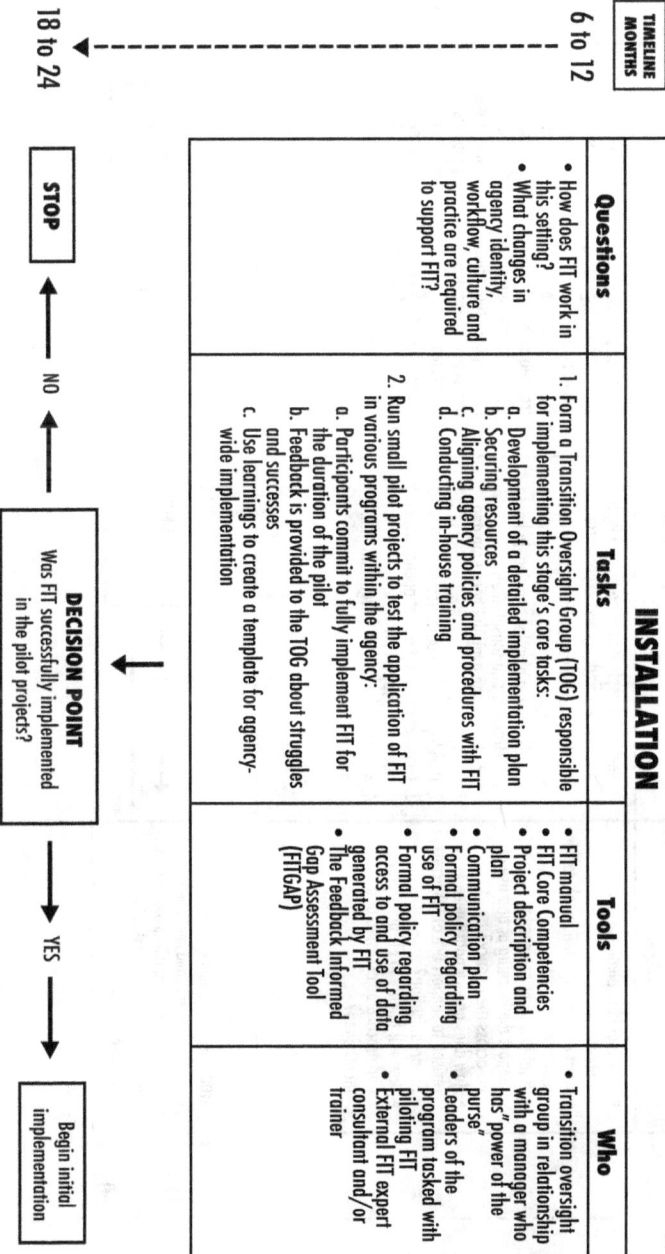

TIMELINE MONTHS

6 to 12

18 to 24

INSTALLATION

Questions	Tasks	Tools	Who

• How does FIT work in this setting?
• What changes in agency identity, workflow, culture and practice are required to support FIT?
	1. Form a Transition Oversight Group (TOG) responsible for implementing this stage's core tasks:
	  a. Development of a detailed implementation plan
	  b. Securing resources
	  c. Aligning agency policies and procedures with FIT
	  d. Conducting in-house training
	2. Run small pilot projects to test the application of FIT in various programs within the agency:
	  a. Participants commit to fully implement FIT for the duration of the pilot
	  b. Feedback is provided to the TOG about struggles and successes
	  c. Use learnings to create a template for agency-wide implementation
		• FIT manual
		• FIT Core Competencies
		• Project description and plan
		• Communication plan
		• Formal policy regarding use of FIT
		• Formal policy regarding access to and use of data generated by FIT
		• The Feedback Informed Gap Assessment Tool (FITGAP)
			• Transition oversight group in relationship with a manager who has "power of the purse"
			• Leaders of the program tasked with piloting FIT
			• External FIT expert consultant and/or trainer

DECISION POINT
Was FIT successfully implemented in the pilot projects?

NO → **STOP**

YES → Begin initial implementation

APPENDIX I: FIT Implementation Flowchart (cont)

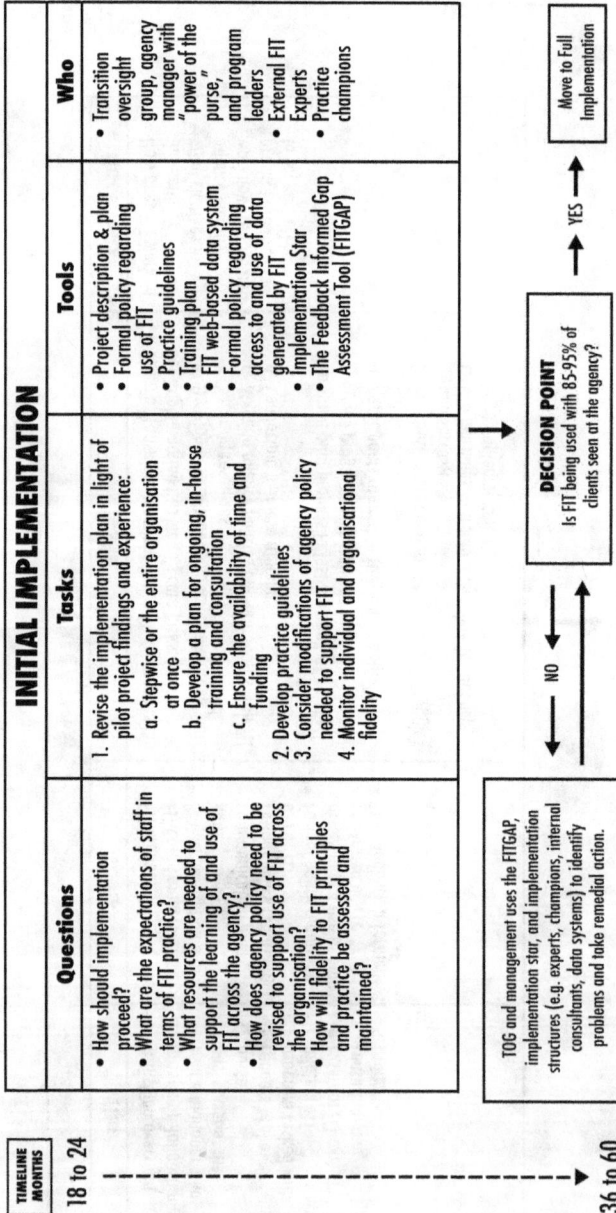

TIMELINE MONTHS

18 to 24

INITIAL IMPLEMENTATION

Questions	Tasks	Tools	Who

• How should implementation proceed?
• What are the expectations of staff in terms of FIT practice?
• What resources are needed to support the learning of and use of FIT across the agency?
• How does agency policy need to be revised to support use of FIT across the organisation?
• How will fidelity to FIT principles and practice be assessed and maintained?
	1. Revise the implementation plan in light of pilot project findings and experience:
	  a. Stepwise or the entire organisation at once
	  b. Develop a plan for ongoing, in-house training and consultation
	  c. Ensure the availability of time and funding
	2. Develop practice guidelines
	3. Consider modifications of agency policy needed to support FIT
	4. Monitor individual and organisational fidelity
		• Project description & plan
		• Formal policy regarding use of FIT
		• Practice guidelines
		• Training plan
		• FIT web-based data system
		• Formal policy regarding access to and use of data generated by FIT
		• Implementation Star
		• The Feedback Informed Gap Assessment Tool (FITGAP)
			• Transition oversight group, agency manager with "power of the purse," and program leaders
			• External FIT Experts
			• Practice champions

DECISION POINT
Is FIT being used with 85-95% of clients seen at the agency?

NO

TOG and management uses the FITGAP, implementation star, and implementation structures (e.g. experts, champions, internal consultants, data systems) to identify problems and take remedial action.

YES → Move to Full Implementation

36 to 60

APPENDIX I: FIT Implementation Flowchart (cont)

TIMELINE MONTHS

36 to 60

FULL IMPLEMENTATION

Questions	Tasks	Tools	Who

• What structures are necessary to sustain FIT culture and practice?
 	
• How does the agency use FIT data for program and professional development?
 	
• What, if any, adaptations or innovations in FIT practice would improve all clients' ability to impact and improve service delivery and outcome?
	1. FIT is integrated into the agency mission statement, hiring decisions, and program development process.
	2. Review program and agency outcome data:
	  a. Identifying performance deficits
	  b. Set performance improvement goals
	  c. Develop and execute a professional development plan
	3. Replace the TOG with the FOG
		• Service Delivery Agreement (SDA) & Progress Note (PN)
		• Ongoing FIT training program
		• The Feedback Informed Gap Assessment Tool (FITGAP)
		• Realtime data system
		• Leadership/management succession plan
			• Feedback Oversight Group
			• Internal/local FIT experts
			• Practice champions

APPENDIX J: Feedback Informed Treatment GAP Assessment and Instructions

The Feedback Informed Treatment GAP Assessment (FITGAP) is a tool for determining the size and nature of the gap between an organization's current culture and practice and one in which FIT is fully implemented. The FITGAP addresses four organizational realms research and experience show are necessary to and impacted by the implementation of FIT:

Realm 1: Clinical (helpers, consultation/supervision, training, client/service users)

Realm 2: Administrative (agency, management and leadership, support personnel)

Realm 3: Documentation & Information Technology (service delivery agreement, progress notes, outcome management software)

Realm 4: Stakeholders (legal, regulatory, accreditation and funding, referral sources).

Completing the scale is simple and straightforward. As can be seen below, each of the 38 items is rated on a scale from 1 to 5 or marked N/A if not applicable.

Not Applicable	No, None, Never	Very Limited, Not Often	Partially. Frequently	Mostly, Regularly	Yes, Fully Always
N/A	1	2	3	4	5

Interpreting the results of the FITGAP depends on the purpose for which it is being used. Agencies typically apply the tool in three different ways, specifically, to:

1. Assess agency readiness to implement FIT;

2. Monitor and track the progress of implementation efforts; and

3. Diagnose and address barriers to successful implementation.

As an example, when completed during the exploration stage, lower scores would indicate a larger gap between current organizational beliefs and practices and an established FIT culture. Such information, in turn, can provide critical information to the IIT and agency management about the scope, feasibility and impact of implementation. Once a decision has been made to proceed, administering the tool at regular intervals would make it possible to gauge progress (e.g., closing gaps in any or all the organizational realms). Additionally, both at the outset of implementation and along the way, lower scores on individual items can be used to identify gaps in the four realms (e.g., clinical, administrative, documentation/IT and stakeholders) in need of attention and remediation. A score of 2 or a 1, for example, would be considered a definite sign of a gap likely to undermine success, while a score of 3 would point to a potential threat to implementation. As a general rule, scores of 4 or 5 indicate alignment with FIT culture and practice.

ICCE | The International Center for Clinical Excellence

Feedback-Informed Treatment GAP Assessment Tool (FITGAP)

Realm 1: CLINICAL (Version 2.0)

Not Applicable	No, None,	Very Limited,	Partially.	Mostly,	Yes, Fully
	Never	Not Often	Frequently	Regularly	Always
	1	2	3	4	5
N/A					

Write in the score that best applies

Helpers:

1. Administer and score the Outcome Rating Scale (ORS) and Session Rating Scale (SRS) together with the client (and/or collateral rater) at each visit or "unit of service."	☐ Score
2. Compare client score on the ORS to the clinical cutoff and discuss with the client at the first visit.	☐ Score
3. Compare client scores on the ORS at each visit to the "treatment response trajectory" (TRT) to determine which clients are making progress and which are at risk for a negative or null outcome.	☐ Score
4. Discuss client progress (ORS) and experience of the relationship (SRS) at each visit.	☐ Score
5. Use the ORS and SRS to develop and refine individualized treatment planning.	☐ Score
6. Use ORS and SRS data to determine which cases need to be discussed in FIT consultation.	☐ Score

Consultation & Supervision:

7. FIT consultants have access to individual helper and program outcome data to facilitate the identification of "at risk" clients.	☐ Score
8. Access to FIT consultation is sufficient to address the number of cases identified as "at risk" for a negative or null outcome.	☐ Score
9. Any supervision beyond FIT consultation is consistent with and friendly toward FIT principles and practice.	☐ Score
10. FIT consultation and other supervision provided encourage flexibility and diversity in methods, approach, and providers in order to accommodate individual client culture, preferences, and worldview.	☐ Score

Training on FIT:

11. Is based on a structured curriculum and training plan consistent with the "Core Competencies of Feedback-informed Treatment."	☐ Score
12. Is available on an ongoing basis to both new and existing staff (i.e., helpers, managers, supervisors).	☐ Score
13. Is offered onsite by "in house" FIT experts/champions.	☐ Score

Client/Service Users:

14. A description of and rationale for FIT (including the process and timeframe for dealing with unhelpful or undesired services) is provided at first contact.	☐ Score
15. Clinical records (e.g., assessments/evaluations, correspondence, FIT SDA, progress notes) are completed in an open and collaborative manner.	☐ Score
16. FIT "Service Delivery Agreement" (SDA) is organized around their priorities, goals, preferences, and progress.	☐ Score
17. Level, intensity, and type of service(s) offered are informed by their initial score on the ORS.	☐ Score
18. Feedback via the ORS and SRS is taken seriously and used on an ongoing basis to inform and adjust service(s).	☐ Score

Feedback-Informed Treatment GAP Assessment Tool (FITGAP)

Realm 2: ADMINISTRATIVE (Version 2.0)

Not Applicable	No, None, Never	Very Limited, Not Often	Partially. Frequently	Mostly, Regularly	Yes, Fully Always
	1	2	3	4	5
N/A					

Write in the score that best applies

The Agency:

19. Client/service user outcomes are a central feature of the agency's "Mission Statement" and strategic plan.	☐ Score
20. Agency has policies and practice guidelines consistent with the principles and practice of FIT including, but not limited to:	
a. How outcome and relationship data are collected, utilized, and shared with clients, staff, managers, and external stakeholders.	☐ Score
b. Using individual client outcome data (i.e., SPI [Success Probability Index] and TRT) to guide care (e.g., intensity, type, provider) and discharge planning.	☐ Score
c. Timing and process of ending services or transferring clients to different providers or service settings when outcome data indicate care is unhelpful.	☐ Score
d. Using outcome data to guide the type and funding of professional development activities.	☐ Score
21. Knowledge about, attitude toward, and experience using FIT are essential qualifications in the hiring of new staff and leadership.	☐ Score

Management and Leadership:

22. Leadership and managers are knowledgeable about FIT and follow the evidence-based steps of implementation.	☐ Score
23. Leadership and managers actively lead the implementation of FIT (e.g., attending the Transition Oversight Group [TOG], establishing an implementation plan and budget, addressing barriers, and establishing an accountability framework).	☐ Score
24. Leadership and managers foster a "culture of feedback" at the agency (e.g., being open and transparent, interested in and receptive to feedback from staff, supervisors, and service users).	☐ Score
25. Leadership and managers ensure client feedback regarding progress and quality of the relationship is included in all clinical discussions.	☐ Score
26. Leadership and managers have secured support for FIT from the governing authorities (e.g., Board of Directors, funders, consumer organization, regulatory and other oversight bodies).	☐ Score
27. Leadership and managers ensure agency personnel have the time available in their schedules to meaningfully and effectively utilize FIT.	☐ Score

Support Personnel:

28. Administrative staff (receptionists, administrative assistants, custodial and other non-clinical employees) have been trained in the principles of FIT.	☐ Score
29. Administrative staff (receptionists, administrative assistants, custodial and other non-clinical employees) embody the "culture of feedback" in their interactions with service users (e.g., are open and transparent, interested in and receptive to feedback).	☐ Score

Feedback-Informed Treatment GAP Assessment Tool (FITGAP)

Realm 3: DOCUMENTATION & INFORMATION TECHNOLOGY (IT) (Version 2.0)

Not Applicable	No, None, Never	Very Limited, Not Often	Partially. Frequently	Mostly, Regularly	Yes, Fully Always
N/A	1	2	3	4	5

Write in the score that best applies

Documentation and IT:

30. One of the three, authorized FIT outcome management systems has been adopted and is being used in all programs and service settings (e.g., inpatient, outpatient, in home, outreach, individual/couple/family, psychiatric and group).	☐ Score
31. A specific staff member has been assigned to oversee and manage access to and organization of the outcome management system (e.g., subscriptions, licenses, and hardware purchases).	☐ Score
32. Staff (e.g., helpers, supervisors, managers) are skilled in using the outcome management system.	☐ Score
33. Support and training on the use of the outcome management system is easily accessible and available on an ongoing basis.	☐ Score
34. Clinical documentation is consistent with and supportive of FIT principles and practice (i.e., FIT service delivery agreement and progress note).	☐ Score
35. Clinical documentation (e.g., administration of the measures, development of the FIT SDA and progress note) is completed in a collaborative manner, together with clients.	☐ Score

Feedback-Informed Treatment GAP Assessment Tool (FITGAP)

Realm 4: STAKEHOLDERS (Version 2.0)

Not Applicable	No, None,	Very Limited,	Partially.	Mostly,	Yes, Fully
	Never	Not Often	Frequently	Regularly	Always
	1	2	3	4	5
N/A					

Write in the score that best applies

Legal, regulatory, accreditation, and funding:

36. Managers and the TOG have identified and addressed potential conflicts between the principles and practice of FIT and legal mandates, accreditation standards, and funding/funder requirements.	☐ Score
37. Managers and the TOG have sought variances from legal, accreditation and funding bodies for mandates or standards representing significant barriers to FIT implementation.	☐ Score

Referral sources:

38. Managers and the TOG have informed referral sources about:	
a. The use of FIT to determine the level and intensity of care.	☐ Score
b. Their potential role as "collateral raters."	☐ Score
c. The formal process and time frame for determining/dealing with care that is unhelpful or undesired.	☐ Score

APPENDIX K: Sample Implementation and Communication Policy and Plan

The implementation plan and policy below was created by a committee of select personnel (e.g., leaders, supervisors, agency staff) from a medium size public behavioral health agency providing diverse services (e.g., children, adolescents, adults, people with substance issues, mandated and voluntary, severe and persistent mental illnesses, cognitive and physical disabilities). Feedback from staff was used to refine the resulting document which was, in turn, formally adopted by each program, professional discipline, agency and municipal leadership.

THE PLAN

Background: We have been searching for a tool to ensure that our clients are directly involved in the planning and delivery of their care and securing their desired outcome.

FIT (Feedback Informed Treatment) has been selected for agency wide implementation as it enables clients to provide feedback on an ongoing basis via two simple scales: (1) the SRS (Session Rating Scale) which measures the client's experience of the helping relationship, and (2) the ORS (Outcome Rating Scale) which measures the client's experience of change (progress).

A chief reason for implementing FIT is to ensure that clients served by the agency experience a culture of openness and receptivity to their input, feedback and critique. In so doing, it is hoped that engagement and effectiveness of the services offered will improve.

FIT is already being used by several agencies in the municipality, specifically by agencies working with children and youth. As such, considerable knowledge and experience about its implementation and application exists locally.

Objectives for the implementation of FIT: In the first year, FIT will be piloted in three different programs within the agency to evaluate applicability and helpfulness of the approach as well as create a template for implementation across the rest of the organization. Specifically:

- The SRS and ORS will be used systematically to determine the effectiveness of the services offered by the programs

- Feedback from clients will be actively used to identify and make adjustments to ineffective services

- Data and experiences from the pilot projects will be reviewed on an ongoing basis by the TOG and adjustments made to services, programs, and agency policies to facilitate the development of an agency-wide culture of feedback.

Time Frame: The agency has secured the financial resources for and is committed to at least a 3-year implementation effort beginning (insert date here). The plan and execution will be supported by external FIT expert (name of person here) who will be available for a minimum of (insert number of days/hours) of training and consultation with staff, management, and the TOG per year.

Implementation Structures: Transition Oversight Group (TOG) consisting of one manager, a leader and representative staff of the programs involved in piloting, a FIT champion, and an administrative or support person.

Pilot groups have been selected to test FIT that reflect the diverse services/ programs offered at the agency. As the programs are large, smaller groups from the following services will participate: (1) child protective services; (2) substance abuse treatment; and (3) long term group homes. FIT will be used with all clients at every visit during the piloting phase. Other programs will be informed about progress of the initiative but should refrain from using FIT until testing is complete.

FIT champions within the organization have been identified and may be consulted and utilized for support. These include (insert names here). Because of their interest and work, time and financial support will be made available for them to: (1) attend advanced FIT courses; (2) provide training and consultation to pilot groups.

Resources: To support the use of FIT during the piloting phase, productivity standards will be changed. For pilot project members, one hour of clinical time per week will be redirected to FIT related activities (e.g., consultation, training, technical and other support). Members will also be given access to an ICCE approved outcome management system and tablet for administering the ORS and SRS and tracking client progress.

All materials related to and supportive of FIT implementation (plan, policies, training manuals, TOG minutes and decision) will be stored on the agency intranet and accessible to all staff.

Communication. Care will be taken to communicate the process and status of implementation to all programs and staff across the agency, including: (1) pilot project findings; (2) minutes of TOG meetings; (3) changes or modifications made to existing policies and programming to facilitate the adoption of FIT; (4) development of and access to FIT-related training resources; (5) revisions of and decisions regarding the implementation plan. The table below summarizes the tasks, timeline, and persons responsible for communication.

Task	Timeline	Target	Person Responsible
FIT Implementation Newsletter	Monthly	All agency staff	Administrative member of TOG
Incorporating FIT into agency culture	Continuous	All agency meetings	Agency leaders and program managers
TOG minutes	Monthly	All agency staff	Administrative member of the TOG
Creation of materials explaining FIT to agency clients	Immediately	Pilot project members	TOG members
Dissemination of materials explaining FIT to clients in pilot programs	Continuous	Agency clients	Pilot project members
Solicitation of and response to feedback from pilot project sites	Continuous	Pilot project members	TOG Program managers for pilot groups External consultant FIT champions
Implementation status update for agency manager/ leader	Quarterly	Leadership group	Leaders of programs piloting FIT

Evaluation: Consistent with the description in the FIT Treatment and Training Manual, the TOG will evaluate progress of the pilot projects, using the resulting information to adjust and refine the plan for the second and third years of implementation. Progress will be tracked and implementation challenges and targets identified via the administration of the FITGAP tool and routinely soliciting feedback from pilot programs regarding staff experience of: (1) the type and amount of training; (2) availability and usefulness of consultation; (3) time available for learning (e.g., computer system, FIT practices, training); (4) support and involvement from management; (5) responsiveness of management and the TOG to concerns and difficulties related to implementation.

APPENDIX L: Sample FIT Data Policy

What is FIT?

Feedback Informed Treatment (FIT) is a method for soliciting feedback from clients regarding their experience of the helping relationship and outcome of care. The process involves the administration of the Outcome Rating Scale (ORS) and the Session Rating Scale (SRS) at each visit or "unit of service." Research documents improved engagement and outcomes when the results of the two scales are discussed and adjustments made to improve the fit between helper, service, and client.

Administration and analyses are facilitated by the use of an ICCE-approved outcome management system offering aggregate reports assessing the outcome of the entire agency, and effectiveness of specific programs, the individual helper, and each episode of care.

How will FIT be used?

FIT will be used in accordance with the principles and practices described in detail in the FIT Core Competencies and FIT Treatment and Training Manual.

Unless a particular program or service has been exempted, the expectation is that FIT will be used with all clients in care and any setting where services/ treatment decisions are being made (e.g., intake, treatment planning, case consultation, FIT consultation, meetings with external stakeholders).

Agency management is expected to provide the time, training, resources, and oversight needed to support the use of FIT.

The data generated by FIT will be used to inform decisions regarding program and practitioner development. For example, the identification of a low effect-size relative to agency norms would result in an offer of training and consultation aimed at improving effectiveness versus disciplinary action (e.g., termination of staff, elimination of specific programs). Aggregate data regarding agency, program, and individual helper effectiveness will be available on an ongoing basis in real time for managers, helpers, and clients.

How will FIT not be used?

Outcome data generated by FIT will not be used in isolation to make employment or salary decisions. Neither is FIT a replacement for performance evaluations routinely carried out by the agency as part of maintaining employment. Unless agreed to by helpers, clients, and management, and accompanied by a context-informed interpretation developed by same, effectiveness data generated by FIT is not shared outside the immediate agency.

How can the FIT data policy be changed?

Amendments to or termination of the FIT data policy must be submitted for review to the Transition or Feedback Oversight Group (TOG/FOG). Staff and management must be notified of all suggested revisions and decisions.

APPENDIX M: FIT Core Competencies

Feedback-Informed Treatment (FIT) is an evidence-based approach for evaluating and improving the quality and outcome of behavioral health services applicable across a wide and diverse range of clients, treatment methods and settings, and cultures.

FIT practitioners demonstrate knowledge and skills in four different areas: (1) empirical foundations; (2) FIT implementation and practice; (3) data collection and analysis; and (4) continuous professional development.

Each competency is summarized below. Detailed descriptions follow.

Core Competency Summaries

COMPETENCY 1: EMPIRICAL FOUNDATIONS

1. FIT Practitioners understand the meaning of terminology commonly used in outcome research.

2. FIT Practitioners are familiar with the empirical evidence regarding the efficacy of behavioral health services (e.g., mental health, substance abuse, and disease management).

3. FIT Practitioners are familiar with the empirical evidence regarding the nature and impact of the therapeutic relationship.

4. FIT Practitioners are familiar with the empirical evidence about "Feedback Informed Treatment" (FIT).

5. FIT Practitioners are familiar with empirical findings on implementation of evidence-based practices (including FIT).

6. FIT Practitioners are familiar with empirical findings on expert performance and its application to professional development.

COMPETENCY 2: FIT IMPLEMENTATION AND PRACTICE

1. FIT Practitioners follow the evidence-based stages associated with the successful implementation of FIT in agencies and systems of care.

2. FIT Practitioners embody the principles of feedback-informed treatment in their daily clinical work.

3. FIT Practitioners use valid, reliable, and feasible measures to obtain client feedback regarding their experience of and progress resulting from care.

COMPETENCY 3: DATA COLLECTION AND ANALYSIS

1. FIT Practitioners have a system in place for ensuring outcome and alliance data are collected consistently and transparently from the beginning (e. g., intake) to the end of service delivery (e.g., discharge).

2. FIT Practitioners are familiar with available, authorized software systems for administering, scoring, aggregating, and analyzing data generated by the outcome and alliance measures they employ in service delivery.

3. FIT Practitioners provide detail sufficient to enable others to assess the accuracy and representativeness of the data collected and any results/ analysis reported (e.g., demographic and descriptive information, frequency of measurement, criteria for choosing which data is included or excluded, and accounting for missing data).

COMPETENCY 4: CONTINUOUS PROFESSIONAL DEVELOPMENT

1. FIT Practitioners work continuously to improve their knowledge about and the effectiveness of the services they provide.

2. FIT Practitioners regularly engage in deliberate practice outside of service delivery.

3. FIT Practitioners continuously assess the impact of their professional development activities by monitoring changes to their baseline level of performance.

Competency 1: Empirical Foundations

1. FIT Practitioners understand the meaning of terminology commonly used in outcome research:

   a. Effect size

   b. Severity adjusted effect size

   c. Relative effect size

   d. Deterioration and dropout rates

   e. Research design (e.g., randomized controlled trial, meta-analysis, direct versus TAU or no treatment control comparisons)

   f. Evidence-based practice, empirically-supported treatments and practice-based evidence

2. FIT Practitioners are familiar with the empirical evidence regarding the efficacy of behavioral health services (e.g., mental health, substance abuse, and disease management):

   a. Behavioral health services are effective in improving well-being and alleviating psychological distress

   b. All "bona fide" therapeutic approaches work about equally well

   c. The effectiveness of behavioral health services is accounted for by a core group of factors, including extra-therapeutic (e.g., premorbid functioning, chance events, existing support network), the therapeutic relationship, therapist allegiance, client hope and expectancy, and the specific treatment method employed (including explanatory rationale and associated techniques)

   d. Strong predictors of the effectiveness of behavioral health services include:

      i. Early positive change

      ii. Improving client ratings of the therapeutic relationship

      iii. High levels of client engagement in the treatment process

      iv. The location and provider of treatment

   e. Weak or non-predictors of the effectiveness of behavioral health services include:

      i. Client age, gender, diagnosis, and prior treatment history

      ii. Clinician age, gender, licensure, professional discipline, degrees earned, participation in personal therapy, and amount of training or clinical supervision

      iii. The degree of match between the client and therapist on personal or demographic qualities

      iv. The therapeutic approach or technique employed (including adherence, competence, and matching technique or approach to diagnosis)

3. FIT Practitioners are familiar with the empirical evidence regarding the nature and impact of the therapeutic relationship:

    a. The therapeutic relationship is comprised of four empirically established components (agreement on the goals, treatment approach or method, bond, and client preferences)

    b. Client ratings of the therapeutic relationship on a standardized measure are more highly correlated with outcome than clinician ratings

    c. Client ratings of the therapeutic relationship are a significant predictor of treatment outcome:

      i. Improvements in client ratings of the therapeutic relationship from intake to termination are associated with better outcomes

      ii. Decreases in client ratings of the therapeutic relationship are associated with higher dropout rates and poorer outcomes

    d. A significant portion of the variability in effectiveness between clinicians is due to differences in their ability to establish therapeutic relationships with a broad and diverse clientele and address ruptures in the relationship when they occur

    e. Monitoring the client's experience of the therapeutic relationship with a standardized measure increases the likelihood of clinicians identifying clients at risk of dropout and poorer treatment outcome

4. FIT Practitioners are familiar with the empirical evidence about "Feedback Informed Treatment" (FIT):

    a. Behavioral health professionals' assessment of their own effectiveness across a variety of metrics (e.g., outcomes, retention, quality of the alliance) are frequently inaccurate and at odds with clients

    b. FIT Practitioners are familiar with the psychometric properties of outcome and alliance measures used to inform treatment and can articulate the trade-offs between feasibility, and reliability, validity, and sensitivity of standardized measurement scale. Longer outcome measures tend to be more reliable and valid, but:

      – Result in lower rates of compliance in real-world

clinical settings

- Provide little additional predictive information if the instrument measures the same single factor (i.e., general distress) as a shorter tool

c. Randomized clinical trials and meta-analytic studies shows routinely monitoring and using client feedback in real time regarding progress and the quality of the alliance can:

   i. Significantly improve client outcomes

   ii. Reduce dropout and deterioration

   iii. Shorten the length of time clients spend in treatment

d. FIT has been successfully applied across a wide range of treatment settings (e.g., outpatient, inpatient, university counseling centers, public mental health, substance abuse treatment, correctional facilities and programs), age groups (adults, adolescents, and children), diverse populations and cultures

e. The impact of FIT varies depending on:

   i. Individual therapist responsiveness to feedback

   ii. The quality and stage of implementation

5. FIT Practitioners are familiar with empirical findings on the implementation of evidence-based practices (including FIT), including:

a. General findings from implementation science:

   i. Implementation occurs in a series of stages (exploration, installation, initial implementation, full implementation)

   ii. Moving through the stages of implementation most often takes between 2 and 7 years

   iii. Success depends on the size of the agency, degree of planning, ongoing onsite training and consultation, an accountable implementation team, management buy-in and support, and focus on organizational change versus the specific evidence-based practice or practitioner development

b. Emerging empirical evidence regarding the implementation of FIT:

   i. The most significant barriers to implementation are:

      - Lack of financial resources (e.g., funding for training and access to computerized feedback systems)
      - Practitioner fears regarding the potential misuse of outcome data
      - Lack of knowledge about, and time (and time-saving

technology), for administering and processing the FIT measures

- Supervisor and management lack of understanding and failure to use and integrate FIT in clinical decision making and agency policy
- The absence of a sustainable implementation plan

ii. FIT is likely to have less impact (e.g., outcome, retention, deterioration, length of stay) during the first two years of implementation

iii. The superiority of FIT over treatment-as-usual (TAU) increases if training and supervision is sustained over time (i.e., 3 or more years)

6. FIT Practitioners are familiar with empirical findings on expert performance and its application to professional development.

   a. Expert performance across a wide range of human endeavors (music, sports, chess, mathematics, etc.) is achieved from ongoing engagement in deliberate practice

      i. To be effective, deliberate practice must be focused on achieving specific targets just beyond a performer's current abilities, guided by the conscious monitoring of outcomes, and carried out over extended periods of time

   b. Behavioral health professionals need to engage in deliberate practice because:

      i. Participation in a host of traditional professional development activities (e.g., continuing education events, attainment of advanced degrees, licensure, supervision, personal therapy) are unrelated to therapeutic effectiveness

      ii. Research on psychotherapy shows the effectiveness of the "average" helper plateaus and begins to decline early in their careers

   c. A deliberate practice program should include the following:

      i. Establishment of a valid baseline of practitioner effectiveness (e.g., effect size, dropout and deterioration rate, treatment length)

      ii. The identification of practitioner performance deficits relative to established norms

      iii. The development of individualized learning objectives aimed at targeting performance deficits

iv. The use of an expert coach to develop remedial practice exercises specific to the individual practitioner and their learning objectives

v. Successive refinement of performance via targeted practice by the practitioner, and ongoing monitoring and feedback from the coach

Competency 2: FIT Implementation and Practice

1. FIT Practitioners apply the evidence-based stages associated with the successful implementation of FIT in agencies and systems of care by:

   a. Encouraging agencies to develop a step-by-step plan for implementing FIT consistent with the stages of implementation (e.g., exploration before installation, installation before implementation)

   b. Securing leadership buy-in and involvement prior to and throughout the implementation process

   c. Setting a realistic time frame and ensure adequate resourcing

   d. Establishing the necessary infrastructure to sustain implementation, including policies, procedures, and an agency culture that actively promotes seeking and using feedback across all levels of interaction within the organization and larger system of care (e.g., clients, practitioners, supervisors, management, funders)

   e. Establishing a policy and process for overseeing and ensuring the quality (e.g., consistency, completeness) of data collection (e.g., entering data for all clients, deactivating at discharge, coding dropout) by FIT practitioners

   f. Using a gap assessment tool (e.g., the Feedback Informed Treatment Gap Assessment Tool [FITGAP]) to assess agency readiness, identify potential barriers, and monitor the implementation progress

   g. Using the experience and data generated by FIT to facilitate transformation of organizational policies and procedures that hinder client engagement and therapeutic effectiveness

2. FIT Practitioners embody the principles of feedback-informed treatment in their daily clinical work, including:

   a. The therapist is responsible for the effectiveness of the care they provide

   b. Client goals, preferences, culture, engagement in and experience of treatment are the central guiding focus of care

   c. The measured effect of care takes precedence over treatment protocols, external mandates (e.g., legal, medical, school, parental), clinicians preferred approaches and agency or payer policies

   d. No one treatment approach, setting, or provider works for all clients

3. FIT Practitioners use valid, reliable, and feasible measures to routinely obtain client feedback regarding their experience of and progress resulting from care by:

   a. Introducing outcome and alliance measures in a manner that secures client engagement and provision of open and transparent feedback about progress and the quality of the therapeutic relationship

b. Seamlessly integrating outcome and alliance measures and resulting feedback (e.g., scores, cutoffs, graphs, trajectories, and aggregate data) into their clinical work across clients, problem types, treatment modalities and settings.

   i. Have a range of options for processing alliance and outcome feedback (e.g., discussion with client, consultation with peers, access to FIT consultation, team meetings)

c. Using outcome and alliance measures and resulting feedback (e.g., scores, graphs, normed trajectories, and aggregate data) to inform treatment planning and decision making for:

   i. Identifying problems/concerns in the therapeutic relationship

   ii. Understanding when and how to seek internal and external collateral ratings (e.g., mandated clients, family therapy, work with children)

   iii. Adjusting service delivery in response to alliance or outcome feedback (e.g., changing the dose, intensity, type, location, and provider)

Competency 3: Data Collection and Analysis

1. FIT practitioners have a system/process in place for ensuring outcome and alliance data are collected consistently and transparently from the beginning (e.g., intake) to the end of service delivery (e.g., discharge):

    a. Familiarity with and abiding by all copyright and licensing terms of the measures they employ

    b. Understanding the psychometric properties and limitations of the measures they employ

    c. FIT practitioners have a clear standard designating how often and from whom measures are gathered and are able to determine the degree of compliance with the standard for administration of measures

2. FIT practitioners are familiar with available and authorized software systems for administering, scoring, aggregating, and analyzing data generated by the outcome and alliance measures they employ in service delivery, including:

    a. Utilizing only authorized systems containing valid formulas and established norms to evaluate the quality of the therapeutic relationship and progress of individual clients in real time and determine therapist, program, and agency effectiveness

    b. Understanding and being able to articulate the meaning, purpose, and limitations of any analysis generated by authorized systems to measure the quality of the relationship, individual client progress, and other treatment benchmarks (e.g., graphs, effect size, relative effect size, dropout rate)

3. FIT practitioners provide detail sufficient to enable others (e.g., clients, supervisors, managers, funders, referral sources) to assess the accuracy and representativeness of the data collected and any results/analysis reported (e.g., demographic and descriptive information, frequency of measurement, criteria for choosing which data is included or excluded, and accounting for missing data)

Competency 4: Continuous Professional Development

1. FIT practitioners work continuously to improve their knowledge about and the effectiveness of the services they provide, including:

   a. Staying current with empirical findings on behavioral health outcomes, the therapeutic relationship, feedback-informed treatment, implementation science, and expertise and expert performance (i.e., Competency 1)

   b. Participating in FIT training, consultation, data analysis and supervision

   c. Engaging with a FIT community of practice

2. FIT practitioners regularly engage in deliberate practice outside of service delivery, including:

   a. Determining their baseline level of performance (e.g., effectiveness [effect size, relative effect size, percentage of clients achieving reliable and clinically significant change], level of engagement [e.g., dropout and retention rates, skipped/missed sessions, intake alliance rating], treatment duration [e.g., length stay, number of treatment sessions])

   b. Comparing their baseline level of performance to the best available norms, standards, or benchmarks to identify performance deficits and professional development opportunities

   c. Developing clear and concrete learning objectives aimed at addressing performance deficits and improving their established baseline performance level

   d. Creating and executing an individualized deliberate practice plan, including practice exercises specific to the individual clinician and their learning objectives

   e. Actively seeking out coaches with knowledge/expertise specific to their performance deficits who can:

      i. Analyze their performance, develop exercises, offer corrective feedback, evaluate the impact of professional development efforts, and refine their deliberate practice plan

3. FIT practitioners continuously assess the impact of their professional development activities by monitoring changes to their baseline level of performance

APPENDIX N: Implementation Star

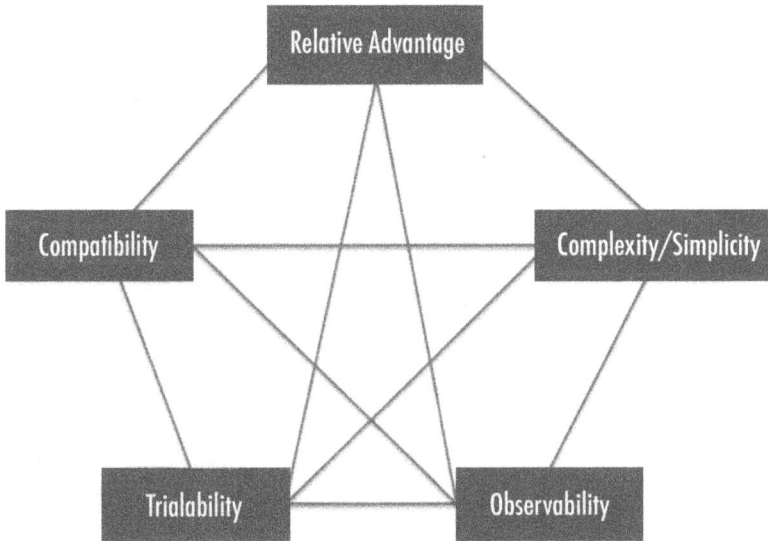

The "Implementation Star" is based on the pioneering research of Everett Rogers (2003) who identified five factors influencing the adoption of new ideas and practices:

1. *Relative advantage,* or the degree to which a new idea/practice is perceived to be better than what it is replacing;

2. *Compatibility,* or the congruence of the new idea/practice with current organizational and individual values and perceived needs;

3. *Complexity,* or how difficult the new idea/practice is to understand and execute;

4. *Trialability,* the ease with which the new idea/practice can be experimented with or "tried out"; and

5. *Observability,* how visible the use and utility of the new idea/practice is to self and others.

Presenting the factors in the shape of a star is purposeful as doing so emphasizes how each of the five is connected to and impacts the others influencing adoption.

REFERENCES

Ahn, H., & Wampold, B.E. (2001). Where oh where are the specific ingredients? A meta-analysis of component studies in counseling and psychotherapy. *Journal of Counseling Psychology, 48*(3), 251–257.

American Psychological Association (2018). *APA Guidelines for Clinical Supervision in Health Service Psychology.* Retrieved December 24, 2024. From: https://www.apa.org/about/policy/guidelines-supervision.pdf

American Psychological Association, Presidential Task Force on Evidence-Based Practice. (2006). Evidence-based practice in psychology. *American Psychologist, 61*(4), 271–285.

Andrade-González N., Rodrigo-Holgado I., Fernández-Rozas J., Cáncer, P., Lahera G., Fernández-Liria A., Rubio G., & Miller, S. (2021). Spanish versions of the outcome rating scale and the session rating scale: Normative data, reliability, and validity. *Frontiers in Psycholology,12*, Article 663791.

Anker, M.G., Duncan, B.L., & Sparks, J. (2009). Using client feedback to improve couple therapy outcomes: A randomized clinical trial in a naturalistic setting. *Journal of Consulting and Clinical Psychology, 77*(4), 693-704.

American Psychological Association (August, 2012*). Recognition of Psychotherapy Effectiveness.* Retrieved October 10, 2024. From https://www.apa.org/about/policy/resolution-psychotherapy

Bachelor A. (2013). Clients' and therapists' views of the therapeutic alliance: Similarities, differences and relationship to therapy outcome. *Clinical Psychology & Psychotherapy, 20*(2):118-35.

Bachelor, A., & Horvath, A. (1999). The therapeutic relationship. In M.A. Hubble, B.L. Duncan, & S.D. Miller (Eds.), *The heart and soul of change: What works in therapy* (pp. 133–178). Washington, D.C.: American Psychological Association.

Baldwin, S.A., Berkeljon, A., Atkins, D.C., Olsen, J.A., & Nielsen, S.L. (2009). Rates of change in naturalistic psychotherapy: Contrasting dose–effect and good-enough level models of change. *Journal of Consulting and Clinical Psychology, 77*(2), 203–211.

Baldwin, S., & Imel, Z.E. (2013). Therapist effects: Findings and methods. In M.J. Lambert (Ed.), *Bergin and Garfield's handbook of psychotherapy and behavior change* (6th Ed.) (pp. 258-297). New York: Wiley.

Baldwin, S.A., Wampold, B.E., & Imel, Z.E. (2007). Untangling the alliance-outcome correlation: Exploring the relative importance of therapist and patient variability in the alliance. *Journal of Consulting and Clinical Psychology, 75*(6), 842–852.

Bargmann, S. (2016). *Feedback informed treatment: En grundbog.* Copenhagen, Denmark: Akademisk Forlag.

Bargmann, S. (2017). Achieving excellence through feedback-informed supervision. In D.S. Prescott, C.L. Maeschalck, & S.D. Miller (Eds.), *Feedback informed treatment in clinical practice: Reaching for excellence* (pp. 79-100). Washington D.C.: American Psychological Association.

Bargmann, S., & Robinson, W. (2012). *Manual 2: Feedback informed clinical work: The basics.* Chicago, IL: ICCE.

Barkham, M., Lutz, W., & Castonguay, L.G. (Eds.) (2021). *Bergin and Garfield's handbook of psychotherapy and behavior change* (7th Ed). New York: Wiley.

Barlow, D.H. (2004). Psychological treatments. *American Psychologist, 59*(9), 869–878.

Bartholomew, T., Kang, E., Joy, E., Robbins, K., & Maldonado-Aguiñiga, S. (2022). Clients' perceptions of the working alliance as a predictor of increases in positive affect. *Journal of Psychotherapy Integration, 32*(3), 310–325.

Bartle-Haring, S., Knerr, M., Adkins, K., Delaney, R.O., Gangamma, R., Glebova, T., Grafsky, E., McDowell, T., & Meyer, K. (2012). Trajectories of therapeutic alliance in couple versus individual therapy: Three-level models. *Journal of Sex & Marital Therapy, 38*(1), 79–107.

Bedi, R., & Hayes, S. (2020). Clients' perspectives on, experiences of, and contributions to the working alliance: Implications for clinicians. In J.N. Fuertes (Ed.), *Working alliance skills for mental health professionals* (pp. 111–136). New York: Oxford University Press.

Behn, A., Davanzo, A., & Errazuriz, P. (2018). Client and therapist match on gender, age, and income: Does match within the therapeutic dyad predict early growth in the therapeutic alliance? *Journal of Clinical Psychology, 74*(9), 1403-1421.

Benish, S.G., Imel, Z.E., & Wampold, B.E., (2008). The relative efficacy of bona fide psychotherapies for treating post-traumatic stress disorder: A meta-analysis of direct comparisons. *Clinical Psychology Review, 28*(5), 746-758.

Bertolino, B., & Miller, S.D. (Eds.) (2012). *The ICCE Feedback Informed*

Treatment manuals (Volumes 1-6). Chicago, IL: ICCE.

Bertram, R., Blase, K., & Fixsen, D. (2014). Improving programs and outcomes: Implementation frameworks and organization change. *Research on Social Work Practice, 25,* 477-487.

Bertram, R., King, K., Pederson, R., & Nutt, J. (2014). Implementation frameworks and MSW curricula: Encouraging pursuit and use of model pertinent data. *Journal of Evidence-Based Social Work, 11*(1–2), 193–207.

Bickman L., Kelley, S.D., Breda, C., de Andrade A.R., &, Riemer, M. (2011). Effects of routine feedback to clinicians on mental health outcomes of youths: Results of a randomized trial. *Psychiatric Services, 62*(12):1423-1429.

Black, D.W., Pfohl, B., Blum N., McCormick, B., Allen, J., North, C., Phillips, K., Robins, C., Siever, L., Solk, K., Williams, J., & Zimmerman, M. (2011). Attitudes toward borderline personality disorder: A survey of 706 mental health clinicians. *CNS Spectrum, 16*(3), 67-74.

Blatt, S. J., Sanislow, C.A., Zuroff, D.C., & Pilkonis, P.A. (1996). Characteristics of effective therapists: Further analyses of data from the National Institute of Mental Health Treatment of Depression Collaborative Research Program. *Journal of Consulting and Clinical Psychology, 64*(6), 1276–1284.

Bodner, E., Cohen-Fridel, S., Mashiah, M., Segal, M., Grinshpoon, A., Fischel, T., & Iancu, I. (2015). The attitudes of psychiatric hospital staff toward hospitalization and treatment of patients with borderline personality disorder. *BMC Psychiatry, 15,* 2.

Bohar, T.A.C., & Wade, A.G. (2013). The client in psychotherapy. In M.J. Lambert (Ed.), *Bergin and Garfield's handbook of psychotherapy and behavior change* (6th Ed.) (pp. 219-257). New York: Wiley.

Bohnet, I. (April 18, 2016). How to take the bias out of interviews. Retrieved December 24, 2024. From: https://hbr.org/2016/04/how-to-take-the-bias-out-of-interviews

Bordin, E.S. (1979). The generalizability of the psychoanalytic concept of the working alliance. *Psychotherapy, 16*(3), 252-260.

Brattland, H., Koksvik, J.M., Burkeland, O., Gråwe, R.W., Klöckner, C., Linaker, O.M., Ryum, T., Wampold, B., Lara-Cabrera, M.L., & Iversen, V.C. (2018). The effects of routine outcome monitoring (ROM) on therapy outcomes in the course of an implementation process: A randomized clinical trial. *Journal of Counseling Psychology, 65*(5), 641–652.

Brattland, H., Koksvik, J.M., Burkeland, O., Klöckner, C.A., Lara-Cabrera, M.L., Miller, S.D., Wampold, B., Ryum, T., & Iversen, V.C. (2019). Does the working alliance mediate the effect of routine outcome monitoring (ROM) and alliance feedback on psychotherapy outcomes? A secondary analysis from a randomized clinical trial. *Journal of Counseling Psychology, 66*(2), 234–246.

Brown, J., Deis, S., & Nace, D. (1999). What really makes a difference in psychotherapy outcome? Why does managed care want to know? In . M.A. Hubble, B.L. Duncan, & S.D. Miller (Eds.), *The heart and soul of change: What works in therapy* (pp. 389-406). Washington, D.C.: American Psychological Association.

Brownson, R.C., Eyler, A.A., Harris, J.K., Moore, J.B., & Tabak, R.G. (2018). Getting the word out: New approaches for disseminating public health science. *Journal of Public Health Management and Practice, 24*(2), 102-111.

Caldwell, B. (2015). *Saving psychotherapy: How to bring psychotherapy back from the brink.* Los Angeles, CA: Benjamin E. Caldwell.

Carlier, I., Meuldijk, D., Van Vliet, I., Van Fenema, E., Van der Wee, N., & Zitman, F. (2012). Routine outcome monitoring and feedback on physical or mental health status: Evidence and theory. *Journal of Evaluation in Clinical Practice,18*(1):104-10.

Casey, P., Patalay, P., Deighton, J., Miller, S.D., & Wolpert, M. (2019). The child outcome rating scale: Validating a four-item measure of psychosocial functioning in community and clinic samples of children aged 10–15. *European Child and Adolescent Psychiatry, 29*, 1089–1102.

Cazauvieilh, C., Gana, K., Miller, S.D., & Quintard, B. (2022). Validation of the french versions of two brief, clinician-friendly outcome monitoring tools: The ORS and SRS. *Current Psychology, 41*(4), 6124-6136.

Chambless, D.L., & Ollendick ,T. H. (2001). Empirically supported psychological interventions: Controversies and evidence. *Annual Review of Psychology, 52*, 685-716.

Chesworth, B., Filippelli, A., Nylund, D., Tilsen, J., Minami, T., & Barranti, C. (2017). Feedback-informed treatment with LGBTQ clients: Social justice and evidence-based practice. In D.S. Prescott, C.L. Maeschalck, & S.D. Miller (Eds.), *Feedback-informed treatment in clinical practice: Reaching for excellence* (pp. 249–265). Washington, D.C.: American Psychological Association.

Chow, D. (2014). *The study of supershrinks: Development and deliberate practices of highly effective therapists* [Unpublished doctoral dissertation]. Curtan University.

Chow, D. (2017). The practice and the practical: Pushing your clinical performance to the next level. In D.S. Prescott, C.L. Maeschalck, & S.D. Miller (Eds.). *Feedback-informed treatment in clinical practice: Reaching for excellence* (pp. 323-355). Washington, D.C.: American Psychological Association Press.

Chow, D.L. (2018). *The first kiss: Undoing the intake model and igniting engagement from the first session in psychotherapy.* Perth, Australia: Correlate Press.

Chow, D.L., Miller, S.D., Seidel, J.A., Kane, R.T., Thornton, J.A., & Andrews, W.P. (2015). The role of deliberate practice in the development of highly effective psychotherapists. *Psychotherapy, 52*(3), 337–345.

Clarkin, J.F., & Levy, K. N. (2004). The influence of client variables on psychotherapy. In M.J. Lambert (Ed.). *Bergin and Garfield's handbook of psychotherapy and behavior change* (5th ed) (pp. 194-226). New York: Wiley.

Colvin, G. (2008). Why talent is overrated. Retrieved December 24, 2024. From https://lionhrt.com/wp2/wp-content/uploads/2015/12/Why-Talent-is-Overrated-by-Geoff-Colvin.pdf

Connolly-Gibbons, M.B., Rothbard, A., Farris, K., Stirman, S.W., Thompson, S.M., Scott, K., Heinz, L., Gallop, R., & Crits-Christoph, P. (2011). Changes in psychotherapy utilization among consumers of services for major depressive disorder in the community mental health system. *Administration and Policy in Mental Health & Mental Health Services Research, 38*(6), 495-503.

Creaner, M. (2014). *Getting the best out of supervision in counselling and psychotherapy: A guide for the supervisee.* Washington, D.C.: SAGE Publications.

Cuijpers, P., Karyotaki, E., Ciharova, M., Miguel, C., Noma, H., Stikkelbroek, Y., Weisz, J.R., & Furukawa, T.A. (2021). The effects of psychological treatments of depression in children and adolescents on response, reliable change, and deterioration: A systematic review and meta-analysis. *European Child Adolescent Psychiatry, 32*(1), 177-192.

Cuijpers, P., Reijnders, M., Karyotaki, E., de Wit, L., & Ebert, D. (2018). Negative effects of psychotherapies for adult depression: A meta-analysis of deterioration rates. *Journal of Affective Disorders, 239*, 138–145.

Cuijpers, P., Sijbrandij, M., Koole, S., Andersson, G., Beekman, A., & Reynolds, C. (2013). The efficacy of psychotherapy and pharmacotherapy in treating depressive and anxiety disorders: A meta-analysis of direct comparisons. *World Psychiatry, 12*(2):137-48.

Davidsen, A., Poulsen, S., Lindschou J., Winkel, P., Tróndarson, M., Waaddegaard, M., & Lau, M. (2017). Feedback in group psychotherapy for eating disorders: A randomized clinical trial. *Journal of Consulting and Clinical Psychology, 85*(5):484-494.

de Jong, K., Conijn, J.M., Gallagher, R., Reshetnikova, A., Heij, M., & Lutz, M.C. (2021). Using progress feedback to improve outcomes and reduce drop-out, treatment duration, and deterioration: A multilevel meta-analysis. *Clinical Psychology Review, 85*, 102002.

de Jong, K., Douglas, S., Wolpert, M., Delgadillo, J., Aas, B., Bovendeerd, B., Carlier, I., Compare, A., Edbrooke-Childs, J., Janse, P., Lutz, W., Moltu, C., Nordberg, S., Poulsen, S., Rubel, J.A., Schiepek, G., Schilling, V., van Sonsbeek, M., & Barkham, M. (2024). Using progress feedback to enhance treatment outcomes: A narrative review. *Administration and Policy in Mental Health and Mental Health Services Research.* Advance online publication. https://doi.org/10.1007/s10488-024-01381-3.

de Jong, K., Segaar, J., Ingenhoven, T., van Busschbach, J., & Timman, R. (2018). Adverse effects of outcome monitoring feedback in patients with personality disorders: A randomized controlled trial in day treatment and inpatient settings. *Journal of Personality Disorders, 32*(3), 393-413.

de Jong K., van Sluis, P., Nugter, M.A., Heiser, W. J., & Spinhoven, P. (2012). Understanding the differential impact of outcome monitoring: Therapist variables that moderate feedback effects in a randomized clinical trial. *Psychotherapy Research, 22*(4):464-74.

de Jong, R., Snoek, H., Staal, W., & Klip, H. (2018). The effect of patients' feedback on treatment outcome in a child and adolescent psychiatric sample: A randomized controlled trial. *European Child and Adolescent Psychiatry, 28*(6), 819-834.

Delgadillo, J., McMillan, D., Gilbody, S., de Jong, K., Lucock, M., Lutz, W., Rubel, J., Aguirre, E., & Ali, S. (2021). Cost-effectiveness of feedback-informed psychological treatment: Evidence from the IAPT-FIT trial. *Behaviour Research and Therapy, 142*, 103873.

Delgadillo, J., Overend, K., Lucock, M., Groom, M., Kirby, N., McMillan, D., Gilbody, S., Lutz, W., Rubel, J., & de Jong, K. (2017). Improving the efficiency of psychological treatment using outcome feedback technology. *Behavior Research and Therapy, 99*, 89-97.

Del Re, A.C., Flückiger, C., Horvath, A.O., & Wampold, B.E. (2021). Examining therapist effects in the alliance-outcome relationship: A multilevel meta-analysis. *Journal of Consulting and Clinical Psychology, 89*(5), 371–378.

Drisko, J., & Friedman, A. (2019). Let's clearly distinguish evidence-based practice and empirically supported treatments. *Smith College Studies in Social Work, 89,* 1-18.

Duda, M., & Wilson, B. (2018). Implementation science 101: A brief overview. *Perspectives in Language and Literacy, 44,* 11-19.

Duncan, B.L. (2010). *On becoming a better therapist.* Washington, D.C.: American Psychological Association.

Duncan, B.L., Miller, S.D., & Sparks, J.A. (2004). *The heroic client: A revolutionary way to improve effectiveness through client-directed, outcome-informed therapy.* San Francisco, CA: Jossey-Bass.

Duncan, B.L., Miller, S.D., Wampold, B.E., & Hubble, M.A. (Eds.). (2010). *The heart and soul of change: Delivering what works in therapy* (2nd ed.). Washington, D.C.: American Psychological Association.

Duncan, B.L., Sparks, J.A., Miller, S.D., Bohanske, R.T., & Claud, D.A. (2006). Giving youth a voice: A preliminary study of the reliability and validity of a brief outcome measure for children, adolescents, and caretakers. *Journal of Brief Therapy, 2*(6):71-88.

Edwards, J., Johnson, E., & Molidor, J. (1990) The interview in the admission process. *Academic Medicine, 65*(3):167-77.

Erekson, D.M., Lambert, M.J., & Eggett, D.L. (2015). The relationship between session frequency and psychotherapy outcome in a naturalistic setting. *Journal of Consulting and Clinical Psychology, 83*(6), 1097–1107.

Ericsson, K.A. (2009). Enhancing the development of professional performance: Implications from the study of deliberate practice. In K.A. Ericsson (Ed.). *Development of professional expertise: Toward measurement of expert performance and design of optimal learning environments* (pp. 405-431). New York: Cambridge University Press.

Ericsson, K.A., Charness, N., Feltovich, P. J., & Hoffman, R.R. (Eds.). (2006). *The Cambridge handbook of expertise and expert performance.* New York: Cambridge University Press.

Fernandez, E., Salem, D., Swift, J., & Ramtahal, N. (2015). Meta-analysis of dropout from cognitive behavioral therapy: Magnitude, timing, and moderators. *Journal of Consulting and Clinical Psychology, 83*(6), 1108–1122.

Fixsen, D.L., Blase, K.A., Horner, R., & Sugai, G. (2009). Readiness for change. *Scaling Up Brief,* Number 3. Chapel Hill, North Carolina: University of North Carolina.

Fixsen, D.L., Blase, K.A., Naoom, S. F., & Duda, M. (2013). *Implementation drivers: Assessing best practices.* Chapel Hill, North Carolina: Frank Porter

Graham Child Development Institute.

Fixsen, D.L., Blase, K., Metz, A., & Van Dyke, M. (2013). Statewide implementation of evidence-based programs. *Exceptional Children, 79*(3), 213-230.

Fixsen, D.L., Blase, K., & Van Dyke, M.K. (2019). *Implementation practice & science.* Chapel Hill, North Carolina: Active Implementation Research Network.

Flor, J. (2016). *"De har i alle fall ikke blitt dårligere, har jeg trodd" - en kvalitativ studie av psykologers perspektiv på forverring i terapi.* [Master's Thesis]. Norwegian University of Science and Technology. https://doi.org/10.13140/RG.2.1.3829.9763

Frank, J.D. (1961). *Persuasion and healing: A comparative study of psychotherapy.* Baltimore, M.D.: Johns Hopkins University Press.

Friedlander, M., Escudero, V., Heatherington, L., & Diamond G. (2011). Alliance in couple and family therapy. *Psychotherapy, 48*(1), 25-33.

Frølich, M. (2017). FIT in a daily context. In S. Bargmann (Ed.). *Feedback Informed Treatment: En gundbog* (pp. 155-166). Copenhagen, Denmark: Akademisk Forlag.

Garcia, J.A., & Weisz, J.R. (2002). When youth mental health care stops: Therapeutic relationship problems and other reasons for ending youth outpatient treatment. *Journal of Consulting and Clinical Psychology, 70*(2), 439–443.

Garfield, S.L. (1978). Research problems in clinical diagnosis. *Journal of Consulting and Clinical Psychology, 46*(4), 596.

Gawande, A. (December, 2007). The checklist: If something so simple can transform intensive care, what else can it do? *New Yorker, 10,* 86-101.

Gleave, R.L., Burlingame, G.M., Beecher, M.E., Griner, D., Hansen, K., & Jenkins, S. (2017). Feedback-informed group treatment: Application of the OQ–45 and group questionnaire. In D.S. Prescott, C.L. Maeschalck & S.D. Miller (Eds.). *Feedback-informed treatment in clinical practice: Reaching for excellence* (p. 141–166). Washington, D.C.: American Psychological Association.

Glebova, T., & Woolley, S.R. (2019). Split alliance in couple and family therapy. In J., Lebow, A. Chambers & D. Breunlin (Eds.) *Encyclopedia of couple and family therapy.* New York: Springer.

Goldberg, S.B., Babins-Wagner, R., Rousmaniere, T., Berzins, S., Hoyt, W.T., Whipple, J.L., Miller, S.D., & Wampold, B.E. (2016). Creating a climate for therapist improvement: A case study of an agency focused on outcomes and deliberate practice. *Psychotherapy, 53*(3), 367–375.

Goldberg, S.B., Rousmaniere, T., Miller, S.D., Whipple, J., Nielsen, S.L., Hoyt, W.T., & Wampold, B.E. (2016). Do psychotherapists improve with time and experience? A longitudinal analysis of outcomes in a clinical setting. *Journal of Counseling Psychology, 63*(1), 1–11.

Goldberg, S.B., Rowe, G., Malte, C., Ruan, H., Owen, J., & Miller, S.D. (2020). Routine monitoring of therapeutic alliance to predict treatment engagement in a Veterans Affairs substance use disorders clinic. *Psychological Services, 17*(3), 291–299.

Greenberg, R., Constantino, M., & Bruce, N. (2006). Are expectations still relevant for psychotherapy process and outcome? *Clinical Psychology Review, 26*(6), 657-78.

Haas, E., Hill, R., Lambert, M.J., & Morrell, B. (2002). Do early responders to psychotherapy maintain treatment gains. *Journal of Clinical Psychology, 58*(9), 1157–1172.

Hannan, C., Lambert, M.J., Harmon, C., Nielsen, S.L., Smart, D.W., Shimokawa, K., & Sutton, S.W. (2005). A lab test and algorithms for identifying clients at risk for treatment failure. *Journal of Clinical Psychology, 61*(2), 155-163.

Hansen, N.B., Lambert, M.J., & Forman, E.M. (2002). The psychotherapy dose-response effect and its implications for treatment delivery services. *Clinical Psychology: Science and Practice, 9*(3), 329–343.

Harmon C., Hawkins, E.J., Lambert, M.J., Slade, K., & Whipple, J.S. (2005). Improving outcomes for poorly responding clients: The use of clinical support tools and feedback to clients. *Journal of Clinical Psycholology, 61*(2),175-85.

Hatfield, D., McCullough, L., Frantz, S., & Krieger, K. (2009). Do we know when our clients get worse? An investigation of therapists' ability to detect negative client change *Clinical Psychology & Psychotherapy, 17*(1), 25-32.

Hill, C., & Knox S. (2013). Training and supervision in psychotherapy: Evidence for effective practice. In M.J. Lambert (Ed.), *Handbook of psychotherapy and behavior change* (6th ed.) (pp. 775-811). New York: Wiley.

Howard, K.I., Kopte, S.M., Krause, M.S., & Orlinsky, D.E. (1986). The dose-effect relationship in psychotherapy. *American Psychologist, 41*(2), 159–164.

Horvath, A., Del Re, A.C., Flückiger, C., & Symonds, D. (2011). The alliance in adult psychotherapy. In J. Norcross (ed.) *Relationships that work* (pp. 25-69). New York: Oxford University Press.

Horvath, A.O., & Symonds, B.D. (1991). Relation between working alliance and outcome in psychotherapy: A meta-analysis. *Journal of Counseling Psychology, 38*(2), 139–149.

Hubble, M.A., Duncan, B.L., & Miller, S.D. (Eds.). (1999). *The heart and soul of change: What works in therapy.* Washington, D.C.: American Psychological Association.

Huppert, J.D., Fabbro, A., & Barlow, D.H. (2006). Evidence-based practice and psychological treatments. In C.D. Goodheart, A.E. Kazdin & R.J. Sternberg (Eds.), *Evidence-based psychotherapy: Where practice and research meet* (pp. 131–152). Washington, D.C.: American Psychological Association.

Imel, Z.E., Wampold, B.E., Miller, S.D., & Fleming, R. (2008). Distinctions without a difference: Direct comparisons of psychotherapies for alcohol use disorders. *Psychology of Addictive Behaviors, 22*(4), 533-43.

Jacobson, N.S., Follette, W. C., & Revenstorf, D. (1984). Psychotherapy outcome research: Methods for reporting variability and evaluating clinical significance. *Behavior Therapy, 15*(4), 336–352.

Jacobson, N.S., & Truax, P. (1991). Clinical significance: A statistical approach to defining meaningful change in psychotherapy research. *Journal of Consulting and Clinical Psychology, 59*(1), 12–19.

Janse, P., Boezen-Hilberdink, L., van Dijk, M.K., Verbraak, M.J.P.M., & Hutschemaekers, G.J.M. (2014). Measuring feedback from clients: The psychometric properties of the Dutch outcome rating scale and session rating scale. *European Journal of Psychological Assessment, 30*(2), 86-92.

Joint Commission (N.D.). Outcome measures standard. Retrieved December 24, 2024. From https://www.jointcommission.org/what-we-offer/accreditation/health-care-settings/behavioral-health-care/outcome-measures-standard/

Jones, D. (January 9, 2015). The 36 Questions that lead to love. Retrieved December 24, 2024. From https://www.nytimes.com/2015/01/09/style/no-37-big-wedding-or-small.html

Kamenov, K., Twomey, C., Cabello, M., Prina, A.M., & Ayuso-Mateos, J.L. (2017). The efficacy of psychotherapy, pharmacotherapy and their combination on functioning and quality of life in depression: A meta-analysis. *Psychological Medicine, 47*(7), 1337.

Kazdin, A.E. (1996). Combined and multimodal treatments in child and adolescent psychotherapy: Issues, challenges, and research directions. *Clinical Psychology: Science and Practice, 3*(1), 69–100.

Kendrick, T., El-Gohary, M., Stuart, B., Gilbody, S., Churchill, R., Aiken, L., Bhattacharya, A., Gimson, A., Brütt, AL., de Jong, K., & Moore, M. (2016). Routine use of patient reported outcome measures (PROMs) for improving treatment of common mental health disorders in adults. *Cochrane Database of Systematic Reviews, 7*(7), CD011119.

Keum, B.T., & Wang, L. (2021). Supervision and psychotherapy process and outcome: A meta-analytic review. *Translational Issues in Psychological Science, 7*(1), 89–108.

Kia, S.A., Wittkampf, L., van Lankeren, J., & Janse, P. (2024). Motives of therapists for using routine outcome monitoring (ROM) and how it is used by them in clinical practice: Two qualitative studies. *Administration and Policy in Mental Health and Mental Health Services Research*. Advance online publication. https://doi.org/10.1007/s10488-024-01374-2

Klein, P., Fairweather, A.K., & Lawn, S. (2022). Structural stigma and its impact on healthcare for borderline personality disorder: A scoping review. *International Journal of Mental Health Systems, 16*(1): 48.

Knox, S., & Hill, C.E. (2021). Training and supervision in psychotherapy: What we know and where we need to go. In M. Barkham, W. Lutz & L.G. Castonguay (Eds.), *Bergin and Garfield's handbook of psychotherapy and behavior change: 50th anniversary edition* (7th ed.) (pp. 327–349). New York: Wiley.

Kopua, D., Kopua, M., & Bracken, P. (2020). Mahi a Atua: A Māori approach to mental health. *Transcultural Psychiatry, 57*(2), 375-383.

Kreiter, C.D., Yin, P., Solow, C., & Brennan, R.L. (2004). Investigating the reliability of the medical school admissions interview. *Advances in Health Science Education, 9*, 147–159.

Krog, C. (September 12, 2023). Patient centered practice and feedback informed treatment. Retrieved December 31, 2024. From https://fysioaalborg.dk/charlotte-krog-patientcentreret-praksis-og-feedback-informed-treatment/

Lambert, M.J. (2010). *Prevention of treatment failure: The use of measuring, monitoring, and feedback in clinical practice*. Washington, D.C.: American Psychological Association.

Lambert, M.J. (2013). Outcome in psychotherapy: The past and important advances. *Psychotherapy, 50*(1), 42–51.

Lambert, M.J. (2017). Maximizing psychotherapy outcome beyond evidence-based medicine. *Psychotherapy and Psychosomatics, 86*(2), 80-89.

Lambert, M.J., & Arnold, R.C. (1987). Research and the supervisory process. *Professional Psychology: Research and Practice, 18*(3), 217–224.

Lambert, M.J., Lunnen, K., Umphress, V., Hansen, N., & Burlingame, G.M. (1994). *Administration and scoring manual for the Outcome Questionnaire (OQ–45.1).* Salt Lake City, UT: IHC Center for Behavioral Healthcare Efficacy.

Lambert, M.J., & Ogles, B.M. (1997). The effectiveness of psychotherapy supervision. In C.E. Watkins, Jr. (Ed.), *Handbook of psychotherapy supervision* (pp. 421–446). New York: Wiley.

Lambert, M.J., & Ogles, B.M. (2004). The efficacy and effectiveness of psychotherapy. In M.J. Lambert (Ed.), *Bergin and Garfield's handbook of psychotherapy and behavior change* (5th ed.) (pp. 139–193). New York: Wiley.

Lambert, M.J., & Shimokawa, K. (2011). Collecting client feedback. *Psychotherapy, 48*(1), 72–79.

Lambert, M.J., Whipple, J., & Kleinstäuber, M. (2018). Collecting and delivering progress feedback: A meta-analysis of routine outcome monitoring. *Psychotherapy, 55*(4), 520-537.

Lazar, E. (2017). *Client deterioration in individual psychotherapy: A systematic review.* [Unpublished doctoral dissertation]. Indiana University.

Lee, S., Rothbard, A.B., & Noll, E.L. (2012). Length of inpatient stay of persons with serious mental illness: Effects of hospital and regional characteristics. *Psychiatric Services,63*(9), 889-895.

Lee, D. J., Schnitzlein, C.W., Wolf, J.P., Vythilingam, M., Rasmusson, A.M., & Hoge, C.W. (2016). Psychotherapy versus pharmacotherapy for posttraumatic stress disorder: Systematic review and meta-analysis to determine first-line treatments. *Depression and Anxiety, 33*(9), 792-806.

Lilienfeld, S.O., & Arkowitz, H. (2012). Are all psychotherapies created equal? *Scientific American, 23*(4), 68-69. Lutz, W. (December 2014). Why, when and how do patients change? Identifying and predicting outcome in therapy. Retrieved December 24, 2024. From https://www.slideshare.net/scottdmiller/lecture-wolfgang-lutz-calgary2014-send

Lutz, W. (June 2016). When, why and how to patients change in psychological treatments. Presentation at the CORC 2nd International Conference. London, England. Retrieved December 24, 2024. From https://www.corc.uk.net/media/1311/2016when_why_and_how_do_patients_change_in_psychological_treatments.pdf

Lutz, W., Hofmann, S.G., Rubel, J., Boswell, J.F., Shear, M.K., Gorman, J.M., Woods, S.W., & Barlow, D.H. (2014). Patterns of early change and their relationship to outcome and early treatment termination in patients with panic disorder. *Journal of Consulting and Clinical Psychology, 82*(2), 287–297.

Lutz, W., Stulz, N., & Köck, K. (2009). Patterns of early change and their relationship to outcome and follow-up among patients with major depressive disorders. *Journal of Affective Disorders, 118*(1-3), 60-688.

Maeschalck, C.L., Bargmann, S., Miller, S.D., & Bertolino, B. (2012). Manual 3: Feedback informed treatment supervision. In B. Bertolino & S.D. Miller (Eds.) *The ICCE Feedback Informed Treatment manuals* (Volumes 1-6). Chicago, IL: ICCE.

Maeschalck, C.L., Prescott, D.S., & Miller, S.D. (2019). Feedback-informed treatment. In J. Norcross & M. Goldfried (Eds.). *Handbook of Psychotherapy Integration* (3rd Ed.) (pp 84-104). New York: Oxford.

MacKrill, K., Groom, K.M., & Petrie, K. J. (2020). The effect of symptom-tracking apps on symptom reporting. *British Journal of Health Psychology, 25*(4), 1074-1085.

Madsen, J.W., Markova, V., Hernández, L., Tomfohr-Madsen, L.M., & Miller, S.D. (2023). Training practices in routine outcome monitoring among accredited psychology doctoral programs in Canada. *Training and Education in Professional Psychology, 17*(1), 98-105.

Malouf, J. (2012). The need for empirically supported psychology training standards. *Psychotherapy in Australia, 18*(3), 28-32.

Martin, D. J., Garske, J.P., & Davis, M.K. (2000). Relation of the therapeutic alliance with outcome and other variables: A meta-analytic review. *Journal of Consulting and Clinical Psychology, 68*(3), 438–450.

Mikeal, C.W., Gillaspy, J.A., Scholes, M.T., & Murphy, J.J. (2016). A dismantling study of the partners for change outcome management system. *Journal of Counseling Psychology, 63*(6), 704-709.

Miller, S.D. (November 22, 2011). Cutting edge feedback. Retrieved October 21, 2024. From https://www.scottdmiller.com/cutting-edge-feedback/

Miller, S.D. (February 2, 2013). SAMHSA designates feedback informed treatment an "evidence-based practice." Retrieved October 24, 2024. From https://www.scottdmiller.com/s-a-m-s-h-a-designates-feedback-informed-treatment-an-evidence-based-practice/

Miller, S.D. (December 11, 2014). Dinner with Paul McCartney. Retrieved October 21, 2024. From http://www.scottdmiller.com/feedback-informed-treatment-fit/1327/

Miller, S.D. (March 17, 2021). Feedback Informed Treatment in Statutory Services (Child Protection, Court Mandated). Retrieved October 21, 2024. From https://www.scottdmiller.com/feedback-informed-treatment-in-statutory-services-child-protection-court-mandated/

Miller, S.D., Chow, D., Malins, S., & Hubble, M.A. (Eds.). (2023). *The field guide to better results: Evidence-based exercises to improve therapeutic effectiveness.* Washington, D.C.: American Psychological Association.

Miller, S.D., & Duncan, B.L. (2004). *The Outcome and Sessions Rating Scales: Scoring and administration manual (Revised).* Chicago, IL: ISTC.

Miller, S.D., Duncan, B.L., Brown, J., Sorrell, R., & Chalk, M.B. (2006). Using formal client feedback to improve retention and outcome: Making ongoing, real-time assessment feasible. *Journal of Brief Therapy, 5*(1), 5–22.

Miller, S.D., Duncan, B.L., Brown, J., Sparks, J.A., & Claud, D.A. (2003). The outcome rating scale: A preliminary study of the reliability, validity, and feasibility of a brief analogue measure. *Journal of Brief Therapy, 2*(2), 91–100.

Miller, S.D., Duncan, B.L., & Hubble, M.A. (2004). Beyond integration: The triumph of outcome over process. *Psychotherapy in Australia, 10*(2), 2-19.

Miller, S.D., Duncan, B.L., & Hubble, M.A. (2007). Supershrinks. *Psychotherapy Networker, 31*(6), 26-35, 56.

Miller, S.D., Duncan, B.L., Sorrell, R., & Brown, G.S. (2005). The partners for change outcome management system. *Journal of Clinical Psychology, 61*(2), 99-208.

Miller, S.D., & Hubble, M.A. (2011). The road to mastery. *Psychotherapy Networker, 35*(3), 22-31, 60.

Miller, S.D., & Hubble, M.A. (2017). How psychotherapy lost its magick: The art of healing in an age of science. *Psychotherapy Networker, 41*(2), 28-37, 60-61.

Miller, S.D., & Hubble, M.A. (2023). Identifying your "what" to practice. In S.D. Miller, D. Chow, S. Malins & M.A. Hubble (Eds.), *The field guide to better results: Evidence-based exercises to improve therapeutic effectiveness* (pp. 7–24). Washington, D.C.: American Psychological Association.

Miller, S.D., Hubble, M.A. and Chow, D. (2018) The question of expertise in psychotherapy. *Journal of Expertise, 1*(2), 121-129.

Miller, S.D., Hubble, M.A., & Chow, D. (2020). *Better results: Using deliberate practice to improve therapeutic effectiveness.* Washington, D.C.: American Psychological Association.

Miller, S.D., Hubble, M.A., Chow, D.L., & Seidel, J.A. (2015). Beyond measures and monitoring: Realizing the potential of feedback-informed treatment. *Psychotherapy, 52*(4), 449-457.

Miller, S.D., Wampold, B.E., & Varhely, K. (2008). Direct comparisons of treatment modalities for youth disorders: A meta-analysis. *Psychotherapy Research, 18*(1), 5-14.

Moggia, D., Fexas, G., Nino-Robles, N., & Miller, S.D. (2020). Psychometric properties of the session rating scale 3.0 in a Spanish clinical sample. *British Journal of Guidance and Counselling, 49*(5), 648-659.

Mohr, D.C. (1995). Negative outcome in psychotherapy: A critical review. *Clinical Psychology: Science and Practice, 2*(1), 1-27.

Morris, Z.S., Wooding, S., & Grant, J. (2011). The answer is 17 years, what is the question: Understanding time lags in translational research. *Journal of the Royal Society of Medicine, 104*(12), 510-520.

Moss, R., & Mousavizadeh, V. (2017). Implementing FIT: Challenges and solutions. In D.S. Prescott, C.L. Maeschalck & S.D. Miller (Eds.). *Feedback informed treatment in clinical practice: Reaching for excellence* (pp. 101-121). Washington D.C.: American Psychological Association.

NIH Guide (2021). *Succession planning: A step-by-step guide.* Washington, D.C.: National Institutes of Health Office of Management. Retrieved December 24, 2024. From https://hr.nih.gov/sites/default/files/public/documents/2021-03/Succession_Planning_Step_by_Step_Guide.pdf

Neimeyer, G.J., Taylor, J.M., & Wear, D.M. (2009). Continuing education in psychology: Outcomes, evaluations, and mandates. *Professional Psychology: Research and Practice, 40*(6), 617–624.

Nelson, P.L., Warren, J.S., Gleave, R.L., & Burlingame, G.M. (2013). Youth psychotherapy change trajectories and early warning system accuracy in a managed care setting. *Journal of Clinical Psychology, 69*(9), 880–895.

Norcross, J.C. (Ed.). (2002). *Psychotherapy relationships that work: Therapist contributions and responsiveness to patients.* New York: Oxford University Press.

Norcross, J.C., & Lambert, M.J. (2019). Evidence-based psychotherapy relationships: The third task force. In J.C. Norcross & M.J. Lambert (Eds.). *Psychotherapy relationships that work: Evidence-based therapist contributions, volume 1* (3rd ed.) (pp. 1–23). New York: Oxford University Press.

Norcross, J.C., & Wampold, B.E. (2019a). Evidence-based psychotherapy responsiveness: The third task force. In J.C. Norcross & B.E. Wampold (Eds.), *Psychotherapy relationships that work: Evidence-based therapist responsiveness, volume 2* (3rd ed.) (pp. 1–14). New York: Oxford University Press.

Norcross, J.C., & Wampold, B.E. (2019b). Relationships and responsiveness in the psychological treatment of trauma: The tragedy of the APA clinical practice guideline. *Psychotherapy, 56*(3), 391–399.

Norton, P. J., Little, T. E., & Wetterneck, C.T. (2014). Does experience matter? Trainee experience and outcomes during transdiagnostic cognitive-behavioral group therapy for anxiety. *Cognitive Behaviour Therapy, 43*(3), 230–238.

Obbekær, H., Rasmussen, K., & Bendtsen, I. (2017). FIT in psycho-social efforts. In S. Bargmann (Ed.), *Feedback informed treatment: En grundbog* (pp. 169-185). Copenhagen, Denmark: Akademisk Forlag.

O'Donovan, A., Clough, B., & Petch, J. (2017). Is supervisor training effective? A pilot investigation of clinical supervisor training program. *Australian Psychologist, 52*(2), 149-154.

Ogden, T., Bjørnebekk, G., Kjøbli, J., Patras, J., Christiansen, T., Taraldsen, K., & Tollefsen, N. (2012). Measurement of implementation components ten years after a nationwide introduction of empirically supported programs: A pilot study. *Implementation Science, 7*, article 49.

Orlinsky, D.E., & Rønnestad, M.H. (2005). *How psychotherapists develop: A study of therapeutic work and professional growth.* Washington, D.C.: American Psychological Association.

Orlinsky, D., Rønnestad, M.H., & Willutzki, U. (2004). Fifty years of process-outcome research: Continuity and change. In M.J. Lambert (Ed.). *Bergin and Garfield's Handbook of Psychotherapy and Behavior Change* (5th Ed.) (pp. 307-390). New York: Wiley.

Østergård, O.K., Randa, H., & Hougaard, E. (2018). The effect of using the partners for change outcome management system as feedback tool in psychotherapy: A systematic review and meta-analysis. *Psychotherapy Research, 30*(2), 195-212.

Østergård, O.K., & Hougaard, E. (2020). The evidence for the partners for change outcome management system is insufficient: Reply to Duncan and Sparks (2020). *Psychological Services, 17*(4), 497-498.

Owen, J., Adelson, J., Budge, S., Wampold, B., Kopta, M., Minami, T., & Miller, S. (2015). Trajectories of change in psychotherapy. *Journal of Clinical Psychology, 71*(9), 817-827.

Owen, J., Miller, S.D., Seidel, J., & Chow, D. (2016). The working alliance in treatment of military adolescents. *Journal of Consulting and Clinical Psychology, 84*(3), 200-210.

Pejtersen, J.H., Jensen, M.T., & Hansen, H. (November 7, 2018). *The effect of feedback-informed treatment in the housing support effort: A randomized controlled trial.* Copenhagen, Denmark: The National Research and Analysis Center for Welfare.

Pejtersen, J.H., & Hansen, H. (2022). Routine outcome monitoring in social service: A cluster randomized controlled trial. *Nordic Social Work Research, 14*(4), 1–15.

Pope, K.S., & Tabachnick, B.G. (1993). Therapists' anger, hate, fear, and sexual feelings: National survey of therapist responses, client characteristics, critical events, formal complaints, and training. *Professional Psychology: Research and Practice, 24*(2), 142–152.

Prescott, D.S., Maeschalck, C.L., & Miller, S.D. (Eds.) (2017). *Feedback-informed treatment in clinical practice: Reaching for excellence.* Washington, D.C.: American Psychological Association.

Pringle, J., & Fawcett, J. (2017). Facilitating therapeutic alliance between pharmacists and patients to improve medication adherence. In D.S. Prescott, C.L. Maeschalck, & S.D. Miller (Eds.) (2017). *Feedback-informed treatment in clinical practice: Reaching for excellence* (pp. 299-320). Washington, D.C.: American Psychological Association.

Prochaska, J.O., Norcross, J.C., & Saul, S. F. (2020). Generating psychotherapy breakthroughs: Transtheoretical strategies from population health psychology. *American Psychologist, 75*(7), 996–1010.

Project MATCH Research Group. (1998). Matching alcoholism treatments to client heterogeneity: Project MATCH three-year drinking outcomes. *Alcoholism: Clinical and Experimental Research, 22*(6), 1300–1311.

Quen, S. (June 18, 2024). Top 5 succession planning tools in 2023. Retrieved December 24, 2024. From https://accendotechnologies.com/blog/top-5-succession-planning-tools-in-2023/

Quirk, K., Miller, S.D., Duncan, B.L., & Owen, J. (2012). Group session rating scale: Preliminary psychometrics in substance abuse group interventions. *Counselling and Psychotherapy Research 13*(3), 194-200.

Reese, R.J., Usher, E.L., Bowman, D.C., Norsworthy, L.A., Halstead, J.L., Rowlands, S.R., & Chisholm, R.R. (2009). Using client feedback in psychotherapy training: An analysis of its influence on supervision and counselor self-efficacy. *Training and Education in Professional Psychology, 3*(3), 157–168.

Rise, M., Eriksen, L., Grimstad, H., & Steinsbekk, A. (2016). The long term effect on mental health symptoms and patient activation using patient feedback scales in mental health outpatient treatment: A randomized controlled trail. *Patient Education and Counseling 99*(1), 164-168.

Robinson, B. (2017). Feedback-informed treatment with couples. In D.S. Prescott, C.L. Maeschalck & S.D. Miller (Eds.). *Feedback-informed treatment in clinical practice: Reaching for excellence* (p. 211-230). Washington, D.C.: American Psychological Association.

Roehrig, M., Thompson, J.K., Brannick, M., & van den Berg, P. (2006). Dissonance-based eating disorder prevention program: A preliminary dismantling investigation. *International Journal of Eating Disorders, 39*(1), 1–10.

Rogers, E.M. (2003). *Diffusion of Innovations.* New York: Free Press.

Rousmaniere, T., Swift, J., Babins-Wagner, R., Whipple, J., & Berzins, S. (2014). Supervisor variance in psychotherapy outcome in routine practice. *Psychotherapy Research, 26*(2), 196-205.

Sachs, J. (1983). Talking about the there and then: The emergence of displaced reference in parent-child discourse. In K.E. Nelson (Ed.). *Children's language, volume 4* (pp. 1-28). Hillsdale, N.J.: Lawrence Erlbaum Associates.

Sakaluk, J.K., Williams, A.J., Kilshaw, R.E., & Rhyner, K.T. (2019). Evaluating the evidential value of empirically supported psychological treatments (ESTs): A meta-scientific review. *Journal of Abnormal Psychology, 128*(6), 500–509.

Saxon, D., Ricketts, T., & Heywood, J. (2010). Who drops-out? Do measures of risk to self and to others predict unplanned endings in primary care counselling? *Counselling & Psychotherapy Research,10*(1),13-21.

Schilling, V.N.L.S., Zimmermann, D., Rubel, J.A., Boyle, K.S., & Lutz, W. (2020). Why do patients go off track? Examining potential influencing factors for being at risk of psychotherapy treatment failure. *Quality of Life Research, 30*(11), 3287-3298.

Schuckard, E., Miller, S.D., & Hubble, M.A. (2017). Feedback-informed treatment: Historical and empirical foundations. In D.S. Prescott, C.L. Maeschalck, & S.D. Miller (Eds.). *Feedback-informed treatment in clinical practice: Reaching for excellence* (pp. 13–35). Washington, D.C.: American Psychological Association.

Seidel, J.A., & Miller, S.D. (2012). Manual 4: Documenting change: A primer on measurement, analysis, and reporting. In B. Bertolino & S.D. Miller (Eds.). *ICCE Manuals on Feedback-Informed Treatment* (Vols. 1-6). Chicago: ICCE.

Seidel, J., Miller, S.D., & Chow, D.L., (2013). Effect size calculations for the clinician: Methods and comparability. *Psychotherapy Research, 24*(4), 470-484.

Shaw, S.L., Lombardero, A., Babins-Wagner, R., & Sommers-Flanagan, N.J. (2019). Counseling Canadian indigenous peoples: The therapeutic alliance and outcome. *Journal of Multicultural Counseling and Development, 47*(1), 49-68.

She, Z., Duncan, B.L., Reese, R.J., Jiang, Q., Wu, C., & Clements, A. L. (2018). Client feedback in China: A randomized clinical trial in a college counseling center. *Journal of Counseling Psychology, 65*(6), 727-737.

Shimokawa, K. (2010). *A patient-focused psychotherapy quality assurance system: Meta-analytic and multilevel analytic review.* [Unpublished doctoral dissertation]. Brigham Young University.

Sibert, N.T., Pfaff, H., Breidenbach, C., Wesselmann, S., & Kowalski, C. (2021). Different approaches for case-mix adjustment of patient-reported outcomes to compare healthcare providers: Methodological results of a systematic review. *Cancers* (Basel), *13*(16), 3964.

Siev, J., Huppert, J.D., & Chambless, D.L. (2009). The dodo bird, treatment technique, and disseminating empirically supported treatments. *The Behavior Therapist, 32*(4), 69, 71–76.

Simon, G.E., Imel, Z.E., Ludman, E.J., & Steinfeld, B. J. (2012). Is dropout after a first psychotherapy visit always a bad outcome? *Psychiatric Services, 63*(7), 705–707.

Slade, K., Lambert, M.J., Harmon, S.C., Smart, D.W., & Bailey, R. (2008). Improving psychotherapy outcome: The use of immediate electronic feedback and revised clinical support tools. *Clinical Psychology & Psychotherapy, 15*(5), 287-303.

Slade, M., McCrone, P., Kuipers, E., Leese, M., Cahill, S., Parabiaghi, A., Priebe, S., & Thornicroft, G. (2006). Use of standardized outcome measures in adult mental health services: Randomized controlled trial. *The British Journal of Psychiatry,189*(4), 330-336.

Slone, N.C., & Owen, J. (2015). Therapist alliance activity, therapist comfort, and systemic alliance on individual psychotherapy outcome. *Journal of Psychotherapy Integration, 25*(4), 275–288.

Slone, N.C., Reese, R.J., Mathews-Duvall, S., & Kodet, J. (2015). Evaluating the efficacy of client feedback in group psychotherapy. *Group Dynamics, 19*(2),122-136.

Smith, M.L., & Glass, G.V. (1977). Meta-analysis of psychotherapy outcome studies. *American Psychologist, 32*(9), 752–760.

Snyder, C.R., Michael, S.T., & Cheavens, J.S. (1999). Hope as a psychotherapeutic foundation of common factors, placebos, and expectancies. In M.A. Hubble, B.L. Duncan, & S.D. Miller (Eds.). *The heart and soul of change: What works in therapy* (pp. 179–200). Washington, D.C.: American Psychological Association.

Social-og-Boligstyrelsen (N.D.). Feedback-Informed Treatment. Retrieved December 24, 2024. From https://sbst.dk/tvaergaende-omrader/virksomme-indsatser/dokumenterede-metoder-voksne-og-handicap/om/feedback-informed-treatment-fit

Solstad, S.M., Castonguay, L., & Moltu, C. (2017). Patients' experiences with routine outcome monitoring and clinical feedback systems: A systematic review and synthesis of qualitative empirical literature. *Psychotherapy Research, 29*(2), 157-170.

Spielmans, G.I., Benish, S.G., Marin, C., Bowman, W.M., Menster, M., & Wheeler, A.J. (2013). Specificity of psychological treatments for bulimia nervosa and binge eating disorder? A meta-analysis of direct comparisons. *Clinical Psychology Review, 33*(3), 460-469.

Stiles, W. B., Barkham, M., & Wheeler, S. (2015). Duration of psychological therapy: Relation to recovery and improvement rates in UK routine practice. *The British Journal of Psychiatry, 207*(2), 115–122.

Swift, J.K., & Greenberg, R.P. (2015). *Premature termination in psychotherapy: Strategies for engaging clients and improving outcomes.* Washington, D.C.: American Psychological Association.

Swift, J.K., Greenberg, R.P., Tompkins, K.A., & Parkin, S.R. (2017). Treatment refusal and premature termination in psychotherapy, pharmacotherapy, and their combination: A meta-analysis of head-to-head comparisons. *Psychotherapy, 54*(1), 47-57.

Swift, J., Owen, J., & Miller, S. (2023). Client factors. In S.D., Miller, D. Chow & M.A., Hubble (Eds). *The field guide to better results* (pp. 47-78), Washington, D.C.: American Psychological Association.

Talmon, M. (1990). *Single-session therapy: Maximizing the effect of the first (and often only) therapeutic encounter.* San Francisco, CA: Jossey-Bass.

Tech Contributor (2008). Definition: Garbage in garbage out (GIGO). Retrieved December 24, 2024. From https://www.techtarget.com/searchsoftwarequality/definition/garbage-in-garbage-out

Thomas, J. (2013). Therapy: No improvement for 40 years. *The National Psychologist, 23*(1), 1.

Thorsteinson, T. J. (2017). A meta-analysis of interview length on reliability and validity. *Journal of Occupational and Organizational Psychology, 91*, 1-32.

Tilden, T., Wampold, B.E., Ulvenes, P., Zahl-Olsen, R., Hoffart, A., Barstad, B., Olsen, I.A., Gude, T., Pinsof W.M., Zinbarg, R.E., Nilssen, H.H., & Håland, Å.T. (2019). Feedback in couple and family therapy: A randomized clinical trial. *Family Process, 59*(1), 36-51.

Tilsen, J., & McNamee, S. (2015). Feedback informed treatment: Evidence-based practice meets social construction. *Family Process, 54*(1), 124–137.

Truscott, D. (2010). *Becoming an effective psychotherapist: Adopting a theory of psychotherapy that's right for you and your client.* Washington, D.C.: American Psychological Association.

Tuff, G., Goldbach, S., & Johnson, J. (September 27, 2022). When hiring, prioritize assignments over interviews. *Harvard Business Review.* Retrieved October 21, 2024. From https://hbr.org/2022/09/when-hiring-prioritize-assignments-over-interviews

U. S. National Institutes of Health (2021). Succession planning: A step-by-step guide. Washington, D.C. National Institute of Health. Retrieved May 27, 2024. From https://hr.nih.gov/sites/default/files/public/documents/2021-03/Succession_Planning_Step_by_Step_Guide.pdf

VanderWal, B L. (2015). *The relationship between counselor trainees' personal therapy experiences and client outcome.* [Unpublished doctoral *dissertation*]. Western Michigan University.

van Oenen, F.J., Schipper, S., Van, R., Schoevers, R., Visch, I., Peen, J., & Dekker, J. (2016). Feedback-informed treatment in emergency psychiatry: A randomised controlled trial. *BMC Psychiatry, 16*, Article 110.

van Oenen, F.J., Schipper, S., Van, R., Visch, I., Peen, J., Cornelis, J., Schoevers, R., & Dekker, J. (2018). Involving relatives in emergency psychiatry: An observational patient-control study in a crisis resolution and home treatment team. *Journal of Family Therapy, 40*(4), 584–601.

Vinther, B. & Davidsen, A.H. (2016). FIT i gruppebehandling af patienter med spiseforstyrrelser. In S. Bargmann (Ed.), *Feedback informed treatment: En grundbog* (pp. 97-113). Copenhagen, Denmark: Akademisk Forlag.

Wainwright, N. (2010). *The development of the Leeds Alliance in Supervision Scale (LASS): A brief sessional measure of the supervisory alliance.* [Unpublished doctoral dissertation]. University of Leeds (United Kingdom).

Wampold, B.E. (1997). Methodological problems in identifying efficacious psychotherapies. *Psychotherapy Research, 7*(1), 21-43.

Wampold, B.E. (2001). *The great psychotherapy debate: Models, methods, and findings.* Mahwah, N.J.: Lawrence Erlbaum Associates.

Wampold, B.E. (2010). The research evidence for the common factors models: A historically situated perspective. In B.L. Duncan, S.D. Miller, B.E. Wampold, & M.A. Hubble (Eds.). *The heart and soul of change: Delivering what works in therapy* (pp. 49–81). Washington, D.C.: American Psychological Association.

Wampold, B.E., & Holloway, E.L. (1997). Methodology, design, and evaluation in psychotherapy supervision research. In C.E. Watkins, Jr. (Ed.). *Handbook of psychotherapy supervision* (pp. 11–27). New York: Wiley.

Wampold, B.E., & Imel, Z.E. (2015). *The great psychotherapy debate: The evidence for what makes psychotherapy work* (2nd ed.). New York: Routledge.

Wampold, B.E., Flückiger, C., Del Re, A.C., Yulish, N.E., Frost, N.D., Pace, B.T., Goldberg, S.B., Miller, S.D., Baardseth, T.P., Laska, K.M., & Hilsenroth, M.J. (2017). In pursuit of truth: A critical examination of meta-analyses of cognitive behavior therapy. *Psychotherapy Research, 27*(1), 14–32.

Warren, J.S., Nelson, P.L. & Burlingame, G.M. (2009). Identifying youth at risk for treatment failure in outpatient community mental health services. *Journal of Child and Family Studies, 18*(6), 690–701.

Warren, J.S., Nelson, P.L., Mondragon, S.A., Baldwin, S.A., & Burlingame, G.M. (2010). Youth psychotherapy change trajectories and outcomes in usual care: Community mental health versus managed care settings. *Journal of Consulting and Clinical Psychology, 78*(2), 144–155.

Watkins, C.E. (Ed.). (1997). *Handbook of psychotherapy supervision.* New York: Wiley.

Watkins C.E. (2011). Does psychotherapy supervision contribute to patient outcomes? Considering thirty years of research. *The Clinical Supervisor, 30*(2), 235-256.

Watkins, C.E., (2015). The evolving nature of psychoanalytic supervision: From pedagogical to andragogical perspective. *Internal Forum of Psychoanalysis,* 24(4), 230-242.

Watkins, C.E., Jr. & Callahan, J.L. (2019). Psychotherapy supervision research: A status report and proposed model. In S.G. De Golia & K.M. Corcoran (Eds.). *Supervision in psychiatric practice: Practical approaches across venues and providers* (pp. 25–34). Washington, D.C.: American Psychiatric Association.

Webb, C.A., Derubeis, R.J. & Barber, J.P. (2010). Therapist adherence/competence and treatment outcome: A meta-analytic review. *Journal of Consulting and Clinical Psychology, 78*(2), 200-11.

Weiner-Davis, M., de Shazer, S. & Gingerich, W. J. (1987). Building on pretreatment change to construct the therapeutic solution: An exploratory study. *Journal of Marital and Family Therapy, 13*(4), 359–363.

Whipple, J., Hoyt, T., Rousmaniere, T., Swift, J., Pedersen, T. & Worthen, V. (2020). Supervisor variance in psychotherapy outcome in routine practice: A replication. *SAGE Open, 10*(1), 2158244019899047.

Whipple, J.L., Lambert, M.J., Vermeersch, D.A., Smart, D.W., Nielsen, S.L. & Hawkins, E.J. (2003). Improving the effects of psychotherapy: The use of early identification of treatment and problem-solving strategies in routine practice. *Journal of Counseling Psychology, 50*(1), 59–68.

Williams, A.J., Botanov, Y., Kilshaw, R.E., Wong, R.E. & Sakaluk, J.K. (2021). Potentially harmful therapies: A meta-scientific review of evidential value. *Clinical Psychology: Science and Practice, 28*(1), 5-18.

Woltmann, E.M., Whitley, R., McHugo, G.J., Brunette, M., Torrey, W. C., Coots, L., Lynde, D. & Drake, R.E. (2008). The role of staff turnover in the implementation of evidence-based practices in mental health care. *Psychiatric Services, 59*(7), 732-737.

Zilcha-Mano, S., Solomonov, N., Chui, H., McCarthy, K.S., Barrett, M.S. & Barber, J.P. (2015). Therapist-reported alliance: Is it really a predictor of outcome? *Journal of Counseling Psychology, 62*(4), 568–578.

ABOUT THE AUTHORS

SCOTT D. MILLER, PH. D., is the founder of the International Center for Clinical Excellence. Over the last three decades his research, writing, and training has focused on helping agencies and professionals improve their effectiveness via feedback and deliberate practice. He's published scores of research articles and numerous books, including most recently *Better Results* (APA, 2020) and *The Field Guide to Better Results* (2023).

SUSANNE BARGMANN, is the incoming director of the International Center for Clinical Excellence. A clinical psychologist with 22 years of experience, her expertise is helping individual practitioners and organizations implement feedback-informed treatment. She publishes regularly on both FIT and deliberate practice, including two best-selling volumes in Scandinavia, *FIT Foundations* and *Getting Better.*

www.ingramcontent.com/pod-product-compliance
Lightning Source LLC
Chambersburg PA
CBHW050342270326
41926CB00016B/3575

* 9 780999 662444 *